RECENT ADVANCES IN PEACE AND CONFLICT RESEARCH

Volume 27, Sage Library of Social Research

SAGE LIBRARY OF SOCIAL RESEARCH

1. **DAVID CAPLOVITZ:** The Merchants of Harlem: A Study of Small Business in a Black Community
2. **JAMES N. ROSENAU:** International Studies and the Social Sciences: Problems, Priorities and Prospects in the United States
3. **DOUGLAS E. ASHFORD:** Ideology and Participation
4. **PATRICK J. McGOWAN and HOWARD B. SHAPIRO:** The Comparative Study of Foreign Policy: A Survey of Scientific Findings
5. **GEORGE A. MALE:** The Struggle for Power: Who Controls the Schools in England and the United States
6. **RAYMOND TANTER:** Modelling and Managing International Conflicts: The Berlin Crises
7. **ANTHONY JAMES CATANESE:** Planners and Local Politics: Impossible Dreams
8. **JAMES RUSSELL PRESCOTT:** Economic Aspects of Public Housing
9. **F. PARKINSON:** Latin America, the Cold War, and the World Powers, 1945-1973: A Study in Diplomatic History
10. **ROBERT G. SMITH:** Ad Hoc Governments: Special Purpose Transportation Authorities in Britain and the United States
11. **RONALD GALLIMORE, JOAN WHITEHORN BOGGS, and CATHIE JORDAN:** Culture, Behavior and Education: A Study of Hawaiian-Americans
12. **HOWARD W. HALLMAN:** Neighborhood Government in a Metropolitan Setting
13. **RICHARD J. GELLES:** The Violent Home: A Study of Physical Aggression Between Husbands and Wives
14. **JERRY L. WEAVER:** Conflict and Control in Health Care Administration
15. **GEBHARD LUDWIG SCHWEIGLER:** National Consciousness in Divided Germany
16. **JAMES T. CAREY:** Sociology and Public Affairs: The Chicago School
17. **EDWARD W. LEHMAN:** Coordinating Health Care: Explorations in Interorganizational Relations
18. **CHARLES G. BELL and CHARLES M. PRICE:** The First Term: A Study of Legislative Socialization
19. **CLAYTON P. ALDERFER and L. DAVE BROWN:** Learning from Changing: Organizational Diagnosis and Development
20. **L. EDWARD WELLS and GERALD MARWELL:** Self-Esteem: Its Conceptualization and Measurement
21. **ROBERT S. ROBINS:** Political Institutionalization and the Integration of Elites
22. **WILLIAM R. SCHONFELD:** Obedience and Revolt: French Behavior Toward Authority
23. **WILLIAM C. McCREADY and ANDREW M. GREELEY:** The Ultimate Values of the American Population
24. **F. IVAN NYE:** Role Structure and Analysis of the Family
25. **PAUL WEHR and MICHAEL WASHBURN:** Peace and World Order Systems: Teaching and Research
26. **PATRICIA R. STEWART:** Children in Distress: American and English Perspectives
27. **JUERGEN DEDRING:** Recent Advances in Peace and Conflict Research: A Critical Study

Recent Advances in Peace and Conflict Research

A Critical Survey

JUERGEN DEDRING

Foreword by ELISE BOULDING

Preface by J. DAVID SINGER

Volume 27
SAGE LIBRARY OF
SOCIAL RESEARCH

A UNITAR Study

SAGE PUBLICATIONS Beverly Hills London

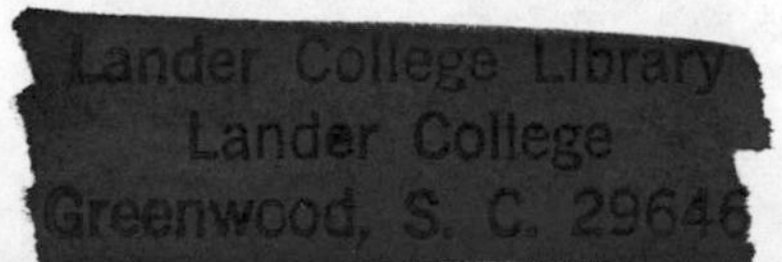

For information address:

SAGE PUBLICATIONS, INC.
275 South Beverly Drive
Beverly Hills, California 90212

SAGE PUBLICATIONS LTD
St George's House / 44 Hatton Garden
London EC1N 8ER

Printed in the United States of America

Library of Congress Cataloging in Publication Data

Dedring, Juergen.
Recent advances in peace and conflict research.

(Sage library of social research ; v. 27) (A UNITAR study)
Bibliography: p.
1. Peace–Research. I. Title. II. Series: United Nations Institute for Training and Research. UNITAR study.
JX1904.5.D43 327'.172'072 76-5849
ISBN 0-8039-0611-0
ISBN 0-8039-0612-9 pbk.

FIRST PRINTING

CONTENTS

FOREWORD

Having lived at first hand for the past ten years with the intense but creative intellectual and moral conflicts within the peace research movement over the issues of how to conceptualize conflict and peace, and over the relevance of evolutionary versus revolutionary processes in bringing about a more just and less violent world, I would not have thought it possible for anyone to write a review of the state of the field that could deal adequately with the variety of existing approaches and still come out with a coherent statement about peace research in policy-relevant terms. Juergen Dedring has done just that, and I think his accomplishment is extraordinary. The book is not simply a review of peace research; it provides a basis for all of us to evaluate the body of knowledge itself. We don't have to go through all those painful sessions so common in the 1960s of "defining peace research" any longer. It is now an established interdisciplinary field, a critical science offering a variety of tools for the analysis of the structures and processes of conflict and peace at global and domestic levels.

As a teacher I am concerned that we share with our students the full range of issues about *how* to study war and peace, yet do so in a way that enables them to choose their own handles for the work they decide to do. We have in this book an analytically sound presentation of all the research models in current use, with a clear statement of the different values and world views on which they are based. There is an underlying compassion in Dedring's approach that I find very appealing. He has moved among us for several years in connection with his duties as a member of the UNITAR research staff. He takes all of us seriously, and expects us to take each other seriously—something we have not always done.

My own primary concerns as a teacher–researcher in the field have to do with optimizing the teaching-learning process itself, both for the apprentice peace researcher in the classroom and for practitioners in the arenas of conflict. The general systems analysis of global systems is tidy and easy to present to students, and is easy to work with in developing indicators of system states, but there is a kind of self-deception in this approach. It gives an appearance of closure to our understanding of system interaction that is not justified, and ignores the issue of how actors in systems *learn.* The assumption is that if feedback loops are working properly, actors will learn what they need to know. The discussion by Dedring in Chapter 2 of Senghaas' work on social autism raises profound questions about that learning. If in fact nations don't make policy in reaction to other nations, but in response to their own inner dynamics, how do we break through that social autism in order to initiate learning processes?

In my view Dedring has brought together the materials in Chapters 4 and 5 in a way that provides us with the basis for better insights about learning than we now have. We must develop better learning theories so we can construct more complete models of international systems. When we have come to the point where we can not only train students to develop good mental models of any particular conflict situation they have to deal with, but also to trigger interactive learning sequences between actors in conflicts, peace researchers will have come a lot closer to their goal of being process enablers and not just researchers.

This type of learning goes far beyond the question of linguistic and cultural misunderstanding and issues of subjectivism. It has to do with learning to respond to the underlying structural and environmental inequities that distort problem-solving behavior and deflect us from the broader agendas that must be dealt with in any objective conflict situation. This type of responsiveness is a skill just as manipulation is a skill, though it is of a much higher order. It is a learning how to learn, and it can be taught. Skill training has not traditionally been thought of as an appropriate concern for peace researchers, who operate at "higher levels" of abstraction. If we are serious about learning processes in the action context, however, we must study the whole range of skills, analytic, perceptual and behavioral, involved in bringing about social change.

One thing that the development of futurism, the first cousin of peace research, has done for twentieth century science is to deal a death-blow to the old discussions about value-free science. In envisioning alternative futures, the first thing futurists have to do is to clarify their values and priorities, and to lay out their working assumptions about the nature of the human condition and the potentials of the social order. The inclusion of a survey of the work on alternative futures in the first chapter of this book, provides a framework for the survey of research paradigms and methodologies that give the student a basis for choosing a way to work.

The world clearly needs women and men who are trained to look at the world and see structures, systems, and processes that are invisible to many policy-makers and practitioners in the international relations field today.

They should be women and men who not only have analytic skills and well-developed critical faculties, but trained imaginations and highly developed moral sensors. Going even beyond imagination and moral sensitivity, the women and men the future is calling for need the faculties for compassion, and for *being present* where we are. I see this book as an unexpected gift to those of us who are committed to working as social scientists with coming generations in an enterprise of becoming the new kinds of people our planet needs. Whether we choose to work in universities or in the streets; whether we opt for local, national, international, or transnational roles and institutional settings, we are all activists, we are all practitioners, we are all researchers, we are all teachers. Some sense of the orchestration of the many tasks associated with the making of peace and justice is needed. No one book could or should try to do that. We don't want a "bible" of peace research. That kind of orchestration has to go on in our own heads. But we can use help, and this book offers us help. I for one intend to use it as a means of sharing with my students an important inventory of many of the tools they will need in working at the peacemaking enterprise.

September 1975
Conflict and Peace Studies Program
University of Colorado

Elise Boulding

PREFACE

Every field of scientific endeavor needs a dose of self-examination and introspection from time to time, but it is difficult to know what the proper amount is and how often it should be administered. It seems to me, however, that the social sciences are more prone to such self-review than are the biological or physical sciences, and that within the social sciences, the more humanly important the area of inquiry, the greater this tendency. A dramatic example of this tendency is seen in the new area known as peace research. If my impression is correct (and it could be checked out rather easily), why should this be so?

For peace research, I suspect that the label ifself is a major factor, and I remember resisting it with some vigor at the outset. My concerns at the time were two. First I feared that, by differentiating ourselves from those who already were at work on the study of international conflict, we might be kept at arm's length from political science, sociology, and the other relevant disciplines. That, in turn, would affect our legitimacy and thus our access to institutional affiliations, university students, and research facilities. While that concern turned out to be more than justified and we now find ourselves in a very weak position from the point of view of institutional arrangements, this is only a minor part of the cost.

More serious, it seems to me, was my second concern: that we would be tempted to redefine the notions of "peace" and/or "research." Since the late 1940s, the peace movement in the West has suffered from a deep division over the proposition that "peace is not merely the absence of war, but the presence of . . ." Needless to say, each of us was free to fill in the personally preferred statement of utopia, ranging from individual physical health to national self-determination. Noble though these other objectives might be, they are hardly the same thing as peace, nor are they—as some would have it—the essential prerequisites of peace. Those who believe that peace comes when no one is any longer disadvantaged or dissatisfied have little appreciation for either the complexity of conflict or the ease with which new asymmetries (real or imagined) can be generated.

Not only did the label help to set us outside the social science mainstream and get us into a morass as to the meaning of "peace," but it also encouraged some foolish argument as to the meaning of "research." In the minds of all too many of those who march under our banner, research can embrace everything from ransacking history for those episodes that will support a given argument, to assembling powerful rhetoric by which to overwhelm or even confuse those with whom we disagree, within as well as without.

My point, then, is that any condition that: (a) places us in an ambiguous position vis-à-vis the relevant mainstreams of research, or (b) creates considerable confusion as to purpose within our ranks, will lead us to much more soul-searching and internal reexamination than is healthy. Rather than getting on with the crucial task of discovering the causes of violent conflict and the possible ways to mitigate and eliminate it, we devote an unconscionable amount of our energies to arguing whether that is indeed our task.

These are, however, merely historical ruminations, and while they may help us understand why we have here another reexamination of the peace research undertaking, my mission is to focus more on the study at hand. Since it is unlike most earlier overviews and evaluations of peace and conflict research, that mission is happily undertaken. In addition to the fact that most prior critiques and evaluations are of article length only, a dominant distinction between Dedring's effort and many of the others is that it provides us with an exceptionally fair and open examination of diverse schools of thought. While much of the critique literature, from the right as well as the left, is highly one-sided, and tends to caricature its intellectual opposition, this author has made a sincere and largely successful effort to clarify and not to confuse.

The virtues of the study are several, and it might be appropriate to single out a few. Particularly refreshing is Dedring's agnosticism regarding the road to human salvation. Whereas all too many of today's peace researchers seem to have already "discovered" both the cause and cure for the world's ills, he appreciates how little we really *do* know, and how important it is to get on with our efforts to find out. Many of those whom he cites not only write and speak as if the necessary research has already been done (often by Karl Marx or one of his disciples), or as if it need not be done, inasmuch as the answers are there for all who are "willing to see."

This appreciation of how little of the necessary knowledge we have acquired so far comes through not only in the modesty and incrementalism of the proposals to which he most responds, but in his rather complete coverage of the more rigorous and quantitative research. Given the unfamiliarity with this work—or the normative and epistemological assumptions behind it—on the part of many radical peace researchers, this is a refreshing change. And, given the public self-confidence that currently characterizes the radical critique school, it is also courageous.

But he is not only independent-minded vis-à-vis those with whom he shares an ideological affinity. He is equally courageous vis-à-vis those who, in this epoch, have the power to legitimize and put into effect, or to discredit and ignore, policy proposals emanating from our work. That is, we get here a competent and careful overview of several schemes and peace proposals that receive little but ridicule from the policy-makers and the academic court astrologers who can be found in or near many of the world's foreign ministries. For example, it was reassuring to see Dedring's thoughtful discussions of disarmament, international organization, functional cooperation, and non-military defense, to mention some ideas that usually produce derision and condescension from our self-styled "realists." I do not want to suggest, however, that we have here an author who seeks to satisfy *all* points of view. While he shows a nice balance of open-mindedness and skepticism toward the several orientations that are found in the peace research literature, he ultimately comes down close to those whom he identified as the "critical and radical students of peace and conflict."

Having noted the thoroughness and thoughtfulness of the book's coverage, let me nevertheless address a few paragraphs to some of Dedring's major conclusions, and suggest why they are best viewed with friendly skepticism. First, as already implied, he ends up generally accepting the unfortunate phraseology of the critical school. Thus, we find frequent use of such phrases as "structural violence" when reference is rather to maldistribution of wealth or health, or we find resort to such pejorative labels as "negative peace," implying that the elimination of international war is a mean and perhaps even contemptible objective, contrasted to the brave vision of "positive peace." I would also fault him for an altogether too casual use of the word "theory." The radical critique literature (along, one might add, with much of the conventional literature on world affairs) tends to apply the label to virtually any polysyllabic argument, no matter how imprecise, inconsistent, and ill-founded it may be. If, by theory, we mean codified knowledge—and I would propose some such label—we would expect a theory to satisfy somewhat more stringent criteria. At the minimum, the label ought apply only to a body of internally consistent and empirically disconfirmable propositions, some fraction of which have stood the latter test. By these criteria, we have no such thing as a theory of the balance of power, no less a theory of imperialism, for example.

Shifting from semantics to substance, another theme that merits closer scrutiny is the author's tendency to equate peace with radical social change within and between national societies. While taking second place to none in my despair over the structure and culture of the contemporary global system, and the belief that radical transformations are essential, I cannot share his jaundiced view of the incremental reformers, especially those who insist on the search for non-violent reform. Not only does it seem to me that we are more likely to get irreversible transformation in the desired directions via incremental reform, but it also seems that by explicitly eschewing violence, we may begin to change the complexion of the struggle itself. Conversely, when we under-emphasize the short run intermediate steps and over-emphasize too heavily the ultimate utopia, we tend to lose those who genuinely worry about how we get from "here" to "there." In this vein, when we encourage or implicitly condone violence (and I use the word in its standard sense), we merely echo and help to perpetuate and legitimize those who now use or threaten violence to *maintain* the status quo.

Closely related is the proposition that peace will remain beyond our reach until social justice is achieved. In addition to my earlier comments on this point, let me also suggest that war, and the recurrent preparation for war, may well be a greater obstacle to the achievement of justice than the opposite. That is, we may be able to reduce the incidence of war while injustice remains, but are quite unlikely to reduce the incidence of injustice while war remains an accepted condition of the human community. As long as war is a regular mode of human problem-solving–and today its legitimacy remains virtually unchallenged–people and resources will continue to be mobilized for war. The material and psychological consequences of such continuing mobilization can hardly be conducive to the growth of civilized discourse, generous cooperation, human liberties, or economic development. Peace and justice are, as Dedring certainly reminds us, highly interdependent, but to think that we can achieve the latter until we are at least on the road to the former strikes me as naive, and perhaps even incendiary.

Another point at which the author seems too responsive to the radical critique school is on the matter of collaboration with policy-makers. Much has been said on this subject already, but from too remote and unempathetic a viewpoint. The social psychology of governmental decision-making is not unlike that of other quasi-collegial associations, including of course those of peace researchers and peace activists. Thus individuals arrive at roles through a great many incremental steps, gradually taking on the intellectual and moral coloration of those with whom they associate. While the more concerned social scientists among us may be very different from those in other roles now, elites and counter-elites probably started out looking rather much alike. Two consequences flow from this proposition. First, by recognizing that "there, but for the fates, go I," we can more effectively empathize with, and thus try to communicate with, those who may appear to be the enemy. Second, if the latter arrived at that role in the manner which I've suggested, they might possibly return to or shift to quite another role and set of viewpoints in quite the same manner, especially if we can bring new ideas and information to their attention. More people, I suspect, become "locked into" their world views by the behavior of their opponents than by that of their associates, and peace workers–like many other dissidents–often do more to reinforce the conventional wisdom of the elites than all the intra-organizational indoctrination to which they may be subjected. To put it in the current metaphor, I would say that "some of my best friends are governmental decision-makers." (I might even add that although they can and do end up condoning all too many acts of barbarism, so do we, and in examining this dreadful dilemma of public and private life, they are often more anguished, insightful, and humane than their detractors and tormentors.) In sum, it is not only more generous, but probably more pragmatic as well, to assume that no one is "beyond salvation and redemption"; experience and new knowledge can often work wonders. When all is said and done, our author seems to concur, but along the way he is, in my judgment, too willing to take seriously the arguments of those who would wage war against those "in power."

This leads, in turn, to Dedring's third major conclusion, that concerning peace education, and here he tends to retreat into a rather passive position, merely calling on us to transcend our national and parochial limits. This is just not sufficient. Peace education, widely conceived, may well turn out to be the most important activity of peace researchers. That is, even if we mount a major and successful research assault on the problems of war and of social justice, of what value will it be if the rest of the world neither believes nor understands our discoveries, even assuming that some of the world's citizens even *hear* about it? My point is that we have a responsibility to not only carry on our research in a creative and inspired, as well as scientifically rigorous, manner. We must also write up our results in language that is clear, spell out our procedures in explicit and reproducible detail, and examine the pragmatic implications carefully yet imaginatively. In so doing, we not only contribute to the body of knowledge that may save us. We also increase the likelihood that those who hear and must act on this knowledge will be able to understand what we have discovered, evaluate it critically, and interpret it intelligently. A corollary is that peace researchers must pass up no opportunity to educate others–in and out of the universities and institutes–on both the possibilities and the limits of the scientific mode in social problem-solving. The bulk of humanity is today deplorably ignorant of the social scientific mode, and among those few who *are* informed, there is considerable–and perhaps even growing–hostility.

While this mix of ignorance and hostility can largely be attributed to the political, economic, and theological elites of the world, the counter-elites have also made their contribution to this sorry state of affairs. By caricaturing science, by posing a dichotomous choice between the scientific and humanistic, and by asserting that science will always be a tool of the establishment, we give up the most potent implement in the repertoire of the peace movement. In my judgment, moral concern and skillful rhetoric just will not suffice. But if we can couple our concern with competence, and our rhetoric with knowledge, we may yet turn the world away from disaster. All too many peace researchers and peace activists do not understand that the most important revolution we can make is an *epistemological* revolution. It is a pleasure to note that Dedring is not, when all is said and done, among them. Having examined these questions with balance and care, he is clearly among those who understand that we may be on the verge of doing what humanity has never done before: bringing *all* of our moral and intellectual faculties to bear on the solution of a menacing human problem. That participants in the peace research movement disagree over orientations and priorities is of less concern than the fact that we are embarked on this critical and exciting voyage. This study should be a major source of guidance along the way.

October 1975 *J. David Singer*
Ann Arbor, Michigan

STATEMENT BY THE EXECUTIVE DIRECTOR OF UNITAR

The United Nations Institute for Training and Research was established by the Secretary-General as an autonomous Institution within the framework of the United Nations. Its purpose is to enhance the effectiveness of the United Nations by means of training and research in achieving the major objectives of the organization–in particular, the promotion of economic and social development and the maintenance of peace and security.

This critical survey of recent advances in peace and conflict research is a part of UNITAR's ongoing research project relating to the peaceful settlement of international disputes. Departing from the principal focus of previous studies published in this area by UNITAR, the book reviews the conceptual and practical significance of recent contributions to the literature. The focus also is on past and present difficulties impeding conflict resolution, taking into account bilateral as well as multilateral levels of international relations.

An earlier draft of the manuscript was distributed to a large number of academic specialists and to several United Nations diplomats and officials with particular experience in the subject. The comments that were received have been of great value for the final revision of the study.

We acknowledge the generosity of the Volkswagen Foundation in providing financial support for this project.

Dr. Juergen Dedring, a scholar from the Federal Republic of Germany, was a UNITAR Research Associate from September 1972 to December 1974, after holding teaching and research posts at Harvard University and at Dartmouth College in the United States. Since January 1975, he has been a Political Affairs Officer in the Department of Political and Security Council Affairs in the United Nations Secretariat.

The ideas expressed in the study are the responsibility of the author alone and do not necessarily reflect those of the staff or trustees of UNITAR. While the Institute takes no position on the matters studied under its auspices, it does assume responsibility for determining whether the study merits publication and dissemination.

Dr. Davidson Nicol
Executive Director

ACKNOWLEDGMENTS

This study grew out of a short background paper on scholarly contributions to conflict analysis which I prepared for a UNITAR Training Seminar on Peaceful Settlement of Disputes in March 1973. After some twelve months of additional research, during which I also had the opportunity to attend several conferences of the International Studies Association (ISA) and the Consortium on Peace Research, Education and Development (COPRED), the manuscript was completed in draft form by the end of August 1974.

The draft was sent to a large number of academic specialists and a few diplomats and UN officials for critical comments and suggestions from a theoretical, or "practical," perspective. I am very grateful to all those who read my manuscript and offered helpful advice, which I tried to follow in the revision of the text during the summer of 1975.

First and foremost, I should thank UNITAR and its Executive Director for enabling me to conduct the research and to complete the manuscript. I am especially endebted to Professor Oscar Schachter, former Director of Studies at UNITAR, who suggested the critical survey of peace and conflict studies as a project and who offered valuable suggestions with regard to its scope, thrust, and content. My thanks also go to Dr. Robert S. Jordan, currently UNITAR's Director of Research, for his vital role in seeing the whole project through, removing obstacles that threatened to delay the completion of the revised draft and its publication. He also convened a panel of UN officials and academic experts whose suggestions proved of great help in the revision of the study and to whom I would like to express my gratitude once again. During my stay at UNITAR, I benefited from many exchanges with my colleagues in the institute and drew information and encouragement from their understanding and knowledge.

My review of recent advances in peace and conflict research is a link in UNITAR's continuing effort to keep abreast of theoretical and practical developments in international conflict management and resolution. That concern is represented in UNITAR's Peaceful Settlement series of publications, especially in Sydney D. Bailey, *Peaceful Settlement of Disputes: Ideas and Proposals for Research* and in Frank Edmead, *Analysis and Prediction in International Mediation.* I am, of course, indebted to these and other UNITAR publications.

I am very glad to see included in this book the brief foreword and introduction by Elise Boulding and J. David Singer, whose leading positions in peace research and education are well known and whose contributions to this volume are a perfect example of the support that I received from the academic community of peace researchers throughout my inquiry into recent advances in the field.

Finally, I want to thank Mrs. Teresita N. Alfonso, whose unfailing secretarial help made the speedy completion of the manuscript in its various stages possible.

Whatever the merits of this study, I am fully aware of its many shortcomings, for which I alone bear the full responsibility.

INTRODUCTION

In 1973, UNESCO published its "International Repertory of Institutions for Peace and Conflict Research" for a second time.[1] At that point, all the available evidence pointed to the rapid growth of this new academic discipline and to its ultimate acceptance into the established structures of teaching and research. Yet there are aspects to current peace and conflict research which demonstrate that its expansion and its heuristic and methodological foundations fall short of what many expect or believe. This is primarily due to the huge span of what is presented as research on peace and conflict, to its interdisciplinary character, and to its ambiguous relevance for the formulation and implementation of foreign policy. International peace is such an important goal and such a pressing need that policy-makers frequently tend to dismiss peace research qua research as too time-consuming and impractical, or they try to utilize it inappropriately by requesting overly narrow and partisan research projects.[2]

Peace Research—A Critical Science

Peace and conflict research is a critical science. This empirical and normative statement is valid for various conceptions of "critical science." A strictly descriptive account, e.g., straightforward diplomatic history, is not really peace research. Normative visions of some future world, such as classical utopias, would also not belong into that category. On the other hand, recent study on conflict and peace comprises areas of concern which apparently are not germane to the scope and substance of peace in its conventional meaning. Herein lies a major source of deep and often sharp disagreement among peace researchers.

The two major antecedents of peace research are the resolve of the international community on the one hand to prevent another world war with its manifold consequences and, on the other hand, to protect mankind against the grave threat of nuclear annihilation. Both these factors have led concerned scholars to view the goal of international peace in dimensions that reach below and beyond the level of interstate diplomacy. Suggestions concerning the domestic political and social order as well as the establishment of transnational non-governmental links loom large in the common statement of several leading social scientists who had come together under UNESCO auspices after World War II.[3] Theo F. Lentz, the "father" of peace research in the United States of America and one of the most far-sighted early advocates of a scientific study of peace, also focused on social-psychological, intrastate, and global factors in his programmatic book *Towards a Science of Peace.*[4]

If we take a brief first look at recent general analyses of peace and conflict, we soon notice that neither conventional diplomacy-oriented treatises[5] nor philosophical essays[6] contribute much to understanding and resolving international disputes or to illuminating the linkages between trans-, inter-, and intranational factors as they affect the current condition of international relations and the evolving system of global politics. General introductions and readers about peace and conflict,[7] published during the last few years, show the new thrust of academic work, but they also reveal the unresolved state of the fundamental discussion about the nature of peace research.

For a clearer insight into the importance of the critical angle in peace and conflict studies, we have to consider the strong tie between the old peace movement and a large group of modern peace researchers and teachers. The peace movement, its pacificist wing as well as its more pragmatic groups, has always viewed government and politics with a very critical eye, and frequently adherents have developed models for internal and international change that have been adverse to the existing sociopolitical conditions in their respective countries. Evidence for the non-conformist role of the peace movement abounds. The question of the stipulated relationship between the peace movement and the students of peace and conflict is still rather unexplored, but efforts are underway to analyze it and to examine its continuities and discontinuities.[8]

A different thrust, supporting the critical stance of peace research, comes from the Gandhian legacy. Gandhi and his followers have always directed their active concern towards the psychological and social condition of man and his communities. This shows in a recent report by an Indian who depicts the dominant trends in Indian peace research as essentially Gandhian in approach, topic, and normative attitude.[9] Gandhi's teaching and political involvement have engendered a whole new school of sociopolitical thinking whose main exponents and representatives today are Gene Sharp[10] and Theodor Ebert,[11] but whose relevance for peace policies is worldwide.

Another crucial determinant for the "critical" (here: scientific) quality of peace research is the question of whether it is conducted according to empirical, quantitative, or behavioralistic methods of inquiry. This dimension of the ongoing debate among students of peace and conflict cuts across the issues which we have just described. The methodological division is more than a mere argument about how to do this kind of research. It also reflects certain conditions of policy research which have troubled many researchers especially in the West European countries and in the United States. For many the question is how to combine "scientific" methods with policy-oriented judgment, especially if norms and values are the subject of their critical examination. This difficult issue is not going to be resolved soon.

Among the various lines of division within the general scope of peace and conflict research, the basic heuristic-philosophical argument is the most prominent cause for a fundamental split within the research community. Many documents and articles speak to that effect and demonstrate the high degree of self-examination typical for a new inter-disciplinary field of study.

The attack on traditional "peace research," i.e., more or less conventional international relations research, has come from two directions. On the one hand, the representatives of the quantitative and empirical approach chide the traditionalists for neglecting scientific precision and for engaging in second-rate journalism or proffering unsolicited policy advice to the practitioners. On the other hand, the radical critics condemn the traditionalist for studying irrelevant issues, for using a much too narrow conception of peace and for serving the powers-that-be internally and internationally by sustaining ideological fixations through the dogma of scientific objectivity.[12] It is clear from this configuration of philosophical and heuristic viewpoints that the fundamental dispute involves at least three parties. To understand fully the implications of research results, it is necessary to be familiar with the major directions and tensions in peace and conflict research.[13]

Quantitative empirical work is still strongest in North America. The underlying normative premises are neutralized by formulating testable hypotheses, which are put through a systematic procedure of empirical verification based on prepared data collections. Recent volumes in peace and conflict research edited by leading quantitative and behavioral scholars indicate the wide range of topics examined with modern tools, the tentative quality of many hypotheses and findings, and the enormous tasks ahead.[14] It is obvious from this short description of empirical peace research that while the methodological gap between empirical and traditional research is self-evident, the philosophical disagreement between them and the radical peace researchers is no less significant.

The sharpest criticism against the dominant trends of peace research has come from Scandinavia. To varying degrees the Scandinavian critics have asserted that peace research will not be able to solve any conflict, subjective or objective, personal or structural, unless it sheds its cautious insistence on its scientific quality and moves toward an action-oriented role in the pursuit of political and social change.[15] Despite the harsh denouncement of prevailing scientific values and endeavors these voices equally reflect unwillingness to be used against the scholarly intent and purpose by the ruling elites for non-scientific objectives. They apparently consider their work as social scientists to be first of all geared toward thorough critical examination of the social and political conditions in their own society and in the international system. This function is concomitant with their open acknowledgment of their personal political values and ideas which lead them to seek involvement in a political movement that best promotes these goals.

The negative judgment about the scientific quality and the policy relevance of peace research, i.e., of its most prevalent type, has been echoed by many younger researchers in Western Europe. The most prolific writer among them is Dieter Senghaas, whose books and articles reflect his sympathy with the Scandinavian critics; his ideas are moderated, however, by his links with major quantitative researchers in the United States and by his own political convictions. He views the researcher as principally committed to his subject of inquiry and to basic heuristic and methodological axioms. The work which derives from his operational hypotheses is supposed to result in crucial insights and arguments that may have an impact on policy. Hence he takes exception to the claim of value-neutrality held by many empirical researchers and to the degree of commitment to radical change postulated by the other side in peace research.[16] Other researchers in West Germany are also affected by the arguments for a critical or radical science of conflict and peace.[17]

It is an interesting phenomenon that little of the quantitative (American) research and even less of the Scandinavian/German radical critique has influenced the study of peace and conflict in the French-speaking parts of Europe as well as in the Mediterranean. Aside from conventional studies in international relations, we find predominantly—at least until very recently—philosophical and heuristic reflections on the ambiguous nature of peace research as pure and applied science,[18] and the massive polemological works by Gaston Bouthoul, who has studied war from a sociological perspective and is unique in approach and provocative in his analysis.[19] The following years will show whether and to what extent an interchange of ideas will occur between this trend in peace research and the empirical and radical-critical groups. What has begun as a confrontation must develop into collaboration, if the students of peace and conflict want their work to be of practical importance.

There are strong indications that the symbiosis of the various types of peace and conflict studies is feasible. Johan Galtung, the Norwegian peace researcher, has shown in his own work that empirical, quantitative, philosophical, and traditional modes of inquiry can be merged into an integrated whole with a socially critical and politically activist perspective. Moreover, his involvement in peace research since the 1950s demonstrates well the growth of the new discipline and its likely development in the near future. His work can indeed be labelled a "critical science."[20] Anatol Rapoport, the famous American game theoretician and peace researcher, who is closer in his outlook to the natural sciences and more reticent to apply the findings of his research to active political involvement, has also contributed significantly to a more comprehensive concept of peace research as applied science.[21]

The study of peace and conflict has so far been undertaken primarily in Western industrialized countries, including Japan. Due to the basic similarity, even homogeneity, of scientific thought and work in this part of the world, we should not put too much emphasis upon the methodological and philosophical disagreements among the various researchers.[22] In view of significant lacunae in research programs and research findings of the past,[23] we neet not attempt to judge conclusively the outcome and merits of the debate among the various camps of peace and conflict researchers. May it suffice to note that a considerable majority of these researchers reject a "science only" viewpoint and support a critical function of their work, but we are not able–nor do we think it necessary or useful–to give a single definition or description of this critical element in the science of peace. Much of the uncertainty can be eliminated as we examine the basic definitions of peace and conflict, since these notions reflect the thrust of the prescientific values and of the research goals underlying the methods and the results of peace research.

Peace and Conflict–Basic Definitions

Terminological skirmishes about the words "peace," "war," "conflict," and "violence" reveal the principal aspects of the current divisions in the field of peace and conflict research. The debate revolves around the polar notions of "positive" and "negative" peace as well as of "personal" and "structural" violence. Representatives of the various dominant camps of peace research have stated their positions on these significant conceptual differences; the evaluation of their viewpoints allows a good preliminary delineation of the various approaches to the resolution and management of international and other disputes, on which we focus in this essay.[24]

The traditional assumption has been that the term "peace" is non-controversial in that it is the counterpart to the state of war; therefore, peace is defined as the absence of war. This conventional conception has recently been reaffirmed vigorously by many peace researchers who consider the prevention of war as the overriding task in the nuclear age.[25] Most of them suggest or imply that such a big assignment does not permit them to pay attention in their research to linkages, including causal relationships, between war and social systems, between international and intrastate factors of conflict. Others see the structural and procedural characteristics of conflict in the international system as the main target of their research and point out that much work has to be done in the analysis of international crises and conflicts. In this context, peace is viewed as "a particular relationship between conflict and cooperation where conflict is channeled into non-violent outlets."[26] It is clear that such a conception of peace does not carry long-range normative implications except for the avoidance of violent conflict or of war in the traditional sense.

Much dissatisfaction has developed over the last ten years concerning the conventional understanding of war and peace. One important reason for this growing dispute is the lively concern of many social scientists that their work, scientifically sound, may have no practical impact on society and politics. The study of peace and conflict is especially weak in this respect, unless the researchers keep the practical importance in mind and choose their subject matters and conduct their study in such a manner that they can come up with credible suggestions as to where and how to change the set-up in the "real world," in order to contribute significantly to the abolition of war and violence structures and to the decisive strengthening of the factors of peace.[27]

Another crucial argument against the simple definition of peace as being an absence of war is the viable claim that behind these words lies an unknown terrain of heterogeneous phenomena which are covered, rather than uncovered, by superficial labels. The concepts of war and peace are inadequate as tools for scientific cognition.[28] Recent studies tend to verify this basic criticism and to render some traditional terms obsolete.[29]

By far the most elaborate attempt to construct a new set of concepts, and with it a new theory, comes from Galtung, who has juxtaposed negative and positive peace and related them to his notions of personal and structural violence.[30] The absence of personal violence constitutes negative peace, whereas the absence of structural violence means the achievement of positive peace. We notice that Galtung has not abandoned the traditional concept of peace as an absence of violence; rather, he proposes to refine the idea and to complement it with the theorem of structural violence and of positive peace.

The crucial problem is the definition and relevance of the key concepts of personal and structural violence. Galtung proposes a broad notion of violence: "Violence is present when human beings are being influenced so that their actual somatic and mental realizations are below their potential realizations"; or put differently: "Violence is here defined as the cause of the difference between the potential and the actual."[31] Personal or direct violence is involved where an *actor* commits the violence, whereas structural violence is present when there is no concrete individual actor and the violence results from the *structure* and is perceived as unequal power, deprivation, and unequal life chances. Galtung also refers to this situation as social injustice.[32] Hence positive peace can only be attained with the abolition of social injustice.[33] In a condition of positive peace or social justice, power and resources are distributed in egalitarian fashion.[34]

The implications of this conceptual framework for research and policy are immense. Galtung cuts across the boundaries of many problem areas and of most social and behavioral sciences in sketching the expanse of peace research. His own work and the publications and projects of PRIO, the International Peace Research Institute Oslo, give ample testimony to this quality. The debate about the validity of Galtung's approach and terminology continues, but his strong emphasis on the inadequacy of the old conception of peace and on the need for the wider perspective of the salience of social systems and of systems change has gained wide acceptance.[35] Since the study of development–economic, social, and political–occupies a prominent spot in academic research and teaching all over the world, even traditional scholars find it difficult to reject or dispute Galtung's basic premise of positive peace.[36]

But the problematic aspects of the theory of structural violence become clearly apparent as we look beyond the realm of scientific research and scientific conclusions. If scholars are committed to policy-relevant work and to an implementation of their findings, the specific qualities of the normative construct of positive peace assume great importance. Does it require drastic changes in the sociopolitical structure of the various modern states? Does it imply a frontal attack upon the international economic system with all its inequities? Does it mandate a revolutionary or an evolutionary course of action? Does it necessitate the globalization of action processes and how is that feasible, or can it be pursued nationally or regionally? The researcher's own beliefs and insights about the current type and level of international conflict and of domestic as well as global social injustice are undoubtedly the decisive determinant for the nature, mode and reach of his active involvement as political reformer. In this respect Galtung retains a moderate stance, despite the unsettling outcome of his social scientific activity.

Many other peace researchers, mostly Europeans, draw from the appeal for social justice a more activist consequence: without explaining the specific details of the new world-to-be, they argue for the revolutionary path to it, or if they do not go so far, they stipulate changes in the political, economic, and social order of such a magnitude that the reader cannot help arriving at a similar conclusion.[37] It is important to notice, however, that in general, the programs for fundamental change lack the necessary specificity to serve as programs for action and to ignite the political imagination of the average citizen.

Senghaas has argued, from a global perspective which he combines with a comprehensive and differentiated conception of prevailing international conflicts, taking into account the economic and social determinants, that positive peace, i.e., social justice, is feasible only if peace research exposes sharply the frequency of asymmetrical conflicts in international relations and the striking prevalence of dependency patterns which characterize the relations in the major military alliances and the interaction pattern between developed and developing countries, in many cases the legacy of colonial connections. He is in agreement with Galtung and others that too much attention has been focused on the military dimension of the arms race of the super powers. Only if socio- and economic-political phenomena are intensively researched will peace research be able to gain a deeper insight into the conflict dimensions of the international system, and propose effective strategies against the conflict-ridden present structure in which even negative peace is unlikely to be preserved.[38] With the help of Marxist social theory one of his colleagues has laid out the critical framework, including its praxeological and didactic dimensions, to fully grasp the phenomenon of international conflict, its domestic and global structures and its far-reaching implications: social, psychological and macro- as well as micro-economic aspects are well integrated into the analytical scheme.[39]

A crucial divisive element emerges from this general review of concepts of peace and conflict: what sets the "critical" school apart is its strong emphasis on the objectivity of conflicts and concurrently its deep suspicion or outright rejection of the subjectivistic conception of conflict. The most outspoken representatives of the anti-subjectivistic viewpoint usually hold disparaging opinions about suggestions for conflict reduction which are based on the premise that misunderstanding is the major source of tension and hostility, and they advocate instead some form of drastic social change.[40] Those who try to join these two perspectives find themselves under attack from both sides. It would be premature—and it is not our intent and purpose —to try to render judgment on the merits of these opposite hypotheses. It may suffice here to emphasize the great importance of these underlying premises for whatever conflict resolution strategies the various schools and individual authors propose as a result of their empirical research and critical analysis. We propose to deal with all these approaches in a truly catholic, i.e., all-encompassing fashion.[41]

A Note on the Methodology of Peace Research

In peace research the debate has been more emphatic and less conclusive than in other more established fields of study as to what kind of research methodology should be adopted. The study of peace and conflict encompasses a huge realm of diverse phenomena and issues, and research is carried out by scholars from many different disciplines; hence the diversity and disagreement regarding methodological questions should not surprise us. Nevertheless, some delimitation is necessary if the peace research is to fulfill the mandate which stems from the urgency of the quest for peace. Some have attempted to circumscribe the field of inquiry. Kenneth Boulding thus suggests to do (1) conflict studies on all levels, using approaches from psychology, sociology, anthropology, economics, game theory, and analogies from epidemiology; (2) international (systemic) studies; (3) strategic studies; and (4) peace research (in the narrow sense). Davis Bobrow has categorized the results of peace research as (1) meta-theory; (2) theory that is scientifically testable; (3) history; and (4) engineering, i.e., social inventions to fit particular needs.[42] The list of what ought to be studied and the list of what has been studied reflect the range of peace and conflict studies and the controversial quality of many of its topics. Both authors would like to exclude some approaches from what they define as peace research. However, a comprehensive view over recent and current research in North America, Europe, and elsewhere makes it practically impossible to exclude a priori anything if it has a direct bearing on peace.

It is much more difficult to judge the strictly methodological dispute over whether to consider other than empirical (quantitative, behavioral) research as legitimate. We find here two principal issues intertwined which have little if anything in common. Eminent scholars, such as M. A. Kaplan, J. David Singer, Bruce M. Russett, R. J. Rummel and others, have argued in varying degrees of determination that strictly empirical work be the sole element of peace research qua research.[43] Yet the nature of the scientific endeavor and the issues and tasks of peace research as an applied social science are such as to refute the claim for the exclusive use of the empirical approach.[44] In many cases, normative, theoretical, or analytical considerations contribute the missing link or open up a new dimension which escapes the quantitative-empirical worker.[45]

Many European peace researchers do not accept the emphasis on a single research technique. The tendency to opt for a broad methodology suited for the purposes of the investigation and less concern for the purity of the analytical instruments is especially apparent among the "critical" Scandinavian and Central European researchers. Most of them openly concede and discuss the values which underlie their research and shape the outcome of their inquiries. Moreover, these values also serve as a basis upon which normative structures for the future order of peace are erected. The arguments of these researchers for their broad conception of the scientific study of peace are convincing, especially in the light of the surge of future-oriented world-order studies.[46] Only an integrative issue-focused methodological approach will enable peace research to consolidate and to expand its contribution in the future. The narrow partisan debate about the quality of *scientific* peace research has not been productive in the past, and the use of any single research tool does not assure success or meaning for the investigation. In the light of large lacunae in the field of peace research[47] and in view of what has been accomplished so far, it seems appropriate to argue for a selective and eclectic research strategy and methodology. However, continued methodological discussions will help to clarify the focus and direction of the study of conflict and peace in all its variations.[48]

About This Study

In what follows, we try to present and to evaluate recent work in the field of peace and conflict research. Our report is not a general survey, but it focuses on those hypotheses and findings that have a direct—or at least a strong indirect—bearing on the problem of conflict resolution in international relations. This emphasis on the peaceful settlement of international disputes could result in a narrow approach to recent peace and conflict research; yet the developments during the last five to ten years suggest a more comprehensive coverage. Many researchers have turned to global and internal dimensions of interstate conflict behavior; others have directed their search for practical solutions to matters which have long been dismissed as irrelevant or utopian. Therefore, we shall include in the following whatever impinges on the short- and long-range prospects of international conflict resolution and conflict management. The relevance of research findings for policy-making is a prime criterion for inclusion in this report. It assures adequate coverage of recent peace and conflict studies, and provides us with a suitable yardstick for the amount and organization of the material to be analyzed.

Initially we intended to include in our report material from Eastern Europe, Asia, Africa, and Latin America, but this proved to be impossible since relevant recent research findings and projects from these regions are nearly inaccessible.[49] Therefore, our survey focuses mainly on North American and West European material. Another limitation arises from the fact that an individual is never able to review everything that has been published or written in this field, even less so as peace and conflict research has gone through an explosion-like expansion in recent years. Not only the amount but also the interdisciplinary range is so enormous that we have to make choices. The major criteria for our selection have been: diversity of approaches and findings on major issues, comprehensiveness in terms of the issues which are examined by peace researchers, and the attempt to bring out those hypotheses and approaches which are not represented in major Anglo-American and French publications. Fascinating work has been done in Scandinavia, in the Netherlands, and in West Germany as well as Switzerland and Austria, work which is not easily accessible to the large majority of policy-makers and diplomats in the international community. If the reader has the impression that a major work or research direction has been omitted while a minor one has been included, he may find the explanation in this criterion for our selection.

Another significant qualification must be recorded here. It would take an inordinate amount of time for the present author to explain and judge major methodological schools and instruments and to evaluate specific research results from that perspective. In general, these tools are so varied and complex that it takes considerably more expertise to evaluate them competently.[50] Moreover, the methodological debate concerns the social sciences as a whole and precedes the emergence of peace research as a full-fledged field of study. The exposition of the various methods used by peace researchers is primarily of interest for the professional social scientists for whom there are other sources of specialized information on these difficult problems. To include any of this material in our study would certainly add to the length of the manuscript without contributing significantly to its usefulness for the student of peace and conflict. Therefore, we have chosen to assume the soundness of the various methodologies unless they are blatantly false or highly questionable. Only in these rare cases shall we try to expose the errors and note the doubtful nature of the research result. We are mainly interested in policy-relevant findings, since these can be tested and applied to further the common search for a more peaceful world.

We have organized this study in such a fashion that systematic, regional, state, group, and individual aspects of conflict resolution are included and that specific theoretical conceptions, e.g., perception, interaction, and game theory, are discussed at greater length. In the conclusion we return to the problem of positive peace, to the quest for research utilization and to the long-range need for comprehensive peace education. By the end, we hope to have shown the vigor of academic peace and conflict research and the high degree of its relevance for present and future approaches to international conflict resolution.

NOTES

1. International Repertory of Institutions for Peace and Conflict Research, Reports and Papers in the Social Sciences, No. 28, (Paris: UNESCO, 1973). The first edition was published in 1966.

2. In the course of our discussion, we shall return to some of these points in greater detail. The issue of research utilization will be briefly analyzed in the conclusion.

3. See Hadley Cantril (ed.), *Tensions that Cause Wars* (Urbana: University of Illinois Press, 1950), pp. 17-21, where the "Common Statement" is reprinted.

4. Theo F. Lentz, *Towards a Science of Peace* (London: Halycon Press, 1955); first published in America in 1954. He warns that mankind will inevitably be engulfed in another world war, a nuclear confrontation, unless a worldwide effort is undertaken to spread the peace movement by engaging in a massive program to study the causes of war and the avenues toward peace, to propagate the results of this research and to insure its application.

5. An example of such a work is F. S. Northedge and M. D. Donelan, *International Disputes: The Political Aspects* (New York: St. Martin's Press, 1971).

6. A recent example of this kind of peace philosophy is Francois Visine, *De la Paix* (Paris: la pensée universelle, 1972). This essay is broad and imaginative, but it does not penetrate the major issues that impede the development of a better foundation of international peace.

7. To name a few, cf. Dean G. Pruitt and Richard C. Snyder (eds.), *Theory and Research on the Causes of War* (Englewood Cliffs, N.J.: Prentice-Hall, 1969); Bruce M. Russett (ed.), *Peace, War, and Numbers* (Beverly Hills, Calif.: Sage, 1972); J. G. Starke, Q.C., *An Introduction to the Science of Peace (Irenology)* (Leyden: Sijthoff, 1968); Daniel Frei, *Kriegsverhütung und Friedenssicherung* (Frauenfeld und Stuttgart: Huber, 1970); Ekkehart Krippendorff (ed.), *Friedensforschung* (Köln: Kiepenheuer und Witsch, 1970); Rainer Waterkamp, *Konfliktforschung und Friedensplanung* (Stuttgart: Kohlhammer, 1971); Dieter Senghaas (ed.), *Kritische Friedensforschung* (Frankfurt: Suhrkamp, 1971).

8. For two recent examples of this self-examination cf. Theodor Ebert, "Friedensbewegung und Friedensforschung–Historische und aktuelle Wechselwirkungen," Jahrbuch für Friedens–und Konfliktforschung, Vol. 2, 1972 (Düsseldorf: Bertelsmann Universitätsverlag, 1972), pp. 156-172; also Hylke Tromp, "Notes sur la science de la paix et le mouvement pour la paix," Science et Paix, No. 1, 1973, pp. 64-70. Similar endeavors, although more sporadic, are found in the United States. It is interesting to note here that Kenneth E. Boulding, a leading American peace and conflict researcher, usually speaks of the "peace research movement," implying the linkage which we have indicated. From initial studies the indications are strong that the peace movement is indeed one important predecessor of current peace researcher, although its traces tend to diminish in the expansion and diversification of the research efforts.

9. See Mahendra Kumar, *Current Peace Research and India* (Rajghat, Veranasi, India: Gandhian Institute of Studies, 1968), esp. Section II.

10. Gene Sharp's most recent work is his massive study *The Politics of Non-violent Action* (Boston: Porter Sargent, 1973).

11. The major recent studies written or edited by Theodor Ebert are his *Gewaltfreier Aufstand: Alternative zum Bürgerkrieg* (Frankfurt: Fischer, 1970); *Ziviler Widerstand.* Fallstudien zur gewaltfreien, direkten Aktion. Aus der inenpolitischen Friedens–und Konfliktforschung (Düsseldorf: Bertelsmann, 1970); and *Wehrpolitik ohne Waffen. Vom passiven Widerstand zur Sozialen Verteidigung* (Opladen: Westdeutscher Verlag, 1972).

12. For this characterization and the following cf. Asbjorn Eide, "Dialogue and Confrontation in Europe," Journal of Conflict Resolution Vol. 16, No. 4, December 1972, pp. 511-522; pp. 512f. See ibid., pp. 519ff. for detailed information about major European institutes and protagonists for the various basic conceptions of peace research.

13. A fine example for the range of axioms and criticisms is the first volume, "Philosophy of peace research," of the Proceedings of the International Peace Research Association (IPRA) Third Conference (Karlovy Vary, September 20-23, 1969), (Assen: Van Gorcum, 1970). The main contributors to this first volume are K. Boulding, H. Schmid, J. Galtung, L. Dencik, B. Röling, van Benthem van den Bergh, and Marion Mushkat.

14. We list a few titles which are representative for the best work done in the quantitative and behavioral mode: J. David Singer (ed.), *Quantitative International Politics* (New York: Free Press, 1968) and his many studies in the "Correlates of War" project, including the recent *The Wages of War;* Charles F. Hermann (ed.), *International Crises* (New York: Free Press, 1972); Russett (ed.), *Peace, War and Numbers.* For an interesting attempt to survey similar literature and to evaluate it in terms of the study of international law cf. Wesley L. Gould and Michael Barkun, *International Law and the Social Sciences* (Princeton, N.J.: Princeton University Press, 1970), esp. ch. I, pp. 3-48.

15. The leading spokesmen for this viewpoint are Herman Schmid, "Peace research as a technology for pacification," Proceedings of the IPRA Third Conference, op. cit., I, pp. 20-69, his "Politics and peace research," Journal of Peace Research, 1968, pp. 217-232, and Lars Dencik, "Peace research: Pacification or revolution," Proceedings, I, pp. 74-89.

16. For principal statements about the nature and function of peace research see Dieter Senghaas, "Friedensforschung–Theoretische Fragestellungen und praktische Probleme," Jahrbuch für Friedens–und Konfliktforschung, Vol. 2, 1972, pp. 10-22; his "Kompositionsprobleme in der Friedensforschung," in: *Kritische Friedensforschung,* op. cit., ed. Senghaas, pp. 313-361, as well as his introduction to this volume; his *Abschreckung und Frieden. Studien zur Kritik organisierter Friedlosigkeit* (Frankfurt: Fischer, 1972), esp. the introduction and the concluding chapter; and his "Conflict formations in contemporary international society," Journal of Peace Research, 1973, No. 3, pp. 163-184.

17. Very close to the position taken by Schmid and Dencik is Krippendorff in his introduction to *Friedensforschung,* op. cit., pp. 13-23, and in "Peace Research and the Industrial Revolution," Journal of Peace Research, 1973, No. 3, pp. 185-202. Fritz Vilmar, "Systematischer Entwurf zur Kritischen Friedensforschung," in: Senghaas (ed.), *Kritische Friedensforschung,* pp. 362-395–a similar line of argumentation is apparent in his other writings–takes a more systematic approach decisively shaped by his socialist outlook.

18. This is demonstrated in the brief conference report by Paul M.G. Levy, Marie-Dominique Simons, Jorge d'Oliveira e Souza, *Le Colloque de Louvain (mars 1971) ou Polémiques de Polémologues.* Extrait de Res Publica 1972, No. 4, pp. 725-744 (Centre de Recherches sur la Paix, Louvain, 1972); also Dominique Simons, "Fondements de la science de la paix," Science et Paix 1973, No. 1, pp. 27-37.

19. Gaston Bouthoul's principal study is his *Traité de Polémologie. Sociologie des Guerres* (Paris: Payot, 1970) first published in 1951 under the title *Les Guerres;* one of his most brilliant, most idiosyncratic works is the recent *L'Infanticide Différé* (Paris: Hachette, 1970). It is easiest to become familiar with his basic thinking through his little introduction *La Guerre* (Paris: Presses Universitaires de France, 1953), a publication in the series "Que sais-je" His most recent work, published in the same series, is *La Paix*

(Paris: Presses Universitaires de France, 1974), in which he further elaborates his own conception of peace and peace research and discusses the other approaches and their heuristic underpinnings from his particular perspective. As an indication of how Bouthoul distinguishes his polémologie from the major conceptions of peace research see ibid., p. 31, where he offers the following objective statistical definition of peace: "La paix est l'état d'un groupe humain, souverain, c'est-à-dire doté d'autonomie politique, dont la mortalité ne comporte pas une part d'homicides collectifs organisés et dirigés."

20. In the subsequent sections Galtung's contributions to peace research as a "critical science" will be considered in detail. For concise statements about the basic premises and hypotheses of his approach see Johan Galtung, "La science de la paix. Historique et perspectives." Science et Paix 1973, No. 1, pp. 38-63; also his "Violence, peace and peace research," Journal of Peace Research 1969, No. 3, pp. 166-192.

21. From among his many articles and books cf. here Anatol Rapoport, "Is peace research applicable?" Journal of Conflict Resolution Vol. 14, No. 2, 1970, pp. 277-286, and his "Les différentes conceptions d'une science de la paix," Science et Paix, 1973, No. 1, pp. 5-26.

22. It comes as no surprise that Western peace research appears to Soviet Russian observers as much more homogeneous than to a Western critic. Cf. here Yuri Barsegov and Rustem Khairov, "A study of the problems of peace," Journal of Peace Research, 1973, No. 1-2, pp. 71-80. Cf. the interesting rejoinder by Kjell Skjelsbaek, ibid., pp. 121f.

23. For recent attempts to present peace research in a comprehensive manner and to poing out lacunae cf. Hanna and Alan Newcombe, *Peace Research Around the World* (Oakville, Ont.: Canadian Peace Research Institute, 1969) and their "Approaches to peace research," Alternative Approaches to Peace Research, Peace Research Reviews, Vol. 4, No. 4, February 1972, pp. 1-23 cf. also Elise Boulding, "Peace research: Dialectics and development," Journal of Conflict Resolution Vol. 16, No. 4, December 1972, pp. 469-473 where she discusses the UNESCO Repertory on peace research (see note 1). Complementary considerations concerning Europe are found in Eide, "Dialogue and Confrontation in Europe," ibid., esp. pp. 521f.

24. Excellent sources for the broad review of terminological positions on peace, violence, and conflict are the Proceedings of the IPRA Third Conference, I, esp. the papers by Boulding, Schmid, Galtung, Dencik, Röling, and van Benthem van den Berg, and Eide, "Dialogue and Confrontation in Europe," op. cit., esp. pp. 514ff.

25. This view has been stressed emphatically by Kenneth Boulding (cf. e.g., his Presidential Address "The Learning of Peace," delivered at the International Studies Association (ISA) convention 1974 in St. Louis, Missouri), by J. David Singer in many of his writings, by Karl W. Deutsch, and also by Alan and Hanna Newcombe, "Approaches to Peace Research," op. cit. esp. p. 10 Betty Crump Hanson and Bruce M. Russett share this view; cf. their "Introduction" to *Peace, War, and Numbers,* op. cit., ed. Russell, pp. 9-17, here esp. p. 9. All these peace and conflict researchers are aware of and sympathetic to the more far-reaching notion of "positive peace."

26. Ibid., p. 16, and the contributions by Rummel and Choucri in the volume. One could add a considerable list of other references which also mirror the primary concern with a phenomenology of war and conflict. For them to understand these events and situations is a promising avenue toward non-violent modes of interstate conflict behavior. Two good examples of such a program underlying specific conflict and crisis research are Oran R. Young, *The Politics of Force. Bargaining During International Crisis* (Princeton, N.J.: Princeton University Press, 1968), esp. pp. 15ff, and Charles F. Herman (ed.), *International Crises,* Introduction et passim.

27. Anatol Rapoport has frequently voiced this line of thinking. Cf. his basic essays

"Is Peace Research Applicable?" op. cit. and "Les différentes conceptions d'une science de la paix," op. cit.

28. Cf. Gaston Bouthoul, *Traité de Polémologie,* p. 535 et passim and his *La Paix.* He has always argued that social science must study war in all its aspects to gain insight into the goal of peace and its necessary and sufficient conditions. In principle, Levy, Simons, and d'Oliveira e Souza, *Polémiques de Polémologues,* op. cit., share Bouthoul's viewpoint in this matter.

29. In the main chapters of this study, this general observation will be bolstered by a lot of evidence from quantitative and óther recent research. That shows the gap between much of the principal theorizing about the criteria of research and the actual research itself. The lack of congruence is marked.

30. From many of his writings we name here only a few basic ones: Galtung, "Violence, Peace, and Peace Research," op. cit.; "La science de la paix. Historique et perspectives," op. cit. and "Theorien des Friedens," in Senghaas (ed.), *Kritische Friedensforschung,* pp. 235-246.

31. Galtung, "Violence, Peace, and Peace Research," p. 168.

32. See ibid., pp. 168ff. This section contains a detailed exposition of the basic conception of peace and violence.

33. A more recent itemization of values which together would constitute "quality of life" or "positive peace" contains personal growth, socioeconomic growth, freedom, equality, social justice, equity, solidarity, autonomy, participation, and ecological balance as "world goals." See, e.g., Galtung, "World indicators program," Bulletin of Peace Proposals Vol. 4, No. 4, 1973, pp. 354-358; here p. 357.

34. See Galtung, "Violence, Peace, and Peace Research," p. 183.

35. For support of Galtung's viewpoint on heuristic grounds cf. e.g., Bengt Höglund and Jörgen Willian Ulrich, "Peace Research and The Concepts of Conflict–Summary and Criticism," in: *Conflict Control and Conflict Resolution,* ed. Höglund and Ulrich (Interdisciplinary Studies from the Scandinavian Summer University, Vol. 17) (Copenhagen: Munksgaard, 1972), pp. 13-36; p. 14.

36. Detailed critical examination of Galtung's hypotheses and findings is scheduled in the subsequent chapters.

37. Two examples in which a religious perspective is used to argue the urgent need for change are *Friede im Atomzeitalter* ed. Walter Dirks, translated from the Dutch, (Mainz: Mathias-Grünewald Verlag, 1967) and Hans-Eckehard Bahr (ed.), *Weltfrieden und Revolution. In politischer and theologischer Perspektive* (Frankfurt: Fischer, 1970). Of special interest in the latter volume are the essays by Hans P. Schmidt (pp. 131-167) and Hans-Jürgen Benedict (pp. 168-217).

38. The basic outline of his approach is found in many of his writings. Cf. Senghaas, "Conflict formations in contemporary international society," op. cit., also his "Friedensforschung–Theoretische Fragestellungen und praktische Probleme," op. cit. For the initial approach cf. his *Abschreckung und Frieden,* esp. part IV.

39. See Fritz Vilmar, "Systematischer Entwurf zur Kritischen Friedensforschung," op. cit. To my knowledge, this is the most comprehensive statement of its kind in the "critical" vein.

40. See here the fundamental essay by Herman Schmid, "Peace Research as a Technology for Pacification," op. cit. Also his "Politics and Peace Research," op. cit. Cf. also Lars Dencik, "Peace Research: Pacification or Revolution" op. cit., and Krippendorff, "Peace Research and the Industrial Revolution," op. cit. and his introduction to *Friedensforschung,* op. cit., pp. 13-23, where he follows a somewhat similar line of argument.

41. For a balanced description and judgment of the major approaches to peace and

conflict cf. Alan and Hanna Newcombe, "Approaches to Peace Research," op. cit.; also Eide, "Dialogue and Confrontation in Europe," op. cit., and Philip P. Everts, "Developments and trends in peace and conflict research, 1965-1971: A survey of institutions," Journal of Conflict Resolution Vol. 16, No. 4, December 1972, pp. 477-510; esp. pp. 477f. Brief comments also in Karl Kaiser, *Friedensforschung in der Bundesrepublik* (Göttingen: Vandenhoeck und Ruprecht, 1970).

42. For further details see Alan and Hanna Newcombe, "Approaches to Peace Research," op. cit., pp. 4ff. and Hanna and Alan Newcombe, *Peace Research Around the World,* op. cit., pp. 6f.

43. Cf. Morton A. Kaplan, "Traditionalism vs. Science in International Relations," in Kaplan (ed.), *New Approaches to International Relations* (New York: St. Martin's Press, 1968), pp. 1-18 for a sharp anti-traditional statement; also Russett (ed.), *Peace, War, and Numbers,* op. cit., esp. the introduction to the volume; further for very pointed remarks Singer, "Modern International War. From Conjecture to Explanation," in Lepawsky, Albert, Edward H. Buehrig, and Harold D. Lasswell (eds.), *The Search for World Order.* Studies by students and colleagues of Quincy Wright (New York: Appleton-Century-Crofts, 1971) pp. 47-71. In "The Correlates of War" project: Interim report and rationale," World Politics Vol. 24, No. 2, January 1972, pp. 243-270, he describes in detail the approach and the main findings of his major project. Rudolph J. Rummel, "The Relationship between National Attributes and Foreign Conflict Behavior," in: Singer (ed.), *Quantitative International Politics,* op. cit., pp. 187-214, and his "U.S. Foreign Relations: Conflict, Co-operation and Attribute Distance," in: Russett (ed.), *Peace, War, and Numbers,* pp. 71-113, are two typical examples of a strictly quantitative research approach. Cf. Raymond Tanter, "The policy relevance of models in world politics," Journal of Conflict Resolution Vol. 16, No. 4, December 1972, pp. 555-583. For a wide-ranging report on empirical peace research see H. and A. Newcombe, *Peace Research Around the World,* op. cit. Quantitative empirical research is still centered in North America.

44. This can be shown in the sociological work which Bouthoul has done (cf. here his *Traité de Polémologie,* pp. 535f.) in the mathematical game theoretical studies by Anatol Rapoport (for principal remarks see his "Les différentes conceptions d'une science de la paid," op. cit.). Cf. the somewhat related argument by Dominique Simons, "Fondements de la science de la paix," Science et Paix, 1973, No. 1, pp. 27-37.

45. For a rather unusual case of highly imaginative analytical-normative peace thinking cf. B. Landheer, "Industrial Society as the Basis of Worldsociety," in Landheer, B., J.H.M.M. Loenen, Fred L. Polak (eds.), *Worldsociety.* How is an effective and desirable world order possible? A symposium (The Hague: Nijhoff, 1971), pp. 166-177.

46. Some major statements for a broadly conceived science of peace are Galtung, "La science de la paix. Historique et perspectives," op. cit. esp. pp. 60ff; Senghaas, "Friedensforschung–Theoretische Fragestellungen und praktische Probleme," op. cit. and his "Kompositionsprobleme in der Friedensforschung," op. cit., esp. pp. 327 and 339 et passim. Also Fritz Vilmar, "Systematischer Entwurf zur Kritischen Friedensforschung," op. cit. Cf. further Herman Schmid, "Politics and Peace Research," op. cit. and his "Peace Research as a Technology for Pacification," op. cit.

47. Elise Boulding, "Peace Research: Dialectics and Development," op. cit. pp. 472f. points out the major gaps in current peace research. Cf. also for the main trends Philip P. Everts, "Developments and Trends in Peace and Conflict Research, 1965-1971: A Survey of Institutions," op. cit.

48. It is in this respect that general reports, such as Levy, Simons and d'Oliveira e Souza, *Polémiques de Polémologues,* are a significant contribution to the continuous

debate about fundamental issues. The least these principal discussions should achieve is a better mutual understanding among the different groups of peace researchers for the nature and merit of their approaches and subject matters.

49. Two circular letters (1973, 1974) to 110 institutions involved in peace research brought very few responses from which we gained only little information. The lack of responses from the East European institutions and from the Third World either indicates that very little work is being done in peace and conflict research or it shows that our request may have been too broad or too specific.

Other reports, e.g., Mahendra Kumar, *Current Peace Research and India,* op. cit., also demonstrate the quasi-exclusive predominance of American and West European peace research and the relative paucity of high-quality innovative research even in Gandhi's India. The leading academic publications which are distributed internationally, contain mostly Western articles and findings. It probably requires a wide network of active contacts and extensive travel to get wider knowledge of what has happened in peace research throughout the world.

50. For a masterful example of a methodological essay dealing with problems of quantitative analysis see Hayward R. Alker, Jr., "The Long Road to International Relations Theory: Problems of Statistical Non-additivity," in Kaplan (ed.), *New Approaches to International Relations,* op. cit., pp. 137-169. Rummel, "The Relationship Between National Atrributes and Foreign Conflict Behavior," op. cit. can serve as a perfect instance of a very complex research set-up, where a detailed examination of a much larger bulk of material would be necessary to enable the reader to judge the approach and the use of data adequately. As we shall see, this applies equally to many other quantitative and behavioral studies.

PART ONE

PEACE AND CONFLICT IN GLOBAL PERSPECTIVE

Chapter 1

PEACE AND CONFLICT SYSTEMS

Peace research is to a large degree shaped by fundamental premises of general systems theory. This scientific conception has deeply penetrated the world of human organization, but a short discussion of specific aspects of the principles of systems theory and recent applications by social scientists helps to eludicate international relations and patterns of conflict and peace in a manner affecting the tasks of the policy-maker.

The Concept of System

THE THEORY

When we talk about systemic aspects of international peace and conflict, we must work with some definition of "system" in general and of the "international system" in particular. The range of concepts is enormously wide. The most basic one is still Ludwig von Bertalanffy's formulation: systems are "sets of elements standing in interaction."[1] Each system must have a specific structure that consists primarily of certain maintained relationships among the constituent parts. Systemic analysis makes sense only if we look at the various elements in the context of the overall pattern of interaction or interrelationship. This approach opens up dimensions of events and linkages which a unifocal perspective on a single individual unit could not detect.[2]

Systems theorists make an important distinction between concrete and abstracted systems; the first notion refers to "a non-random accumulation of matter-energy, in a region in physical space-time, which is organized into interacting, interrelated sub-systems or components," while the second concept describes "relationships abstracted or selected by an observer in the light of his interests, theoretical viewpoint, or philosophical bias."[3] Leaving aside the intricate details of these two definitions, we notice that a key concept such as "the international system" may be either a concrete or an abstracted system. If we talk of the international system in global or transnational terms, we are dealing with a concrete system, while a bipolar or a multipolar deterrence system can be categorized as an abstracted system.[4] Even if we assume that the systems we describe are concrete systems, there are a number of concomitant conditions in supranational systems for which the empirical evidence is in doubt. This should not surprise anybody since it is generally known that the systems theoretical approach derives from the natural sciences where the establishment of the empirical givens has had a longer, more rigorous tradition.

The criterion of non-randomness is a crucial condition for the systemic quality of political, in particular, international systems. Non-randomness refers to the need for a "reduction of entropy," i.e., for a maintenance of the organizational structure within the system for which energies are continually consumed and–as it is necessary–replenished to forestall its breakdown. The ability of the system to prevent entropy is by far the most important factor making for dynamic stability and peacefulness. This situation is called a "steady-state."[5] If this situation–also called homeostasis–exists, the various components or sub-systems are in balance and the system is in equilibrium. This perpetually changing dynamic equilibrium extends in living systems to the sub-systems and to the environment(s).[6]

The interactions and interrelationships within the system are classified as energy processes or information processes. Basic concepts of communications and cybernetic theory are of great significance for the analysis of the structure and process of systems in general and of the international system in particular. They help to organize and systematize our attempt to gain knowledge[7] about previously neglected aspects of international relations, e.g., the boundaries of systems (open or closed), the fragility of the steady-state, the finiteness of all sources of system-sustaining energy, and the crucial role of adequate communications networks and information processes for the self-maintenance of the system and of its interdependent units. Anti-system behavior, grave inequities in available energy, overload, or other malfunctioning of the communications networks are a few major dangers which can only be recognized through a systemic perspective.

SYSTEMS THEORY AND INTERNATIONAL RELATIONS

Systems theory pays most of its attention to so-called "natural systems," which are defined as "open systems in a steady-state."[8] The characteristic of openness is present even in a global international system, since the system draws energies for its maintenance from the environment surrounding it. Whereas the human body clearly fits the idea of a "natural system," including the processes of self-maintenance and aging, we have some initial difficulties in conceptualizing the international system in a similar manner. However, there are familiar patterns, procedures, regulations, and laws that express and sustain the self-maintaining, self-repairing property in human groups up to the level of the international community; the far-reaching changes in political and social structures (groups, states, the international system) over the last fifty years–to take a relatively short period–are testimony to this pattern of systemic development.

Put into more specific terms, non-randomness, "entropy," and "homeostatis," which are highly abstract but central characteristics of systems, can become lucid and real for the practitioner and student of international politics. While the notion of equilibrium has been used throughout the centuries to depict a major goal of international politics, the other two symptoms are much more difficult to illustrate and explain, although they are even more decisive for the process of global interaction. Non-randomness, or a certain regularity of the interrelations between the various actors in the system, as expressed in the rapidly growing body of international law and diplomatic practice, has shaped international relations throughout many periods of world history. The danger of entropy, of self-exhaustion and self-destruction in the system, has also been a constant threat, the stark reality and imminence of which finally becomes apparent to all of us in the face of food, energy, and resource shortages accompanied by the worldwide population increase and the undiminished danger of nuclear confrontation.

As long as man exists, there will be no consensus about the best form of system maintenance, but the fact that schemes for stable world order have been proposed indicates that man is aware of the feasibility of systemic rules and structures for the peaceful conduct of interstate relations, although the perspective of the individual state (or unit) has been dominant for a long time.[9]

Taking its cue from systems theory and from empirical data about natural organisms, one school of thought has proposed that the best method of system maintenance is a unified "decider" or central decision-making unit.[10] That is, in systems theoretical terms, the long-standing idea of a world government, based on the assumption that the separate systems tend to coalesce into more complex supersystems and that this phenomenon in natural organisms applies equally to social systems.[11] Another more heterogenous group of scholars de-emphasizes the world government conception and regards the structural characteristics of biological and social systems as the key to more coherent and reliable notions of system maintenance and conflict resolution in the international system. Morton Kaplan, a leading representative of the systems approach, has based his research on certain abstracted interaction patterns, drawn from history, e.g., the balance of power model, the bipolar model, and some variations of these basic models;[12] others have used different hypotheses to arrive at empirical results about the processes of system preservation and change, and to formulate tentative suggestions for the organization of the future system of world order.[13]

Diverging from the systems approach, some scholars have developed alternate models of the structure and process of international relations, but what these models amount to is, in the judgment of this author, not so much a drastic break with the main systems theoretical conception as a revision of some of its premises and an emphasis on elements neglected so far. "Field theory," originating with the late Quincy Wright and further elaborated by Rudolph J. Rummel, is an example of how close these alternatives are to systems theory. Rummel has tried to visualize the sum total of all relations between every conceivable pair of actors in the international system as a "field." These relations, which can range from extremely hostile to very friendly behavior, are measured for certain attributes along a compatibility-incompatibility scale between the partners in dyadic relationships. Rummel uses vector analysis, in which the direction and strength of the chosen attribute can be given in precise numerical terms and which enables him to establish for each attribute the distance between the actors in the dyad. In Rummel's own language, "the relative behavior of one nation to another is a function of the distance vectors between them on the dimensions of attribute space."[14] The "field," or the vector space, is the universe of the behavior attributes of individual states.

In a recent research effort Rummel used the following measures for his analysis: economic development, size, political orientation, geographic distance, power and status, sociocultural orientation. His examination revealed that power, political orientation, sociocultural orientation (Catholic culture in United States and West European cases), geographic distance, and economic development are the most meaningful attributes to use in explaining state behavior.[15] Despite the fact that this kind of field theoretical analysis works with available empirical data, the main issue remains whether it does indeed replace systems theoretical approaches. The answer, according to fundamental system theory, is negative because field theory operates solely from the level of the individual unit within the system, whereas the system as a whole hardly ever has the same characteristics as its components. If that axiom of systems theory is correct, field theory is inadequate for the systemic examination of the international system, even though the component units, i.e., the states and other non-global actors, are dominant.[16] Considering the complexity of the total system and of its component sub-systems, field theory is, however, very useful in broadening our knowledge about vital interrelation patterns in segments and on lower levels of the overall structure; hence its relevance for a systemic approach to peace and conflict.[17]

Superficially, field theory seems to differ considerably from systems theory, but as we have seen, a more thorough look at its premises and in particular its results reveals its similarity and complementarity. Recent, seemingly slight, variations of general systems theory have had much more important consequences for the orientation of peace research. The major policy-relevant revision is the emphasis on the decisive negative effect of asymmetric interrelations on "homeostasis," i.e., a stable equilibrium in the international system or in parts thereof.[18] The distinction between symmetric and asymmetric types of interaction is a fully developed integral part of Galtung's peace and conflict theory.[19] He starts from the simple stipulation that relations are symmetric only if the actors are of roughly equal rank. Now, whether we consider social systems or international systems, it is clear that inequality of rank and hence asymmetry is more prevalent than symmetry. Galtung and other peace researchers criticize traditional students of international relations and many gaming experts for studying international interaction exclusively in terms of symmetric equality. Once this premise is abandoned, social science is able to investigate social and political interrelationships in a more meaningful manner. Galtung himself has argued that asymmetric patterns involve structural violence, while conflict in symmetric conditions amounts to personal violence. The repercussions of this classification in the normative policy-related sense are far-reaching. The concern here is not for "homeostasis" in the abstract sense of systems theory, but for avoidance of war and for establishment of a peace order in which equality between the unit states of the system is the criterion for stability. In some way, we can say that Galtung looks at "entropy" from an actor-oriented as well as structural angle and argues for a radical overhaul of the structure to achieve homeostasis.

A major need in this approach is a thorough description of what constitutes inequality in the international system. Political scientists have struggled long and hard, but in vain so far, to find operational standards that can be unified into a single quantitative measurement—absolute or relative—of "power" in international relations, even if they have limited their efforts to the so-called political sphere. Intuitively we recognize rank inequalities immediately, but we are hard put to translate this knowledge into hard data of a comprehensive quality. That is a major limitation of Galtung's basic concept of structural inequality in the international system and its sub-systems. Even if rough indicators can be given, the much more challenging task is to arrive at a full picture of all relations and linkages between the units of the system and at an overall rank order. It constitutes a large field of inquiry in which current work is still fragmentary.[20]

From these brief remarks the specific merits and problems of a systemic approach to international relations and to peace and conflict behavior emerge somewhat more clearly. For our purposes it is sufficient to operate with this limited set of terms and conceptions, as most research on peace and conflict does not require a more detailed analytical framework for understanding. The image of the dynamics of international systems that we get from the three major variations helps to evaluate in a critical manner the following peace- and conflict-related theorems, hypotheses, and findings. The merits of the systemic level of analysis can become apparent only as it is applied in the construction of models or in empirical case studies, although it is difficult to substantiate many of the systems theoretical propositions.

Peace and Conflict—the Global Approach

Attempts to conceptualize the nature, occurrence, and interrelationship of peace and conflict in a systemic manner, from a birds'-eye perspective so to speak, are few and recent. This is not surprising due to the magnitude of such an effort and to the difficulties entailed in assembling enough data that support the theoretical construct. Looking at patterns of integration and of conflict, Robert C. North has suggested that various kinds of data have to be used to build and to prove relevant hypotheses. In his judgment, the study of integration requires large data collections from anthropological and historical sources containing information about the nature and transformation of decision and control systems in different societal contexts; if other factors are included that help define the functioning of the socio-political systems, e.g., geographical location, climate, population and its density, level of technology, and the techniques to exploit the environment to ensure survival, hypotheses can be formulated about trends of peace and conflict. A small population with low density, a low level of technology, and a low level of political organization will affect the environment only minimally. More specific figures, such as trade relations, weapons systems and military behavior, and GNP data series, will help complement and complicate estimates about the disposition of state actors toward war and about probable outcomes. These data can be refined for the purpose of using them in the analysis of perceptual issues as they affect conflict or peaceful behavior.[21]

The major problem with this approach is the thorny issue of how to translate all the data from the level of the single actor or of a dyadic relationship to that level of the total system at which all the figures can be linked and evaluated as to their relative significance. The quantity and quality of available or constructed data is a crucial prerequisite for the extraction of findings that go beyond narrow empirical statements about specific conditions and consequences of interstate conflict behavior in a particular type of international system between certain national actors. Any claim that such limited data permit general conclusions about universal perennial characteristics of state conflict behavior is, in the final analysis, based on the same intuitive insight that characterizes most traditional studies of war and peace.[22]

In an effort to understand the basic sequence of war and peace and to grasp their linkage from the global perspective, Karl Deutsch and Senghaas have distinguished three basic conditions of international relations: war, acute danger of war, and relatively stable peace. The guiding question for their inquiry is whether states that are in one of the three conditions at Time 1 (let us assume 1959) find themselves at Time 2 (c.g., 1961) in the same situation or have moved into either of the other two conditions.[23] There are nine conceivable transitions[24] within any time span chosen by the researcher[25] for which he has to find adequate data. The search for the data is not overly complicated, although it is time-consuming. A first step is a clear definition of the three conditions; here the major difficulty is a precise and workable delineation of the situation of risk or acute danger of war. The best way to achieve this is to use some measurement of interstate tensions, e.g., level of armaments, diplomatic tension or rupture of relations, exchange of hostile notes, ultimatums, military moves, public demonstrations, etc. What Deutsch and Senghaas provide is a set of simple numerical figures; these are drawn from aggregate data prepared according to the particular indicators which they have chosen. In addition, they have translated them into percentages of the sum total of measured conditions at Time 1 and of those transitions that have been counted at Time 2. The set of figures thus reveals the incidence of wars and the transitions from and to relative peace during a certain period of history. Abstracting from the historical background that supplies the data the researcher can view the resulting numbers and percentages as a matrix of transition probabilities for the international system as a whole, beyond the spatial and temporal limits of the particular case.

If the number of such studies is multiplied for many other periods and for many other constellations of the system or its sub-systems, the opportunity is likely to arise for social scientists to relate the data to the particular historical circumstances and to draw from that step conclusions about the causes and consequences of wars in the international system. The tentative nature of these conclusions would be outweighed by the cumulative quality of the data base supporting the analytical findings. This is especially true as the statistical data used by Deutsch and Senghaas can be changed and varied nearly endlessly in terms of the number and the kind of actors, the number of years (or months) in the transition period, the level of measurement (global, regional, dyadic, or between groups of states), and in terms of other parameters.[26] The authors themselves propose as an important next step to differentiate between "all-out war" and "limited war." That would increase the number of stages to four (all-out war, limited war, risk of war, and peace) and would result in sixteen transition probabilities.[27] It is clear that this differentiated pattern complicates the data compilation and analysis considerably, but it also allows a more credible approach to the vital aspects of peace and war in the global systemic perspective. Unfortunately, not enough work has been done in this direction so that policy-relevant findings are not yet available. The potential of this analytical mode is great due to the accessibility of the data and to the relative ease of data-processing and data evaluation.[28]

Morton A. Kaplan also takes a truly global approach to the conflict and peace potential of international politics. On the basis of his historical analyses and computer experiments he ranks the pre-nuclear balance of power system highest in terms of systemic equilibrium and stability, while bipolar conditions are held to weaken the prospects for system equilibrium and maintenance. The full range of constellations and factors of the international system (number of actors, military capabilities, alliance patterns, presence or absence of ideologies, non-alignment and neutralism, status differential between the "great powers" and the small states, etc.) is linked in Kaplan's framework of hypotheses to certain outcomes, i.e., the rise or decline in overall equilibrium.[29]

The principal problem with this kind of peace and conflict scheme is the scarcity of adequate systemic measures and of source material for empirical verification of basic causal and linkage propositions. Another more immediate difficulty is the delineation among the different types of systems, especially true since the introduction of nuclear weapons. The traditional rules for the maintenance of the balance of power system—assuming power can be defined and measured—are obsolete for the post-war system. The bioplar nuclear deterrence strategy is a main factor in the remarkable loosening of the international structure; a multipolar international system emerges that does not conform to the principal models formulated by Kaplan. If this is continued, none of his various sets of rules of conduct could be applied and hence predictions about the conflict potential of the present international system could not be based on the previous historical record. Nevertheless, Kaplan's approach is important because it puts customary speculations on a more solid data base.

Other American students of international conflict work with hypotheses of a similar universal dimension, although they prefer to take their data from the body of measures for single states, which are then combined for systemic trends and patterns. Singer and his colleagues, in the Correlates of War project, have pursued this analytical strategy in preparing and evaluating their data. They have examined the power and behavior of states and found out that during the nineteenth century peace was achieved and maintained essentially through a condition of parity in the system, while preponderance of the leading actor or coalition usually constituted the condition for peace in the twentieth century. They have stipulated that the intrusion of domestic political considerations into the traditional diplomatic process at the turn of the century is responsible for the sharp contrast between the two periods.[30] Michael Wallace has concluded from the same data that status inconsistency (here measured in terms of the difference between a nation's power base–achieved status–and the prestige or recognition–ascribed status–that it enjoys in the international system) is strongly related to the outbreak of war, i.e., the higher the status inconsistency, the greater the likelihood of war. He also found that there is a strong positive link between the level of military preparation and the beginning of war.[31]

A somewhat similar analysis of the discrepancy between two measures of status, power and economic development, also revealed that such a discrepancy is to some extent connected with the occurrence of international conflict.[32] Other researchers have posited that past levels of alignment are the main indicators for future cooperative behavior in the international system,[33] or that severe domestic, economic, and demographic pressures affect the external behavior of states and thus shape the international conflict and peace system; for example, evidence showed that high rates of population growth are positively related to military preparation and expansion, whereas high rates of technological growth tend to have a negative link with military preparation.[34] All these hypotheses and findings point to environmental and structural factors that constrain state behavior, both on the level of the state as political and social system and on the level of the international system.[35]

From a sociological point of view, Galtung has developed a more systematic theory of conflict and peace, in which he points to status differences as a major structural element that determines the evolution of a given system and is of crucial significance for the quality of the global order.[36] Taking the two-fold conception of peace as a starting point, he distinguishes international relations as follows: (a) symmetric relations between topdogs; (b) asymmetric relations between topdogs and underdogs; (c) symmetric relations between underdogs. Since he posits that in a conflict there are incompatible goal states in the system of interaction, it is clear that an asymmetric relationship must always be one of conflict, i.e., involving structural and possibly also personal violence. Hence in order to advance toward conflict resolution, it is not enough to prevent violent conflict; an effort toward the abolition of the asymmetric patterns of interaction is indispensable. This latter goal can be achieved only if the unequal distribution of resources and of the power to decide over their distribution is abolished.[37]

From that set of axioms description and projection of the patterns of conflict and peace in the international system derive logically. Moreover, the theory enables the observer to detect indicators for potential conflict without overt violence. It also follows that the strategy for a regional or global peace order does not succeed by simple amalgamation; such an indiscriminate merger policy would simply transplant the germs of violent conflict in asymmetric relationships. If we leave out for the moment the very difficult aspect of general empirical documentation of the presence and relevance of the components of inequality as structural violence, it is not an exaggeration to say that Galtung's approach in the systemic perspective is among the most fruitful suggestions for the analysis of peace and conflict.[38]

As we noted before, the crucial difficulty with this type of global modelling is the inclusion of structural linkages into the analysis of the empirical data that are generally derived from and focused on the single state actors. Some scholars have tried to subject the theoretical propositions to systematic examination on the systemic level with the aid of large-scale simulations, but the results of this analytical procedure are rather inconclusive.[39] Since our purpose is mainly a critique of hypotheses, models, and findings in terms of their relevance for understanding and mastering interstate disputes, the heuristic and methodological issue does not concern us here directly.

Another mode of approaching the transitions from peace to war to peace has recently been systematized; although it focuses on the event, the crisis in international relations, it allows the researcher to take the systemic viewpoint in his data collection and analysis. The difference between classical diplomatic history, case studies, and the study of international crises is essentially one of the underlying research problem and of the specificity of focus. The student of international crises concentrates on those situations that register very high levels on the crisis barometer or that will likely develop into major tensions or hostilities. On the basis of previous work and of specific crisis studies, the analyst seeks to acquire the skill to decipher, measure, and analyze configurations in the international system that constitute an explicit or implicit threat to international peace and security. If hopes for the crisis approach prove to be justified, it may become a useful instrument in deciding on those policies that promote peaceful relations and prevent ruptures in the international interaction process.

Starting from the general definition of systems, crisis has been defined as a "process of interaction occurring at higher levels of perceived intensity than the ordinary flow and characterized by: a sharp break from the ordinary flow of politics; shortness of duration; a rise in the perceived prospects that violence will break out; and significant implications for the stability of some system or sub-system (or pattern of relationships) in international politics."[40] This broad concept shows that there are at least two aspects for its study; we can examine, on the one hand, the impact of the given international system on the crisis and, on the other, the impact of the crisis on the system.[41] Below the systemic level, other research areas include the decision-making process and its structure.[42] Issues such as time, communications, surprise, and abatement are of great importance for both the system and the decision-making focus.[43] Specific systemic conclusions for conflict and peace are still rather random, but as more research is done in this framework, we can expect new significant findings that might sharpen or change our perceptions about the flow of events and about levels of stable peaceful interaction in the international system.[44]

A different angle of analysis should also be mentioned here. The school of polemology and in particular its head, Gaston Bouthoul, have viewed the global system from the perspective of war, the violent rupture of regular interaction. In their view the knowledge of the causes and symptoms of war allows them to describe the dimensions of the various systems throughout history and to recognize more precisely the main factors for the recurrence of war and violent conflict. Moreover, Bouthoul holds that war has been the most significant motor for large-scale domestic and global change and that we have to study this phenomenon in much greater depth before we can develop feasible strategies to lessen its occurrence or even to avoid it.[45]

Using a sociological approach, Bouthoul sees a close interrelationship between domestic demographic and economic conditions and the global interaction patterns. Technological factors are obviously of great relevance since they have always been responsible for the arms levels and military capabilities of state actors, out of which rank orders, alliances, dependency structures, and inimical conditions have evolved. If we take a look at just the development after World War II, we have abundant material supporting the arguments proposed by Bouthoul and other war researchers.[46] The array of linkages is wide. Work on these problems continues.

For the policy-maker and for the researcher the multiple perspectives on peace and war in the international system stimulate their thinking and encourage the development of world order models that transcend the image of sovereign states and of diplomaticopolitical interaction among them. There is still much room for creative conceptualization at the global systemic level, as long as the intertwining of global forces and of pressures and events within each unit of the system is taken into account. We must attempt to make the theoretical concepts and models more transparent by explicating them in terms of specific systems of the past, the present, and the projected future.

The Changing International System

In discussing the endeavors of scholars to describe various international systems of the past and present or to sketch the outlines of the evolving international system we pursue two objectives: we hope to juxtapose global conceptions of peace and conflict, and empirical accounts of concrete systems of international interaction, and thereby to arrive at a firmer judgment about the merits and deficiencies of both types of systemic analysis; and we intend to bring out the remarkable diversity in viewing and mapping the specific global or regional systems under consideration. This diversity is consonant with that of the global systemic approaches and reflects the wide range of contemporary peace and conflict research.

From among the many descriptions of international global and regional systems of the past, most of which have focused on Europe and its colonial territories since around 1600, we need not consider any in particular since these historical systems have formed the basis for traditional university and diplomatic training. Moreover, the relevant insights from that period underlie a large number of models that have been proposed for the international system of our time. Nevertheless, as two applications of Kaplan's balance of power model show, the true significance of these historical systemic factors for peace and war remains in the realm of conjecture which might give way to more certain knowledge only after many more such case studies.[47] What is most revealing here is that in both cases, in the Italian city–state system of the fifteenth century and in the Chinese warlord system during 1918-1928, a major cause for the final collapse of the balance of power systems was the personalities of the major actors involved. It stands to reason that the presence of the personality variable may be the most difficult impediment to a systemic explanation of war and peace trends in international systems of the past and present. Despite this severe limitation, historical case studies on the basis of Kaplan's hypotheses help to shed light on those aspects of the structure and process of international relations that give rise to violent conflicts or lay the foundations for a relatively stable equilibrium among the major actors. The number of actors, their relative capabilities, and the degree of outside involvement (other actors, the environment) are the crucial determinants in those analyses.

Attemtps to analyze the war and peace perspective of the international system as a resultant of economic and social conditions in the human communities constitute a rejection of the independent explanatory merits of the systemic level of analysis as well as a rejection of the personality of the decision-maker. According to premises from Marxist socioeconomic theory, the requirements of the mode of economic production and the concomitant division of society into social classes are seen as the forces that have shaped global and regional interaction especially since the first industrial revolution.[48] It follows that the international system has again gone through large-scale ruptures because its base still contains the germs for the war disease: namely, economic and social imbalances, and oppression. Even in the light of the historical record of the modern industrial age, it is difficult to accept this socioeconomic causal focus as the exclusive analytical instrument for the tracing of war and peace factors in the various international systems of the past.[49]

THE PRESENT INTERNATIONAL SYSTEM

Accounts of the current international system are of course numerous and wide-ranging in emphasis. The main issue which most analysts and commentators discuss is the question of whether the present structure is bipolar or multipolar and which of the two situations promotes peaceful relations among the actors, given the political, military, ideological, and economic dimensions of international interaction. The specific world-view and methodology of the individual authors inevitably shapes their judgment on the crucial effect of the different factors and variables on the danger of war and the chance for peace.

The time since 1945 has properly been labeled the nuclear age. The repercussions of atomic weapons for the military and political structure of the world have not yet been felt to the fullest extent. It is no wonder that many observers have proclaimed for the last quarter century that because of this phenomenon the global political pattern is essentially bipolar, with the Soviet Union and the United States as key actors. Some analysts have gone as far as to make the possession of nuclear weapons the single criterion for the hierarchical order in the international system.[50] Due to the paradoxical effect of nuclear arms on the political and military action range of the states that wield this weapon, this unidimensional classification of states makes little sense, especially in light of the most recent developments. Exceptions might possibly be at the top levels of the two superpowers who have the capability to continue the expensive qualitative arms race.[51] The duopoly of these two antagonists is neither a guarantee for the prevention of war nor a warranty for ultimate ruin and death.

If we take a broader look at the rather diverse strands and issues of postwar international relations, we notice that the bipolar constellation, characteristic of the period from 1945 to around 1962, comprised a broad compass of global interactions of a strategic, political, economic, and social nature. Beginning in 1958, the strict bipolarization has slowly given way to a very complex pattern that contains bipolar, multipolar, regional, and pluralistic structures of global interaction.[52] The linkages between the various categories of interstate activity are now far more tenuous; i.e., a predominance of certain actors in the military-strategic field does not result in their economic hegemony or in their political superiority, thus allowing for an increase in non-alignment policies throughout large parts of the world. It is clear that this new situation in global politics does not permit unequivocal forecasts about the relative increase or decrease in the probability of war in the system as a whole or in one of its parts.

Although most of the available research data fail to give us definite clues about this crucial question, some quantitative studies are helpful for preliminary clarifications or for seeing old questions in a new light. McClelland's World Event Interaction Survey (WEIS) data show that in terms of all interactions a few actors participate much more than the rest: in 1966, the United States, the Soviet Union, China, England, and France were responsible for 40% of the total; from 1967 to 1972, the United States, the Soviet Union, Israel, Egypt, North and South Vietnam accounted for 50% of the interactions. The difference between these two periods is due to the sharp increase in conflict activity in the Middle East and in Indochina.[53] Despite the limited relevance of these findings, we can infer that the system as a whole is affected by local conflicts and that in all the interactions the United States and the Soviet Union have occupied a predominant position.

To conclude from these basic data that the duopoly of the rival superpowers is still dominant is, however, not warranted. A study of the Arab-Israeli conflict has shown that the influence of the Soviet Union and of the United States has been limited, compared with other determinants of the conflict behavior of the Middle Eastern antagonists.[54] This does not mean that the strength of the superpowers counts for nothing, but it proves that their influence depends on the specific nature of their relationship with the parties in the conflict area and on the context of their involvement. It seems justified to postulate that the impact of the superpowers is essentially a negative one: they can usually sharpen and intensify a dispute among client and neutral states, but they are unable, except if they employ their gravest threat, to reduce the overt or covert tensions and promote a peaceful settlement.[55]

The insight that the power of the leading actors in the system is limited, and to some extent non-applicable, helps in taking a critical look at the claim of radical peace researchers that the current international system, seen in its military and economic dimensions, is a structure of "global dominance" in which the Western capitalist states are involved in the effort to keep the Third World and the socialist countries in a state of relatively marked dependency.[56] The system perspective is useful in this issue, since it stresses the mutual linkages among all actors of the global system and the systemic environment.[57] To argue in terms of a global dependency framework without taking these crucial features into account must lead to somewhat distorted images, although the concern with the economic stratum of global interaction is a most desirable and necessary addition to the systemic analysis.

A major feature that has great relevance for the stability of the international system is the existence of alliances and their particular structures. Regardless of whether they are offensive or defensive–something that is impossible to establish accurately anyway–the incidence of alliance commitments reveals the state and the evolutionary trends of the international system. On the basis of diplomatic capabilities and alliance data, Singer and his colleagues have proposed as preliminary findings that a fluid equilibrium of capabilities and numerous alliances strengthened the peace in the nineteenth century, whereas the same pattern has resulted in war in the twentieth century. Explained differently, the empirical record so far indicates that the best avenue to peace in our time would be a sharp reduction in the number of alliances (alliances encompassed approximately 80% of all states in 1965) and a stable preponderance of a few main actors, i.e., a continuation of the bipolar system.[58] Singer suggests that the major reason for this amazing reversal of the causal links between the characteristics of the system and the incidence of war lies in the radical change in the domestic political and social situation at the turn of the century; the collapse of autocratic regimes and the rapid expansion of widespread popular participation and expectations destroyed the classical diplomatic process.

The emphasis on the potential crucial effect of alliances and capabilities is supported by another examination of alliances. In this case, informal alignments[59] between great powers and between most active states were measured and linked to several national characteristics and to major kinds of interstate bonds. The analysis revealed that among these indices only past levels of alignment, and to a limited degree shared membership in formal alliances as well as trade exchanges in the case of great powers, are significant and positively related to present alignments. Indicators such as sociopolitical similarity, similar economic capability, and similar region are negatively related, especially in the case of great power collaboration.[60] To avoid drawing unwarranted conclusions, we should emphasize that this study was narrowly limited to a small number of powerful and active states and to their informal alignments. With this caveat we can, however, propose that traditional assumptions about the determinants of alliance behavior, namely ideological, political, social, economic, or even regional proximity of similarity, are not verified empirically, whereas past patterns of cooperation and alignment explain to a significant degree present and–presumably–future joint endeavors. In the light of Singer's findings about the war-prone characteristics of alliances in the twentieth century, and in view of the continued erosion of the bipolar structure of the international system (in Singer's judgment this process has a destabilizing effect on the interaction not only among the superpowers) the current web of alliances and alignments and the expansion of non-alignments are imponderable variables that are likely to be of crucial relevance for war and peace in the future.[61]

THE FUTURE INTERNATIONAL SYSTEM

Speculations and projections of how the international system will develop in future years have always occupied the human mind, but especially now, in an age when global peace is indispensable and its preservation most precarious. During the last five to ten years the scholarly concern with the future world order has grown substantially; at the same time it has become much more systematic and comprehensive in the projection of trends and alternatives. Concurrently, many scholars have abandoned the exclusively empirical conception of their research task and have adopted a carefully reflected normative approach to these decisive problems. The range of such reflections has widened in this recent development without lessening the traditional mode of future-oriented thinking.

The main dividing line is still between the advocates of a world government, world federation, or other effective management structures, and the proponents of changes in the processes among the decisive actors, i.e., at present mainly sovereign states, but also international organizations, regional groupings, and non-governmental actors. The first group envisages drastic changes in the overall structure of interaction, while the second is in favor, or resigned to the need, of preserving the status quo of national sovereignty. The line between the two orientations is, however, extremely thin since quite a few students of the future world order perceive links between the two approaches to the common goal.

In the search for world order,[62] John W. Burton has from early on denied the practicality of ideas of world government or other forms of transnational decision-making. Instead, he has urged that a peace structure will emerge only on the basis of the current system of nation-states, which should associate in regional and functional bodies.[63] More recently, he has shifted his emphasis slightly to a world society focus, due to the erosion of the state monopoly on political decision-making and to the diversification of authority structures away from national governments, but his thinking about the future system still revolves around expectations of functional as well as regional arrangements as the framework of the "world society."[64] The underlying premise of the decline of the nation-state is at present the subject of a sharp academic debate, while the belief in the merits of functional and regional groupings is also under severe attack. Hence it is impossible in the context of this study to offer more than a very subjective estimate of the relevance of Burton's conjectures.

An equally cautious but much more innovative projection of current trends into the future has been proposed by Almond, who points to so-called "consociational democracies," states that are internally deeply divided and fragmented, but hold together in considerable stability since a breakup would result in a worsening of their situation in the hostile environment of the present international system. Almond believes that a similar development might change the state system of the past into a consociational structure in which the sub-systems would differ sharply from each other and within themselves, but they would increasingly adopt habits of restraint and co-operation in the wake of the spreading nuclear technology and science. The giant menace of nuclear destruction and the rewards for scientific cooperation would become more compelling. On the other hand, he argues that the decisions of the political elites have become much more visible, while the differences in rank and capability of the states have not changed and in many cases have even widened, so that the international system will turn more pluralistic and tutelary. This dialectical development is due to the ability of small states to manipulate great powers to some extent, and to the need of developing countries for large-scale technical and economic aid from developed states. These two trends are likely to bring about a system that is consociational, tutelary, and pluralistic, and that will develop norms to manage conflicts in a non-violent manner.[65]

What is most remarkable in this projection is the mix of factors which together allow for the construction of the future system. If we were to account only for the great powers, the important actors, the scientific-technological dimension, the immense changes in communications and in public opinion, or the menace of nuclear destruction, the resulting configuration would lack in comprehensiveness and hence would fail to provide relevant foresight. Some of Almond's premises, however, are questionable in that they imply an unbroken growth pattern in which the relationship between developed and developing states will not change, or in that they project a continued nuclear threat, the avoidance of which would moderate the policies of all states, small or great, to accept conflict management schemes and to submit to the tutelage of the powerful states. In the end, the future order rests either on the prolongation of the status quo or on the acceptance of rather striking innovations, the acceptability of which is in grave doubt in view of recent history. However, this image of the future order contains rich material for further exploration.

Carl Friedrich von Weizsäcker, the noted German philosopher and physicist, (who coined the phrase "Weltinnenpolitik," i.e., global domestic politics, in which structures and processes are so closely linked that the formal boundaries between nation-states are no longer significant in economic, social, technical, and ideological respect) has nevertheless concluded that, at present, hope for a liberal democratic world state or federation is in vain and will remain so for years and decades to come, although such an order would be best suited for world peace.[66] The danger that the governing elite would abuse and destroy the constitutional guarantees of such a world system is actually the least of Weizsäcker's worries, considering the huge obstacles and impediments that make the erection of this kind of world organization most unlikely. Drastic quasi-revolutionary changes that are required to bring about that state will neither start nor will they succeed as long as the major states and their supporting economic and social elites continue to oppose any significant change. Moreover, those substitute arrangements that could help maintain some stable peace, e.g., a duopoly of the two superpowers, or the domination by a single state over the world, as well as strategies that try to reduce the crucial role of sovereign states, such as transnational governmental and non-governmental links and organizations, have intrinsic defects out of which conflict will grow and damage the peace. States and governments resist any impairment of their ultimate decision authority in matters of war and peace. All these limiting factors lead to the conclusion that the present structure will not evolve into a new future peace order and that only active measures at all levels and in all directions, measures which hold some promise for peace, will enable mankind to steer clear of nuclear self-annihilation and other kinds of self-destruction.[67]

This view of the future international system is characterized by its unmitigated disillusionment and by its avowal of incremental gains to be made from the current status quo. It is spelled out in recognition of the short-term impossibility of far-reaching changes and in the light of the long-term importance of the relevant utopia of a worldwide order of stable peace. To weld these two elements together is a difficult operation and has given rise to misunderstandings and attacks from both sides, from the advocates of the continuation of the current condition and from the proponents of revolutionary change. Nevertheless, the merits of this approach are evident, since it enforces rigorous thinking and reveals the doubtful quality of practically all the major remedies to cure the world of the war disease. Useful policy-making has to begin at such a point of critical reflection.

Under the impact of the long history of East-West tension in Europe, many European scholars tend to conceive of avenues toward greater security and more peaceful interaction in a specifically European context. One line of argumentation that has found special favor with the progressive group of peace researchers is the policy of cooperation, distinct from integration or convergence. The advocates of this policy point to the asymmetrical condition of intra-European contacts and to the questionable value of a full-fledged assimilation that would wipe out the social diversity and ideological pluralism of the current state system. Moreover, due to the low level of current interactions in vital areas of broad political concern, cooperation is seen as the more likely trend of development for the European region.[68] An expansion of the cooperative scheme of interaction beyond Europe does not foreclose the regionalization of political order and the formation of sub-systems of peaceful interaction.[69]

The world order thinking of this group of peace researchers is predominantly normative, although the empirical underpinnings for their recommendations are still quite strong. The general policy advice of cooperation is, nevertheless, not any more easily applicable, as it raises difficult issues about the nature of cooperation compared with peaceful co-existence and with political integration.[70] However, the suggestive quality of the cooperation formula is helpful in judging other conceptions of world peace systems.

World Order Models

As a consequence of rising concern about the future of the globe and of mankind, symbolized in the current food, population, resources, and environmental crises, a growing number of scholars have begun to view the world as a whole in a value-oriented manner and to formulate relevant utopias for a new world order over the long range rather than to concentrate on conventional interstate relations or to focus exclusively on the goal of peace defined as the absence of war. These novel transnational approaches are quite different from concepts of world government or world federation.[71] They also have little in common with the highly important research examining recent peace systems within states or regions, and deriving those parameters for war behavior and for peace that can be applied in global conflict management schemes.[72]

Antecedents for the world order conception are infrequent and diverse. A significant role is played by those supporters of the United Nations Organization who are dissatisfied with the severely reduced impact of the world organization under the adverse conditions of postwar international politics. They place their hopes in a drastic restructuring and strengthening of the United Nations, which they expect to result in the final demise of the era of national interest and power politics.[73]

In this connection we might note long-standing proposals to seek under the auspices of the United Nations a universal agreement not to use violence in the settlement of divisive issues. Such a pledge would not necessarily prejudice the outcome of international conflicts.[74] It is feasible, if we weigh the practical consequences of a quasi-binding ban of nuclear weapons or of territorial acquisitions through overt violent means. To ensure the implementation of such universal agreements one could and should enlist important transnational forces with a special ethical legitimation, e.g., the major religious organizations, which would help to strengthen the peaceful facets of global interaction and to disparage the employment of sovereign military might.[75]

In the past most programs and suggestions regarding the creation of a peaceful and just world were incremental or intermediate. Due to the experience of World War II and the recently growing global interdependence, the insight has spread that there is a large need for a comprehensive organizing scheme to stabilize and to expand the structures of international interaction and of conflict management. The main question nowadays is whether supranational governmental institutions are necessary or whether economic or social organizing principles and mechanisms are sufficient to achieve that goal.

Recently the editors of a symposium on world society concluded that any effective structure of world order presupposes a system of regulatory law, without a formal centralized control system.[76] In an "ecological" analysis one of the editors argues that the global social system, like any other social system, must take care of its natural environment by preserving adequate supplies of life-sustaining resources, and that it must assure a certain degree of social cohesion to survive. The maximization of material capability, a major source of international friction, is seen as just one of three functions of social systems: too much emphasis on this objective leads to failure in the other two. This is how the author supports his contention that world society is in danger due to multiple lags in effectiveness and that a global system of organization and regulation is indispensable for progress towards a global structure of peace.[77]

In an examination of economic development as an indicator for the prospects of a world society, another participant in the above-mentioned symposium has clearly shown that the patterns of interdependence are such that measures by individual states or even by regional organizations are inadequate to remove major inequities and imbalances or to further the developmental process and that they are likely to provoke or to exacerbate sharp tensions, even violent confrontations among the members of the global system. In the light of these dire prospects the enactment of worldwide regulatory norms for development as well as for other vital areas of global concern becomes an urgent need arising out of the logic of the present situation.[78]

Similar analyses and action programs, e.g., ones dealing with environmental monitoring, food storage and distribution, population control, and resources management, are often accompanied by general calls for the adoption of transnational approaches in the endeavor to build a moral consensus among the peoples of the world, and to deal with the common needs in a spirit of collective solidarity. These appeals are truly the focus of the first full-fledged project to develop and analyze world order models.[79] The World Order Models Project (WOMP), conceived in 1966 and conducted under the direction of the World Order Institute in New York, has by now reached a high level of conceptual design and of detailed research, so that a more extensive presentation and discussion of its main features is fully warranted. It is at present the most ambitious and seriously transnational intercultural venture in future- and value-oriented world order modelling. The first major results of this project have just been published in book form, and additional studies will follow soon.[80]

The research team assembled by the World Order Institute comprised social scientists from all parts of the world, including scholars from the Soviet Union; Chinese participation was also sought. They were asked to develop a model of world order for the 1990s, in which five basic values were to be implemented, and to project the transition processes from the contemporary international system to their preferred world. They should take into consideration the ideological, cultural, and socioeconomic standards prevailing in their own region and at the same time express their personal beliefs as citizens of the world. A juxtaposition of these conceptions of preferred worlds would reveal convergences and divergences in the design and in the methods needed to get to the new world order. On the basis of those results scholars, educators, and policy-makers might be able to collaborate to agree on a common set of world order goals and on steps to implement that scheme.

The fundament of the World Order Models Project is the basic values which the researchers adopted as cornerstones of their "relevant utopias" and which reflect the essence of what scholars and intellectuals throughout most of the world pronounce as the guiding norms for a world of peace and justice. The five values are peace, ecological stability, economic well-being, social justice, and participation. A brief look at the meaning of these broad concepts is necessary in order to grasp the thrust of the world order idea.

Peace constitutes a norm without which no preferred world is conceivable. Here the world order programmer remains committed to the original purpose of peace research, namely, the absence of war and the management of conflicts without overt organized violence. As indicated above, a recent trend in peace and conflict research has been to move beyond the study of this so-called "negative peace."

Ecological stability is nearly self-explanatory after what we have witnessed in the last five years in terms of environmental concern. The UN Conference on the Environment (1972), the lively debate about "the limits to growth" are just two milestones for the awakening of the public and for the wide scope of the many issues that require urgent attention. WOMP supports the call for a drastic reevaluation of man's place in the ecology of the globe.

Economic well-being is another general goal which expresses a long-cherished hope of mankind without specifying how this worthy goal can be attained. The WOMP scholars are agreed in their rejection of the present world economic system as being a structure of inequality favoring the industrialized countries of the West, and in their open call for a comprehensive reorganization of the present monetary and trade system that would enable the underdeveloped regions to rapidly improve their conditions.

Closely related to the value of economic well-being is the postulate of *social justice.* Though it is difficult to fill this category with meaning, the WOMP team lists life, health, freedom, basic material comforts, and equal social status as components of social justice. In this manner, severe discrimination and deprivation for peoples, groups, and individuals are brought into focus and the need for their rectification is rightly stressed. If we try to establish a rank order of the constituent elements of social justice, we soon recognize that the consensus ends at that point. The differences in life experience and cultural orientation render it difficult, if not impossible, to formulate a specific as well as universal concept of social justice. WOMP is a beginning in the overdue search for that standard.

Participation is the last of the five basic values. Participation in the decisions shaping human communities is part and parcel of social justice and human dignity. Lack of participation renders the individual and the group subject to illegitimate dominance by a few and deprives man of the opportunity for self-realization. An adequate scheme of participation and representation may take many forms, depending on the history and function of the specific community, be it local or regional. Ultimately, the thinker who is concerned with a viable order in the future must come to grips with the supreme challenge: to propose a global structure of participation which will prove its viability and dynamism in the reality of political decision-making processes.

It is easy to see that the five categories chosen for the catalogue of WOMP norms have built into the exercise the required amount of intellectual and ideological pluralism without which the global research team could not have functioned. But it also shows that relatively controversial and ambiguous principles can be embraced by a diverse group of scholars for the reflection and promotion of truly worldwide objectives. A brief review of the major contributions by members of the group will enable us to obtain a closer insight into the present state of world order thinking and into the prospects for a unified global approach—as far as scholars are concerned—to the actual endeavor to construct the preferred world for the 1990s or for the twenty-first century.[81]

In his essay "World Culture and the Search for Human Consensus," Mazrui, an African scholar, offers his aims and depicts the instruments he would choose to realize them. He places the emphasis on the establishment of a world culture as a consequence of which the other main goals, namely social justice, economic welfare, and reduced violence, would be realized. To move toward a world culture, mankind must reach a consensus on the far-reaching reforms that will further the envisioned world order. Mazrui believes that the first priority is an extensive intercultural transmission of ideas and their internalization by individuals and societies, rather than the formation of global institutions for external (quasi-governmental) control.

He envisages four stages of global interrelationships; they would range from (1) bare co-existence, to (2) contact, (3) compromise, and (4) coalescence. The coalescence of cultural identities would not require a coalescence of interests. The transition from contact to compromise always involves violent confrontation. In this context he sums up the history of the economic and cultural dependency in which Europe has kept the colonial peoples and which is still strong in the cultural field. He posits that the path to a world culture will lead through intra- and intercultural conflict, and will necessitate large-scale mobility which will remove old structures of stratification impeding the coalescence of world society. A model for the destruction of antiquated stratification to him is postwar Europe.

In line with his main concern he proposes a world cultural organization (a restructured UNESCO) with three world languages, several regional languages, a federal structure of representative assemblies, and other instruments for cultural homogenization. His suggestions for the achievement of economic welfare and social justice are vague and mirror his nearly exclusive attention to the world cultural dimension of his world conception. We should add that the socioeconomic goals must in his judgment be implemented primarily within each society and in an evolutionary mode.[82]

Mazrui's vision of the coalescence of cultural traditions in a global framework and his vehement denunciation of the legacy of European colonialism in sociocultural terms prove to what a degree his world order model is intimately connected with the past and present situation, especially in Africa. Moreover, it demonstrates his belief in the feasibility of global unity, although in diversity, in the realm of human culture, formalized in a system emphasizing the crucial role of regional structures. This is complemented by his conviction that the norm of social justice and economic welfare is basically a domestic priority; that allocation is correct insofar as intrasocietal inequality is indeed a grave problem, but it bypasses the question of international inequities as well as the issue of how to counter the unwillingness of domestic elites to abandon their positions of privilege. There is no clear sign whether Mazrui omits these critical points because of his emphasis on the cultural angle or whether he avoids them out of a feeling of resignation facing the harsh realities of internal politics.

As we turn to Kothari's article, "World Politics and World Order: The Issue of Autonomy," we perceive a noticeable shift in the emphasis on core values and in the scope of his world order image. He focuses on the values of autonomy, non-violence, and justice, and contrasts these principles with the present system of a hierarchical pattern of power distribution in the world, exemplified in the military, economic, and social disparities under which the countries of the Third World have suffered so long.

His vision of the future revolves around the principle of individual, social, and political autonomy, which subsumes the values of equality, identity, participation, dignity, and economic welfare. This set of principles must be converted into guidelines for the drastic restructuring of the present international system: Kothari calls for the abolition of the structure of dominance, and for the establishment of a new global system comprising as its units about twenty-five states which would be economically and politically equal and further organized by means of regional and global forms of government. Adhering to his principle of autonomy, Kothari suggests that the basic state units and the regions should be autonomous and complementary, thereby free of imperialism and exploitation.

In depicting his vision for the internal organization of the basic units in the global system, he places little emphasis on ideologies and instead focuses on democratic participation as the guiding standard. However, he does not go into great detail in sketching that important dimension.

Instead he pays considerable attention to the transition from the present to his preferred world. He would rely on available UN machinery, primarily ECOSOC, to initiate the first changes. ECOSOC for instance would be significantly strengthened and endowed with global policy-making tasks. In addition he would like to see a WPA (World Parliamentary Assembly) come into existence in which delegates from national parliaments would learn to think in terms of global rather than parochial dimensions. He would expect a major impulse for the large-scale restructuring of the international system from a strengthened association of Third World countries, similar to the Group of 77. These and other instruments would help to assure the defeat of the "reactionary" model of a five-power world and instead contribute to the emergence of a world order of autonomy, equality, and justice.[83]

It is noteworthy how a long-term abstract vision such as Kothari's turns out to be drawn from and meant for the immediate situation in which the world finds itself. The postulates formulated by him are the direct outgrowth of his justified anger about the lack of justice and equality in the contemporary system of world politics. This results on the one hand in the familiarity of his assessment of the major symptoms and causes of the existing stratification of the globe, and on the other hand in his overly cautious approach to the design of his preferred world, which is unlikely to implement his core values within the institutional framework that he envisages. This weakness also affects his fascinating proposal to erect a new community of approximately two dozen states of equal size and wealth on the ruins of the existing fragmented and hierarchical system. He does not go beyond the general normative postulate, thereby weakening the foundation of his extraordinary recommendation. Moreover, Kothari shares with Mazrui the reluctance to supplement his global perspective of values and reforms with a more specific prescriptive analysis of the necessary changes in the internal politics of states and regions.

Speaking as a Latin American, Gustavo Logos, in his essay "The Revolution of Being," pursues a highly philosophical line in his world order modelling. The underlying premises revolve around such individualistic values as self-realization and liberation. He stresses the standard of rationality and seems to treat equality, welfare, and participation as subordinate norms. His conception about global politics is little developed and fits into the general mold of the WOMP outlook with special Latin American features relating to the hemispheric hegemony of the United States and its political and economic repercussions.

The prescriptive part of his contribution entails a broad scheme for the creation of a free, enlightened, gregarious individual in a self-managed society under the rule of reason and social justice. To build such a community he recommends the addition of a few new powers to the three classic powers of the state: (1) an independent controlling agency to be charged with the testing of the legality of the acts of the executive; (2) an agency for the defense of human rights, a kind of human rights ombudsman with independent rights for the prosecution of wrongdoing; (3) a constitutional tribunal to settle differences between the executive and legislative powers. This machinery could be complemented by the constitutional exercise of the popular right to co-determine the affairs of the society directly through referenda on principal issues.

His suggestions for the international dimension of the "revolution of being" as he calls it, are elaborate without really penetrating the complexities of their adoption and implementation. Together with the common general norms of global solidarity, equality, and welfare he stresses national and regional autonomy, the need to eradicate direct and structural violence, and the goal of universal cultural interchange. To destroy the feudalism of capitalist societies he proposes the formation of numerous global agencies transcending the United Nations, which would administer the economic, social, cultural, ecological, communications, and other questions in a supranational fashion. The United Nations would be replaced by a community of peoples in which regional communities would be represented. He concludes the description of his world order vision by demonstrating the manifold impediments and complications in the way of urgently required reforms in

Latin America, where internal as well as regional solidarity and cooperation are lagging.[84]

Lagos' thinking exemplifies very well the dilemma of world order modelling: how to steer clear of the Scylla of incremental institutional engineering and the Charybdis of abstract unreal appeals for a new universalism as the basis of the envisaged world order. His conception appears to be affected by both defects. Beyond this basic flaw, we must take note of the sweeping rejection of the UN machinery and its substitution with a scheme of federal world government for which the social foundations are practically non-existent, and which are not likely to emerge unless severe ruptures in the present system of international relations will give urgency to the message Lagos and his WOMP colleagues are trying to communicate to the ruling elites and to the general public.

Needless to say, Lagos represents clearly the preoccupations of Latin America. He refrains from addressing himself explicitly to the pertinent class-ridden structure of the Latin American societies and to its immense impact on the sharp division between a small rich minority and the large poor majority. The remedies he suggests would expand the governmental apparatus without substantially promoting the end of discrimination and unequal life conditions. The hope he places in the rise of a large middle class throughout the region is a most inadequate alternative to the formulation of a concrete program for the achievement of social justice and equality. This applies, of course, to most societies in the world.

A last point for which Lagos' essay is a good example, is the close proximity of the global and regional design to the current constellation of forces: regional units seem to grow in importance, especially in the United Nations, where regional and quasi-regional groupings participate to an ever increasing extent in the decision-making processes. Even if Lagos' far-reaching ideas are not implemented, there are strong indications that the ongoing process will strengthen the regional presence in global organizations.

Carl Friedrich von Weizsäcker, the West German member of the WOMP team, diverges sharply from the purpose and direction of the effort to design the preferred world in his "A Sceptical Contribution." Starting out from the thesis that world peace, i.e., avoidance of a nuclear confrontation, is the first and most urgent objective and that all signs at present speak for the eventual outbreak of that dreaded conflagration, his argument is thoroughly permeated with deep-felt scepticism that is antithetical to the core idea underlying the modelling of preferred world order schemes. He explains his sombre prediction by pointing to global political and economic conditions and to anthropological-ontological givens of human nature, both of which tend to negate hopes for the achievement of a peaceful and just world order through ethical insight and rational agreement.

While Weizsäcker's essay deals extensively with these fundamental factors that are decisive for the future of mankind, he also offers some thoughts on the kind of world order he would like to see emerge. This prescriptive vision entails the widely accepted notion that the gap must be closed between the developed and the developing countries, that governments must turn from the foreign policy of the national interest to a conception of the global concerns as "domestic" policies and that a sound world order must rest on the principles of liberal socialism, i.e., of a socialism that does not abrogate human freedom. The welding together of collective solidarity and individual liberty is a precondition for human self-realization, a value that is of central significance to Weizsäcker. He does not restrict its relevance to the realm of ethics, but proposes instead its universal application in political, economic, and other spheres of human action.[85]

Whatever the merits of his basic philosophical argumentation, there is no denying the fact that Weizsäcker's world order projection is really not commensurate with the scope of the WOMP goal. To acknowledge the dire realities of world politics does not absolve one from the commitment to liberate the mind from today's afflictions and to construct normatively the image of the preferred world and the route to it. If the creative thinker is convinced that global war is the gravest and liveliest threat for mankind, he should at least propose a "relevant utopia" as an alternative to motivate his fellow man to do whatever is in his power to avert the catastrophe. The withdrawal into the sphere of ontology is nothing less than an escape, even if the philosopher tries to camouflage it. If we have the impression that the world races towards doomsday, are we not obliged to work even more forcefully for its avoidance, despite all our premonitions and against all probabilities? Man cannot achieve self-realization in a global Hiroshima.

Since our study returns again and again to the work of Johan Galtung, we can try to give only a brief summary and evaluation of his WOMP contribution, "Non-territorial Actors and the Problem of Peace," in which he offers a future-oriented perspective on the place of non-territorial actors in a world peace order. He starts from the major premises concerning lack of symmetry and structural violence in world politics and contrasts the presence with an envisaged structure that would significantly strengthen the function of universal non-territorial agencies and reduce the range of authority of territorial actors. He sees the new global organizations as complementary elements within a refurbished and expanded UN system short of a world government. He compares the interrelationship among the numerous parts of the projected world system with the complex pattern of central, regional, and local power and responsibility in the Indian federation, where the central government is normally not empowered to wield absolute authority over the sub-units of the community.

From a realistic point of view Galtung considers likely the rise of specialized global organizations, as the nature of most political and economic issues will increasingly require global or at least regional handling due to the rapid growth of what we commonly call interdependence. As a consequence of global decision processes the major social forces will also organize transnationally and are bound to participate eventually as such on the universal and regional levels. In the last stage, military problems will also become transnationalized, although it is by no means clear what shape this evolution will take.[86]

It is clear from our short survey that Galtung has fulfilled the requirements of vision and relevance in his world order design. His goal of the control and elimination of structural and direct violence accords with the core values of WOMP and with the shape and function of the scheme of functional non-territorial global bodies that he proposes. He succeeds in his endeavor to render his preferred world realistic, although it is sufficiently removed from the contemporary international system.

Sakamoto's "Toward Global Identity" presents a modern Japanese conception that strikes a fascinating balance between specific concrete concerns and the fundamental issue of identity and alienation. He subordinates the other four world order objectives, namely ecological balance, economic well-being, communication development, and peaceful change, to the value of positive identity, manifested in participation, autonomy, and self-realization. Identity in Sakamoto's understanding is the core of human development. The term has gained wide acceptance especially through Erik Erikson's psychological works. What Sakamoto does is essentially to refine the term and to emphasize its sociological angle.

Having established identity as his core value, he examines the trends in world politics (depolarization, denationalization, and increasing interdependence), in world society (depersonalization of society, development of a new type of racial or ethnic discrimination in which both the privileged and underprivileged groups are fragmented and unable to articulate their objectives, and the increasing dysfunction of democratic majority rule), and concludes that the nation-state will lose its unique historical position as it increasingly fails to provide for the population in an adequate manner. Where can man turn to seek the realization of those values that define the core of his existence?

Sakamoto suggests various organizational and procedural innovations which would put the United Nations into the crucial position to promote the realization of the principal values of man. Thus he recommends strengthening the rights of social, economic, and cultural groups to participate in the deliberations and decisions of major UN assemblies. In this way the formation of transnational links of a non-governmental quality could be significantly expanded. To assure representation of internal minorities and of the political opposition, the United Nations could create a Consultative Assembly composed of representatives of the major political parties of each country. Yet in these organizational changes the danger still looms large that the underprivileged will not be able to shake off the chains of their deprivation due to their financial and organizational weakness, especially compared with the powerful forces that already wield decisive influence nationally and transnationally.

This is why Sakamoto develops another program, one in which the United Nations would sponsor and assist local community-building efforts in order to help the underprivileged overcome their unfortunate condition and to involve the global organization in comprehensive and visible endeavors to restructure the social, economic, and political environment where the individual and his community are most affected. As a consequence of this local involvement, the United Nations could arrive at a new system of world order in which the individual could identify with his local community and embrace at the same time the global values implemented in the successful community-building exercise.[87]

The astonishing thing about Sakamoto's world order design is his attempt to erect an elaborate program of action on the basis of a core value that is highly ambiguous because its realization is by necessity subjective. To broaden its meaning into a social-psychological category raises great difficulties which become apparent in Sakamoto's reflections on the political and social dimensions of the identity problem. In the final analysis the focus on the local community does not guarantee the fulfillment of the longing for identity any more than human adherence to his smallest community, i.e., his family, or to his largest community, i.e., the global society. It just demonstrates that identity is not an absolute norm since its direction and intensity depends on the ethical and intellectual disposition of the individual.

Another point that deserves our attention concerns Sakamoto's noticeable inclination to work with the present UN system in his preferred world. His suggestions for action would require only a few modifications of the existing UN machinery. We deal here with a very limited vision which emphasizes relevance rather than utopia. This is even more astonishing because the indicators he has given for wide-ranging ruptures in human societies would seem to demand a far stronger response from the world organization.

Richard A. Falk's "Toward a New World Order: Modest Methods and Drastic Visions" is far more commensurate in this respect. His essay offers the strongest affirmation of the WOMP core values and expresses his belief that their implementation is not only necessary, but also feasible. Moreover, he is guided by the clear conviction that the present state system is bound to collapse soon and that the new world order must emerge from this collapse, whereas recent efforts to devise "realistic" conflict management systems, such as the five-power variant of the existing international system, cannot but fail.

Based on his well-known analysis of "this endangered planet,"[88] Falk develops his relevant utopia of a new world order which will provide global mechanisms for a disarmed world, for a sound environment, for a fair and equitable world economy, and for the realization of social justice. He holds that the new world order will not arise before the twenty-first century and that man will have to invest all his energy in order to make it possible. In a fascinating series of models juxtaposing his preferred world to the present system and to major alternatives, e.g., world empire, world government, regional actor system, transnational corporate system, and functionalist system, he shows that his design envisages an intermediate system dividing the execution of vital global functions between global, regional, and to a small degree state actors. The regional and state actors would work under the limited direction of the global government and its network of autonomous global agencies. The regional sub-systems would fulfill important functions implementing and complementing the global policy decisions. The states would not disappear but administer the action programs in fulfillment of the core world priorities. True to the norms of participation and representation, Falk's world order would be characterized by intricate procedures for checks and balances and for maximum involvement of the social forces on all levels of decision-making.

In an elaborate analysis of aspects of the transition to the envisaged world order system Falk indicates the sequences and levels of the transition. Proposing a decade of consciousness raising, another decade of mobilization, and a third one of transformation, he puts great emphasis on world order education to inform the public about the urgency of global change and to engage its participation in the phase of mobilization. He recommends social and political actions that serve to initiate and to sustain the processes of change within societies and in the world at large. He also expects certain transformations in West European regional integration and in global functional bodies that will become antecedents for the administration of political affairs in the new world order.[89]

We can restrict our comments to a few observations comparing Falk's contribution to those of the others. His model is least influenced by local and regional biases and he captures best the global spirit of the WOMP values. He also penetrates the ambiguities inherent in the assignment to construct a preferred world model and makes its specific features transparent by describing it in terms of major alternatives of world order. In this way we learn how far the Falk model diverges from other views and designs. We are able to estimate the probability and the time span of the mobilization and transformation phases and the most likely shape of the eventual world order. This is to a large extent due to Falk's willingness to face all the hard questions without abandoning the vision of his preferred world. It shows that the world order modeller can combine normative postulates with sober realism. In our judgment, Falk's essay is exemplary of what should become the foundation of further explorations of the available options for world order and of action programs to promote its principal values.

Lin's exposé entitled "Development Guided by Values: Comments on China's Road and Its Implications" is the last essay in the WOMP volume. The author presents a short survey without much analysis of the principles guiding China's internal development and her role in world society. He organizes the basic values of Chinese development along the lines of the WOMP values and demonstrates that the Chinese leadership has pursued a political course consonant with these principles. In addition he informs about the Chinese position in the international system where China quietly pursues a strategy against the dominance of the superpowers and for a reorientation of world politics toward the real needs of the people rather than what the ruling elites pretend are these needs.[90]

It is regrettable that the Chinese perspective is not elaborated for the scope and time of the World Order Models Project. The information about the current values and actions is useful, but a detailed picture of the objectives and expectations over the long range would have been far more relevant as we anticipate a continuous increase in China's global influence and as we reckon that there exists a Chinese version of the preferred world that differs substantially from those we have dealt with above. Of particular interest would be the Chinese conception of the United Nations and of a possible successor organization and of regional structures in the future world order. How would the Chinese proceed to organize and administer programs of social justice, economic well-being, ecological balance, etc., on a transnational scale, given a functioning global system? Lin's essay gives us a little guidance in our speculations, but that is far from what we wish for. Here is an area for considerable expansion and specificity.

A consistent theme of nearly all world order models we have considered so far is the allocation of significant tasks to regional structures and organizations, even if they are subordinated to global decision-making and administrative bodies. This indicates a general belief among most world order planners that a central world government is neither feasible nor desirable and that instead political responsibility is to be diffused among numerous semi-autonomous or autonomous forces. The commitment of principal WOMP participants to regionalism is strikingly apparent in a collection of essays on regional politics and world order, in which regional structures are viewed as crucial building blocks for the emerging world order.[91]

A second feature common to practically all WOMP members is the explicit or implicit persuasion that the United Nations or a world organization of its type will play a crucial role in the future world order of their choice. Considering the frequent harsh criticism voiced against the United Nations in many parts of the world, it is encouraging to observe this thrust of the WOMP conception. It indicates the continuous commitment of scholars to the idea of global deliveration and management of global issues and to the expansion and consolidation of the universal machinery. At the same time we should emphasize that they opt for a strengthened United Nations or something analogous to it, thereby setting it clearly apart from the concept of world government. This element in the WOMP designs is of central significance as it constitutes a strong endorsement of what we might call a "pluralist" approach to world order.

A last question, with which we have dealt already, must be raised once again. As we review the WOMP designs we repeatedly ask ourselves whether the proximity of key elements in their models to the present constellation signals the durability and suitability of these factors for the future world order, or whether it simply reveals the intrinsic limits of the human effort to look and plan ahead into an unknown future. WOMP was conducted as an exercise in prescriptive thinking or normative prediction. But is it indeed realistic or imaginative to posit that dominant patterns and trends of past and present world politics will remain basically the same even though certain evolutionary changes are, of course, expected, or would it not be more appropriate to break loose from the constraints of the present and develop a radically different image of the future? We confront here a principal issue in future-oriented modelling. Do we extrapolate present trends into the future, or should we make a conscious decision to view the development over the next decades in terms of ruptures and discontinuities and to assume the unlikely to happen?

The WOMP participants are aware of this difficulty in their designs. They regard their contributions as preliminary "footsteps into the future" and expect that others will be encouraged or provoked to chart different world order plans and thereby help to improve the design.[92] If the WOMP work fulfilled no other purpose than that, it still would be truly invaluable. The most important lesson is indeed the challenge to engage in a systematic exploration of as many world order models as possible and in the vital task to determine which of these would best lead to a durable, just world peace.

At this point we conclude our survey over truly global systemic approaches to the problems of conflict and peace. We have seen that the systemic perspective helps to rise beyond the limited and inadequate traditional focus on the nation states as exclusive actors in world politics. The best illustration for the superiority of the global systemic approach is the development of the world order models which would otherwise be unthinkable. We can state that the results that have been obtained so far are most helpful and that further work along these lines is not only urgently required but also highly promising. Intensive research on a wide scale would quickly advance our knowledge with regard to global and systemic structures and processes and their impact on the prospects for a new peace order.

NOTES

1. Ludwig von Bertalanffy, "General Systems Theory," *Yearbook of the Society for General Systems Research* I, 1956, pp. 1-10; p. 3. See here the very detailed recent article by James G. Miller, "The nature of living systems," Behavioral Science Vol. 16, July 1971, pp. 277-301. He suggests a slightly different definition: "A system is a set of interacting units with relationships among them." The term "set" implies some common proportion among the units. The condition of each unit is dependent on that of other units. The units are coupled. This basic definition is generally accepted with a few minor exceptions.

2. Cf. here Ervin Laszlo, *The Systems View of the World. The Natural Philosophy of the New Developments in the Sciences* (New York: Braziller, 1971), pp. 12f. et passim. This book is a good introduction to the principal elements of general systems theory.

3. For these definitions see Miller, "The nature of living systems," op. cit., pp. 282f.

4. Easton's political system, Parsons' social system, or Kaplan's balance of power system are clearly abstracted systems, whereas the West European Community is a concrete (political) system.

5. Cf. Laszlo, *The Systems View of the World,* pp. 37ff.

6. Cf. ibid., esp. pp. 41ff., and Miller, "The nature of living systems," p. 202.

7. The major notions here are information, input, output, feedback, etc. For a general description and discussion of important communications and cybernetic concepts see Robert C. North, "The Behavior of Nation-States. Problems of Conflict and Integration," in: *New Approaches to International Relations* ed. Kaplan, op. cit., pp. 303-356, esp. pp. 305ff. Also Miller, "The nature of living systems," pp. 289ff.

8. See Laszlo, *The Systems View of the World,* p. 37 et passim.

9. Cf. ibid. pp. 44ff. Also Gould and Barkun, *International Law and the Social Sciences,* pp. 61ff. for relevant observations on international law and international system. Cf. here also Richard A. Falk, "New Approaches to the Study of International Law," *New Approaches to International Relations* ed. Kaplan, pp. 357-380; esp. pp. 375f. for relevant remarks.

10. For the term and concept of "decider" see Miller, "The nature of living systems," pp. 282, 289f.

11. Cf. for the general theorem Laszlo, *The Systems View of the World,* pp. 50ff. and 65ff. We shall return to specific axioms from the social sciences further below, when we discuss world order and integration proposals.

12. The basic work by Kaplan is still his *System and Process in International Politics* (New York: Wiley, 1957); for a recent discussion of the major theses see his "The Systems Approach to International Politics," *New Approaches to International Relations* ed. Kaplan, pp. 381-404. For an innovative exercise in "opposed-systems" design, a highly abstract systems theoretical paper, see Albert Wohlstetter, "Theory and Opposed

Systems Design," ibid., pp. 18-53. He tries to answer questions "affecting a choice of ends and of means to accomplish ends that stand a good chance of being opposed by other governments" (p. 21). For an interesting critique of Kaplan's system rules see Alan Dowty, "Conflict in war–potential politics: An approach to historical macro-analysis," Peace Research Society (International) Papers, XIII, 1970, pp. 85-103, who cautions against ascribing system-oriented behavior to states in the systems and argues that those "system rules" which are empirically supported are not system-specific but are part of the topic of strategic interaction.

13. Cf. here the fundamental essay by North, "The behavior of nation-states: problems of conflict and integration," ibid., pp. 303ff., where he constantly refers to general systems theory and to findings from the study of biological and social systems to put conflict and integration patterns into a systemic framework. For a skillful adoption of Talcott Parsons' theory of social systems in an international systemic analysis of pattern maintenance, adaptation, goal attainment, and integration see Paul Smoker, "Nation-State Escalation and International Integration," in: Kriesberg (ed.), *Social Processes in International Relations* (New York: Wiley, 1968), pp. 486-504; esp. pp. 488ff.

14. See Rummel, "U.S. Foreign Relations: Conflict, Cooperation, and Attribute Distances," *Peace, War, and Numbers* ed. Russett, pp. 83ff., esp. p. 84. For a critical description and evaluation of field theory in relation to systems theory see Charles A. McClelland, "Field Theory and System Theory in International Relations," in: *The Search for World Order* ed. Lepawsky et al., pp. 371-385; esp. pp. 373f.

15. See Rummel, "U.S. Foreign Relations: Conflict, Cooperation, and Attribute Distances," op. cit., pp. 89ff., esp. pp. 101ff. for the hypotheses and the results of the evaluation of empirical data.

16. For these critical remarks cf. McClelland, "Field Theory and System Theory in International Relations," pp. 378f. He stresses the complementary quality of the two theoretical approaches.

17. Conflict behavior has been the main concern of the work of Wright and Rummel. We will return to some of the propositions and findings by the latter.

18. Cf. here in general Anatol Rapoport, "Directions in Peace Research," *Conflict Control and Conflict Resolution* ed. Höglund and Ulrich, op. cit., pp. 217-238; esp. pp. 223f., and his "Les différentes conceptions d'une science de la paix," Science et Paix, 1973, No. 1, pp. 11f.

19. For a detailed exposition of this theory see Galtung, "Peace Thinking," *The Search for World Order* ed. Lepawsky et al., pp. 120-153 and his "Theorien des Friedens," *Kritische Friedensforschung* ed. Senghaas, op. cit., pp. 235f. et passim.

20. The inevitable shortcomings of what has been done so far are apparent in quite a few of Galtung's writings and in those of his associates. The categories "topdog" and "underdog" are not sufficient to depict the complex patterns of inequality in the international system. Cf. here Galtung, "East-West Interaction Patterns," Kriesberg (ed.) *Social Processes in International Relations,* op. cit., pp. 272-307. Cf. also Kjell Skjelsbaek, *Peace and the System of International Organizations* (Magister's thesis, Institute of Political Science, University of Oslo; International Peace Research Institute, Oslo, 1970), and Sivert Langholm, "On the concepts of center and periphery," Journal of Peace Research, 1971, No. 3-4, pp. 273-278.

21. See on these points and on their elaboration North, "The behavior of nation-states: Problems of conflict and integration," op. cit., esp. pp. 332-341. The work done by him and by his associates is an excellent demonstration of the importance of these axioms and hypotheses and of the tremendous difficulties involved in carrying out the empirical research to substantiate them.

22. These critical remarks are not directed against North's work that is distinguished in its exemplary caution and precision in the generalization of empirical findings. Nevertheless, the givens of this approach to systemic aspects of conflict and peace tend to give rise to severe misunderstandings about the applicability of its results to different circumstances.

23. See Karl W. Deutsch and Dieter Senghaas, "A Framework for a Theory of War and Peace," *The Search for World Order* ed. Lepawsky et al., op. cit., pp. 23-46, esp. p. 37 et passim.

24. The nine possibilities are (1) from war to war; (2) from war to risk; (3) from war to secure peace; (4) from risk to war; (5) from risk to risk; (6) from risk to secure peace; (7) from secure peace to war; (8) from secure peace to risk; (9) from secure peace to secure peace. See ibid., p. 39.

25. Deutsch and Senghaas have used the figures for the development from 1959 to 1961 in this paper. See ibid., p. 39.

26. See ibid., pp. 41f.

27. See ibid., pp. 42f.

28. This is a good example of what kind of research could be carried out in many institutions throughout the world, if governments and the academic community supported it.

29. See here Kaplan, *System and Process in International Politics* and for more recent developments his "The Systems Approach to International Relations," op. cit., esp. pp. 389ff.

30. See, e.g., Singer, Stuart Bremer, and John Stuckey, "Capability, Distribution, Uncertainty, and Major Power War, 1820-1965," *Peace, War, and Numbers* ed. Russett, op. cit., pp. 19-48. Cf. esp. pp. 46f. for their discussion of the tentative nature of the data and for an attempt to explain the differences between the nineteenth and twentieth centuries in the incidence of war. For a related examination of alliances see Melvin Small and Singer, "Formal alliances, 1816-1965: An extension of the basic data," Journal of Peace Research, 1969, No. 3, pp. 257-282. For principal comments on the theory of war and peace cf. Singer, "The 'Correlates of War' project: Interim report and rationale," World Politics, January 1972, pp. 243-270, and his "Modern International War. From Conjecture to Explanation," *The Search for World Order,* op. cit.

31. See Michael D. Wallace, "Status, Formal Organization and Arms Level as Factors Leading to the Onset of War, 1820-1964," *Peace, War, and Numbers* ed. Russett, pp. 49-69, esp. pp. 68f.

32. See Rummel, "U.S. Foreign Relations: Conflict, Cooperation and Attribute Distances," ibid. esp. pp. 89, 106.

33. See, e.g., John D. Sullivan, "Cooperating to Conflict: Sources of Informal Alignments," ibid., pp. 115-138. This is essentially an analysis of dyadic relations; hence its applicability for the system as a whole is in question.

34. See Nazli Choucri's contribution in the same volume: Choucri with the collaboration of Robert C. North, "In Search of Peace Systems: Scandinavia and the Netherlands; 1870-1970," ibid., pp. 239-274.

35. Cf. here Hanson and Russett, "Introduction," to ibid., esp. p. 17.

36. See here mainly Galtung, "Peace Thinking," *The Search for World Order* ed. Lepawsky et al., pp. 120-153, see also his "Non-territorial Actors and the Problem of Peace," *On the Creation of a Just World Order,* ed. Saul H. Mendlowitz (New York: Free Press, 1975), pp. 151-188, esp. 151-157.

37. For this definition of "structural violence" see Galtung, "Violence, peace, and peace research," Journal of Peace Research, 1969, pp. 170f.

38. For a similar conception of peace and conflict in the international system see Senghaas, "Conflict formations in contemporary international society," Journal of Peace Research, 1973, pp. 165ff. and his "Kompositionsprobleme in der Friedensforschung," op. cit. pp. 347f. Adam Curle, *Making Peace* (London: Tavistock, 1971) also views the world much in Galtung's manner, but he expressly takes exception with Galtung's notion of symmetry, since it implies too high a degree of similarity; he prefers to talk of balance as an approximation of such similarity (pp. 5f.). Senghaas uses symmetry and balance interchangeably.

39. A comprehensive analysis of simulation is contained in Paul Smoker, "International relations simulations," Peace Research Reviews III(6), 1970. One of many examples for a global systemic simulation and the subsequent formulation of hypotheses is Kenneth W. Terhune and Joseph M. Firestone, "Global war, limited war and peace: Hypotheses from three experimental worlds," International Studies Quarterly Vol. 14, No. 2, June 1970, pp. 195-218. In chapter 6 we discuss the conceptual validity and policy relevance of simulations for international conflict resolution.

40. Oran R. Young, *The Politics of Force. Bargaining During International Crises,* op. cit., p. 15, Cf. ibid., p. 23 for the various types of crisis: positive feedback crisis, overload crisis, starvation crisis, steering crisis, adaptation crisis. These concepts from systems theory strengthen the systemic quality of the crisis perspective. For an intensive discussion of Young's and other concepts of crisis and of the wide-ranging applications of this approach see Charles F. Hermann, "Some Issues in the Study of International Crisis," Hermann (ed.) *International Crises,* op. cit., pp. 3-17.

41. Cf. ibid., pp. 11f. for some remarks about both aspects. Also Hermann, "International Crisis as a Situational Variable," *International Politics and Foreign Policy* ed. James N. Rosenau. (New York: Free Press, 1969), pp. 409-421.

42. We deal with these issues in chapter 5. In the volume *International Crises* ed. Hermann, several contributions focus on decision-making in crisis situations.

43. Cf. here the contributions by Ole Hoslti, McClelland, and Hermann, ibid.

44. We return to various aspects of the crisis approach in subsequent chapters.

45. Cf. e.g., Bouthoul, *Traité de Polémologie,* pp. 6 et passim. Cf. also p. 470 where he points out that even the superpowers have not been able to suppress war. Under their rule, proxy wars and civil wars have mushroomed.

46. Cf. the various cited works by Bouthoul, also his "Les baromètres polémologiques . . . ," Etudes Polémologiques 4, April 1972, pp. 30-54, and the essay by d'Oliveira e Souza, "Les Métamorphoses de la guerre," Science et Paix 1973, No. 2-3, pp. 3-19; esp. pp. 14ff. on the "new war." Hopefully, it has become clear from these brief remarks that we find in Bouthoul's approach a rather different perspective from that in Singer's war studies, to mention one example.

47. Cf. Hsi-sheng Chi, "The Chinese Warlord System as an International System," Kaplan (ed.), *New Approaches to International Relations* pp. 405-425, and Winfried Franke, "The Italian City-State System as an International System," ibid., pp. 426-458.

48. For this radical thesis see e.g., Krippendorff, "Peace research and the Industrial Revolution," Journal of Peace Research, 1973, pp. 185-202. Cf. also his "The state as a focus of peace research," Peace Research Society (International) Paper, XVI, 1971, pp. 47-60.

49. The number of peace and conflict researchers who follow the neo-Marxist conception of the nature of the international system is quite large in Europe and also in developing countries. However, broader historical arguments or specific historical case studies in this vein are at this moment still infrequent. There is much material for further

research on these issues. Judgment on the merits of this approach has to await considerably more research results specifically on the causes of war and peace.

50. Cf. here the special French view of Pierre M. Gallois, *Paradoxes de la Paix* (Paris: Presses du Temps Present, 1967), pp. 184ff.

51. We discuss the problem of the arms race in greater detail below.

52. For an attempt to describe the bipolarization of the international system since 1946 with a time series of various interaction data (trade, diplomatic relations, alliances, arms, economic aid) see G. R. Wall, Bipolarization and the International System 1946-1970, Research Report U1-72-2 (Stockholm: The Swedish Institute of International Affairs, 1972), esp. the summary on pp. 71ff. For a brief survey over the political-military evolution after World War II cf. Young, *The Politics of Force,* pp. 42-53. Cf. also his "Political Discontinuities in the International System," *Regional Politics and World Order,* eds. Richard A. Falls and Saul H. Mendlovitz (San Francisco: W. H. Freeman, 1973), pp. 34-48, and Roger D. Masters, "A Multi-Bloc Model of the International System," ibid., pp. 10-29. For a fine analysis of the global structure from the angle of U.S. foreign policy see Stanley Hoffman, "Choices," Foreign Policy, No. 12, Fall 1973, pp. 3-42; he argues convincingly against the unified classical multilateral balance-of-power model that is the cornerstone of Kissinger's foreign policy. Wolfram F. Hanrieder, "The international system, bipolar or multibloc?" Journal of Conflict Resolution Vol. 9, No. 3, September 1965, pp. 299-307, made an earlier imaginative effort to break loose from the simple bipolar-balance of power dichotomy by differentiating levels and types of system interaction.

53. For reports on the WEIS project and its findings–the data are taken from the New York Times and then classified and measured–see Charles A. McClelland and Gary D. Hoggard, "Conflict Patterns in the Interactions Among Nations," *International Politics and Foreign Policy* ed. Rosenau, pp. 711-724, and Gary Hill, General Patterns of Interaction Throughout the International System (Annual Report: World Event; Interaction Survey–WEIS, 1972). Cf. also John H. Sigler, "Cooperation and conflict in United States-Soviet-Chinese relations, 1966-1971: A quantitative analysis," Peace Research Society (International) Papers, XIX, 1972, pp. 107-128. The truly significant aspect of the WEIS project is that nobody had begun such a comprehensive systematic interaction data collection previously and that the team tries to bring out global measures for conflicting interaction, cooperative interaction, and other routine participation.

54. This fascinating result is submitted by Jeffrey S. Milstein, "American and Soviet Influence, Balance of Power, and Arab-Israeli Violence," *Peace, War, and Numbers* ed. Russett, pp. 139-166. For background information and for comparison of the quantitative and non-quantitative results cf. the discussion of the Middle East conflict and of the involvement of outside powers in Galtung, "The Middle East and the theory of conflict." Journal of Peace Research, 1971, No. 3-4, pp. 173-206 and in the debate about the article by Charles Boasson, Galtung and Adnan Amad, ibid., 1973, No. 1-2, pp. 133-154.

55. Two recent examples for this "negative" influence are the Vietnam and the Middle East conflicts. It would be worthwhile to examine this problem much more thoroughly.

56. While Helge Hveem, "The global dominance system," Journal of Peace Research, 1973, No. 4, pp. 319-340, is mainly concerned with global economic structures of the world capitalist center, Senghaas, "Conflict formations in contemporary international society," ibid., 1973, No. 3, pp. 163-184, focuses on the political and social aspects of the global dependency pattern. Neither of the two authors pays attention to the possible divergences between military, political, and economic ranking orders and degrees of influence.

57. Cf. here the Brief remarks by Hanson and Russett in their introduction to *Peace, War, and Numbers,* p. 17.

58. For these interesting results see the more recent papers by Melvin Small and J. David Singer, "Formal alliances, 1816-1965: An extension of the basic data," Journal of Peace Research, 1969, No. 3, pp. 257-282, and by Singer, Stuart Bremer, and John Stuckey, "Capability Distribution, Uncertainty, and Major Power War, 1820-1965," *Peace, War, and Numbers,* pp. 19-48.

59. Informal alignment is here defined as the tendency for two nations to share a common conflict and to cooperate in the pursuit of their common policy.

60. See John D. Sullivan, "Cooperating to Conflict: Sources of Informal Alignments," ibid., pp. 115-138.

61. I have chosen Singer's findings as a point of reference, due to the rich data basis on which he arrives at judgments. Spokesmen for the opposite viewpoint, that a multipolar balance-of-power system would be a more stable guarantor of peace, although often eloquently argued, lack empirical substantiation for the contemporary system that is still based on the nuclear deterrence.

62. *The Search for World Order* is the title of a "Festschrift" for Quincy Wright, edited by Albert Lepawsky, Edward H. Buehrig, and Harold D. Lasswell. Quincy Wright was not only one of the first to study war in a systematic and quantitative fashion, but was also a "founding father" of the group of scholars concerned with world order.

63. For these views see John W. Burton, *Peace Theory. Preconditions of Disarmament* (New York: Knopf, 1962).

64. A concise exposé of his most recent thinking is found in The study of world society: A London perspective. A discussion among J. W. Burton, A.J.R. Groom, C. R. Mitchell, A.V.S. De Reuck. Occasional Paper No. 1 (International Studies Association, 1974), esp. Burton's short introductory paper, "International Relations or World Society," pp. 3-29.

65. See Gabriel A. Almond, "National Politics and International Politics," *The Search for World Order,* op. cit., pp. 283-297; esp. pp. 295ff.

66. See Carl Friedrich Frhr. von Weizsäcker, "Bedrohungsvorstellungen als Faktor der internationalen Politik. Eine Einführung, Jahrbuch für Friedens–und Konfliktsforschung Vol. I, 1971, pp. 15-29. For a critical, somewhat misdirected, attack on Weizsäcker's idea of "Weltinnenpolitik," which is falsely interpreted as a call for a universal technocratic regime cf. Hans-Eckehard Bahr, "Frieden ohne Revolution?" Bahr (ed.), *Weltfrieden und Revolution,* op. cit., pp. 7-22. It is clear that Weizsäcker never implied such an elitist technocratic rule, but referred simply to the sharply intensified patterns of global interaction and interdependence.

67. See Weizsäcker, "Einleitung," in Weizsäcker (ed.), *Kriegsfolgen und Kriegsverhütung,* (Munich: Hanser, 1971), esp. pp. 17-21, and his "Bedrohungsvorstellungen als Faktor der internationalen Politik," op. cit., p. 29.

68. See, e.g., Galtung, "Europe–bipolar, bicentric, cooperative?" Journal of Peace Research, 1972, No. 1-26; also Ulrich Albrecht, Johan Galtung, Pertti Joenniemi, Dieter Senghaas, and Sergiu Verona, "Is Europe to demilitarize?" Instant Research on Peace and Violence, 1972(4), pp. 181-246; esp. the introductory remarks, pp. 183-186. Gerda Zellentin, "Intersystemic regionalism and peace in Europe," Journal of Peace Research, 1973, No. 3, pp. 235-244, offers a good example of a detailed examination of European conditions and likely cooperative developments with special regard to the potential for a system of peace.

69. This emerges very clearly from Galtung's stimulating article "Japan and the future world politics," Journal of Peace Research Vol. 10, No. 4, 1973, pp. 355-385, in which

he portrays Japan as an emerging partner to dominate the Asian sub-system together with China.

70. These issues will be further discussed in subsequent sections.

71. To give just two prominent examples for the advocacy of world government see Arnold J. Toynbee, "War in Our Time," *The Search for World Order,* op. cit., pp. 3-22, and Jean Molimart, *Sauver la Paix* (Paris: Promotion et Edition, 1966). The latter advocates the creation of a world federation. Both works are remarkable for the political acumen, soberness, and "realism" of the authors' thinking. This is strikingly different from the often illusionary idealism of less recent writings in this vein.

72. The important example for this kind of global peace research is Nazli Choucri with the collaboration of Robert C. North, "In Search of Peace Systems: Scandinavia and the Netherlands, 1870-1970," *Peace, War, and Numbers,* pp. 239-274, using population dynamics, technological development and alternative paths to military preparedness as a data base and showing the effects of these variables on the pattern of peace and conflict behavior in these communities. Similar research efforts for other areas and other periods are currently in progress.

73. One of the earliest and most significant programs for the overhauling of the UN system is that of Grenville Clark and Louis Sohn, *World Peace Through World Law* (Cambridge: Harvard University Press, 1966), the introduction to which has recently been revised by the latter. Cf. Clark and Sohn, *Introduction to World Peace Through World Law* (Chicago: World Without War Publications, 1973).

74. To give just one example we refer here to Arthur I. Waskow, "Nonlethal Equivalents of War," *International Conflict and Behavioral Science* ed. Roger Fisher (New York: Basic Books, 1964), pp. 123-141; p. 135, who arrives at his suggestion on the basis of the examination of four cold war conflicts.

75. Cf. here Ulrich Duchrow, " 'Gerechte Gewart,' Gewalttätigkeit und Gewaltlosigkeit im B-Waffen-Zeitalter," *BC-Waffen und Friedenspolitik* ed. Ernst von Weizsäcker, Studien zur Friedensforschung, Vol. 5 (Munich: Kösel; Stuttgart: Klett, 1970), pp. 112-136; p. 132. He points to some precedents in which the churches clearly criticized governmental actions, and proposes a principal withdrawal of church approval for current conflict behavior of states and governments. Other transnational organizations, such as labor unions, scientific and academic associations, professional and business organizations, could also play similar roles enhancing peaceful mechanisms in global politics.

76. See Landheer, Loenen, and Polak, "Editorial Introduction," *Worldsociety,* op. cit., pp. 3f. They point out that these views are still disputed by some. They argue that stability is necessary to produce an *effective* world order.

77. See B. Landheer, "Industrial Society as the Basis of Worldsociety," ibid., pp. 168-177; esp. pp. 171f. What is new and interesting about this essay is the deliberate application of sociological and ecological standards to the conceptual framework of a global social system.

78. See Bruno Fritsch, "The Problem of a Global Social Order," ibid., pp. 148-154; esp. pp. 153f., and the legal study by Wil D. Verwey, *Economic Development, Peace, and International Law* (Assen: Van Gorcum, 1972), who stresses the continuing need for the elaboration of UN charters and programs and their legal codification to assure peaceful economic development.

79. For some of the immediate antecedents cf. here Richard A. Falk, "Bipolarity and the Future of World Society," *Worldsociety* ed. Landheer et al., op. cit., pp. 102-114, esp. pp. 113f. Cf. also Falk, "The Trend Toward World Community: An Inventory of Issues," *The Search for World Order* ed. Lepawsky et al., op. cit., pp. 353-370. Quincy Wright, "Building a Social System for Mankind," *Worldsociety,* op. cit., pp. 178-196;

p. 194 also emphasizes education as a major instrument for globalizing the awareness and the peaceable inclinations of the average citizen. For an interesting attempt to formulate a basic conceptual proposition about the theory of collective goods in its relationship to international organization cf. Bruce M. Russett and John D. Sullivan, "Collective goods and international organization," International Organization, Vol. 25, No. 4, Autumn 1971, pp. 845-865, and the comment by Mancur Olson, "Increasing the incentives for international cooperation," ibid., pp. 866-874.

80. For basic information on the history of the World Order Models Project see Saul H. Mendlovitz, "Introduction" *On the Creation of a Just World Order.* Preferred Worlds for the 1990s, op. cit., pp. vii-xvii, also Mendlovitz and Thomas G. Weiss, "Toward Consensus: The World Order Models Project of the Institute for World Order," Clark and Sohn, *Introduction to World Peace Through World Law,* op. cit., pp. 74-97. For a more teaching-oriented paper on the project cf. Norman W. and Thomas G. Weiss, *A World Order Framework for Teaching International Politics* (New York: Institute for World Order, 1974).

On the Creation of a Just World Order, the lead volume, consists of essays by the various members of the WOMP research team from different regions of the world. Full book-length studies by several of these individual scholars, reporting their views and issues in greater detail, are already available: Rajni Kothari: *Footsteps in the Future: Diagnosis of the Present World and a Design for an Alternative* (New York: Free Press, 1975) and Richard A. Falk, *A Study of Future Worlds* (New York: Free Press, 1975). Additional volumes by Mazrui and Galtung are to follow in the near future.

81. In the following we shall discuss the main points proposed by the contributors to *On the Creation of a Just World Order.*

82. See Ali A. Mazrui, "World Culture and the Search for Human Consensus," ibid., pp. 1-37.

83. See here Rajni Kothari, "World Politics and World Order: The Issue of Autonomy," ibid., pp. 39-69. For an extended version of his ideas consult his *Footsteps into the Future,* op. cit.

84. For these points see Gustavo Lagos, "The Revolution of Being," *On the Creation of a Just World Order,* pp. 71-109.

85. See Carl Friedrich von Weizsäcker, "A Sceptical Contribution," ibid., pp. 111-150.

86. See John Galtung, "Non-territorial Actors and the Problem of Peace," ibid., pp. 151-188.

87. See Yoshikazu Sakamoto, "Toward Global Identity," ibid., pp. 189-210.

88. Richard A. Falk, *This Endangered Planet: Prospects and Proposals for Human Survival* (New York: Random House, 1971).

89. See Falk, "Toward a New World Order: Modest Methods and Drastic Visions," *On the Creation of a Just World Order,* pp. 211-258. For a detailed exposition of his world order design consult his *A Study of Future Worlds.*

90. See Paul T.K. Lin, "Development Guided by Values: Comments on China's Road and Its Implications," *On the Creation of a Just World Order,* pp. 259-296.

91. See Falk and Mendlovitz (eds.), *Regional Politics and World Order* op. cit., esp. the essays by Masters and Young and the introductory and analytical comments by Falk and Mendlovitz. We shall return to the role of regional integration for world peace in ch. 2.

92. George Kent of the University of Hawaii has analyzed the whole issue of design for the future and of world order designs in particular. Cf. here his "Plan for designing the future," Bulletin of Peace Proposals, 1972, pp. 280-285, his "Political design," The Dimensionality of Nations Project, Research Report No. 63, 1972, and his "World Order Design: What Could Be More Practical?" (unpublished manuscript). On the specific characteristics of the WOMP design as defined by its director cf. Mendlovitz, introduction to *On the Creation of a Just World Order,* especially pp. VIII-XVI.

Chapter 2

DIMENSIONS OF INTERNATIONAL PEACE AND CONFLICT

New Aspects of Strategic Deterrence and of the Arms Race

Any attempt in this paper to deal with the full range of either the study of modern strategy or the debate about the arms race would be futile, mainly due to the infinite complexity of the issues and conceptions and to the sheer mass of material published since World War II. It is in this area that communication and interaction between the policy-makers and those who execute their decisions on the one hand and the researchers and critics on the other have been most intensive and consequential. The highly technical nature of the subject matter restricts the possible audience considerably and lends itself to easy and frequent distortion, misinformation, and manipulation. Moreover, the discussion of most of the problems relating to strategy and disarmament, arms race, and arms control is inevitably politicized to a considerable degree, and unfortunately, aside from a few recent cases, the advocates of disarmament and effective arms control have not really been able to advance their cause by straightforward practice-related scholarly work emphasizing the opportunities and impediments of the implementation of their program.

All these factors force us to propose a tentative and limited examination of some of the new aspects that peace researchers have introduced into the discussion. Opinions will be presented that are critical of the mainstream of strategic thinking, which, however, is merely alluded to. In addition, we are trying to give at least a glimpse of the extent and diversity of the work of peace and conflict researchers in the whole field. Last, since the questions are of immediate policy relevance, the debate has been carried on with much calculation and fervor, but so far with little empirical foundation. This makes it utterly hard to state anything in other than speculative terms.

The most important single factor causing deep concern among the advocates of détente and disarmament is the continuing nuclear arms race between the two superpowers, and the impact this development has on the various efforts to adopt some kind of arms control measure that would liberate the states from the vicious cycle of arms acquisition and arms development. Many hold that the Soviet-American competition has affected the growth of the arms sector in many countries, in that outdated equipment has been handed down to less powerful and less resource-rich states, and in that the arms industry of the two superpowers and of other major actors has sought to expand its market for cost and profit reasons.[1]

The phenomenon of the arms race has been the subject of considerable attention, partly owing to the availability of data that allow for quantitative analysis. The characteristics of the arms race and the nature of the specific interrelationship between those involved in the race, as well as their impact on the overall stability and cooperation in the international system, have been demonstrated on several occasions.[2] It is relatively simple to collect military budget data, but the reliability of the findings is somewhat uncertain because the direct translation of the budget data—or other similar figures—into the conflict behavior dimension is subject to considerable doubt, due to the impact of many other elements that enter into the cognitive and perceptual screening process of the decision-makers in the interaction.[3]

As is well known, the special qualities of nuclear weapons and nuclear warfare, as strategic thinkers view them, tend to complicate the assumptions we hold about military preparations and the likelihood of open war. The main causes for this uncertainty are the erosion of pre-nuclear standards of the calculability of the consequences of military action, and the constant danger for both the nuclear power and the non-nuclear vassal state that the one may be held accountable for the measures taken by the other; both these factors give the non-nuclear states considerable leeway and tie the superpowers in a paradoxical fashion.[4] If these factors are indeed significant for the current military constellation, the main credo of strategic deterrence focusing exclusively on the superpowers needs correction to forestall severe crises that could lead to a fatal collapse of the present global system.

Some authors have criticized the theory of strategic deterrence on principal conceptual grounds. Thus Rapoport has argued persuasively that strategic thinkers have tended to simplify *and* to misrepresent the problems involved in making the decision problems more tractable; he has tried to show in particular the fallacy of the assumption of rational thinking that is basic to strategic analysis.[5] Seen from various angles, the inadequacy of the strategic theorem is easily demonstrated. Unilinear definitions of what is rational in a constellation of strategic deterrence are practically impossible. One author showed that the common assumption that a hard-line foreign policy provides the opponent with an incentive for a negotiated agreement is highly questionable, and that in arms control negotiations intrinsic factors in the negotiations proper weighed equally or more heavily than the influences deriving from the international environment.[6] In another study the thesis that increased trade with a rival will result in rising levels of arms production proved to be nearly inapplicable in the American-Russian threat system.[7] If we try to measure the power of the parties in a crisis situation, we face an endlessly difficult task. Military, economic, geographical, or resource data are each not sufficient; such elusive notions as "national morale" or the unwillingness to suffer or the cost-tolerance are usually given some weight, but a recent essay on the possible connection between cost-tolerance, wealth, and defeat or victory in war shows that the willingness to suffer is by far too weak to overcome the disparities in wealth or in population size of the war parties.[8] Despite the uncertainty of this finding in its policy relevance, it demonstrates the impossibility of defining the composite standard of power and establishing a scale of relative significance. However, a high level of precision is assumed—and is necessary—in the calculations of strategic theory.

A West German research team has used strategic data for a substantive examination of recent developments (ABM) and of the future implications of new programs, such as MIRV. The main focus has been to establish quantitatively the likelihood either of a decline in stability or of its maintenance; the spokesmen for continued strategic arms development claim that the latter results from a further build-up. The German researchers have acknowledged that the system of deterrence has so far proven its overall stability; yet in several detailed analyses, e.g., computer simulations, they arrived at the conclusion that MIRV and ABM will destabilize the future strategic relationship and will sharply reduce the calculability of the risk which has been the main guarantor of the relative peace. The proliferation of nuclear weapons is bound to exacerbate this process.[9]

Although the recent qualitative advances in weapons technology may not be reflected by increases in the military budgets of the superpowers,[10] it is undeniable that a discontinuation of the ABM and MIRV programs would result in considerable savings for the governments and societies involved, and it would be a great bonus in the long search for effective disarmament, a search that has long been delayed for reasons of so-called security. Moreover, a lessened emphasis on strategic analysis would enhance the study of possibly more important issues, such as the goals of international interaction and better ways of preventing and resolving violent conflict.[11]

On this list of significant but neglected topics we also include the under-researched problem of partial and complete disarmament. It has been the custom to link these questions with that of arms control. In this way the fundamental difference between these two objectives has been obscured. Disarmament is not an idealistic or utopian suggestion; its crucial characteristic lies in its arms-reducing direction, while arms control amounts to controlled arms build-up or at best to a termination of weapons acquisition without requiring the discarding of the available arms holdings. If we accept this distinction, it is clear that the study of disarmament involves a host of problems that are of no concern in arms control and have been neglected by most traditional and modern peace and conflict researchers. From available records it appears that the socialist countries have devoted considerable time and attention to many of the primary and secondary aspects of disarmement, including projections as to the nature of different political, social, and economic systems in a disarmed condition.[12] In America and in Western Europe disarmament problems have figured in research and not just in advocacy primarily in studies of the process of conflict resolution, while little room has been given to long-range social and political aspects. Most serious researchers have rejected the strategy of unilateral disarmament in particular as long as an effective procedure for the settling of grievances is not agreed upon.[13]

Two interesting suggestions that transcend the customary range of disarmament discussions and have a long-term perspective deserve special mention at this point. In 1963, John C. Polanyi proposed that specially sealed records caches on arms stockpiles and production should be established immediately in order to be available at later stages for a disarmament program to check declared inventories. He indicated specific techniques to make those records secure against tampering and detailed the nature of the material to be deposited and the likely results of such an agreement.[14]

A farther-reaching proposal that still seems eminently practicable envisages the transfer of code-locked nuclear weapons from the individual states to a Weapons Transfer Agency, which would station these stockpiles at random locations throughout the territory of the member states or elsewhere, and could not use these weapons unless authorized by a majority vote of the members' council. In this manner, the nuclear weapons could no longer be used by single states, but the members would be able to prevent each other from misuse or threats by unlocking their own weapons for use by the collective force of the council. The emphasis here is not on the usage but rather on mutually agreed de facto de-nuclearization and on gradual increase in mutual trust and confidence, with a built-in guarantee against unilateral misuse. The proposal also includes an elaborate inspection scheme, a stipulation that could be a considerable impediment to implementation of this program.[15]

Despite some intrinsic weaknesses in both proposals (the reliability of the information; the need for elaborate inspection; the possibility of collusion of a majority of the participants to get rid of a member or outside rival by employing the procedures provided for in the principal weapons transfer agreement; the problem that important nuclear and near-nuclear states refuse to join either of the two schemes) it is urgent that such practical measures be intensively studied and considered for political adoption as soon as the exact provisions of these schemes have been worked out. The two proposals could be implemented successively or concurrently, depending on the initial level of mutual cooperative thinking among a sufficiently large group of states. These problems could benefit from the kind of careful and detailed research that at this moment goes mostly into issues of strategic deterrence and threat systems. Policy-makers have an excellent opportunity here to redirect the whole research effort without abandoning the criterion of policy relevance.

In recent years, an effort has been made to look at the whole deterrence and arms race problem from a basic critical angle; in which linkages are tested between the behavior of states in the arms field and domestic social-psychological and socioeconomic conditions. The theory of the pathology of organized peacelessness has been the work of Dieter Senghaas, the West German political scientist, whose views have given rise to a lively and important debate, the outcome of which is still completely open. Due to the comprehensive quality of his critical approach it is necessary, even in our limited endeavor, to examine a wide range of contended issues and hypotheses, some of which may initially have little connection with the strategic problem in its global dimension. It would appear most suitable to give a concise summary of Senghaas' position and then to engage in the analysis of major points of interest for our purposes.

Against the dominant assumption that strategic interaction in the threat system follows the action-reaction scheme, Senghaas has posited, on theoretical grounds as well as in recognition of a number of empirical observations, that governments and political elites base their armaments and deterrence policies to a large degree on autonomous inner-directed motives and goals that derive from and focus upon domestic groups and needs rather the moves of the external opponents. This hypothesis is not too different from the viewpoint of the critics of the "military-industrial complex." Moreover, it is related to the Marxist principle that behavior of states and societies is foremost the consequence of the respective social systems and of the processes of societal interaction.[16]

What sets Senghaas' analysis apart from this approach is his attempt to introduce psychological theorems, in particular the notion of *autism,* into the analysis of arms race and deterrence problems. Autism may be defined as "absorption in need-satisfying or wish-fulfilling fantasy as a mechanism of escape from reality."[17] This refers primarily to a pathological condition in individual psychology. But Senghaas shows that a few social psychologists have employed the concept in the social context of communication and interaction among groups or individuals. Theodore M. Newcomb and Erich Lindemann were interested in the development of hostile attitudes of groups or individuals against others who are seen as actual or potential opponents. What is remarkable is that both these scholars posited that if the actors perceive the outside in an autistic manner, the hostility level will remain the same or increase, since the lack of communications will exacerbate the self-oriented quality of the perceptual process; and as Lindemann suggested, aside from a distorted view of the real world, the actors will begin to see the others as scapegoats who are held responsible for all the evils in their conflicting relationship.[18] Three features emerge as significant elements of the pathology of social autism: a highly unreal map of the outside world; a severely disturbed communication pattern; finally the strong concomitant inclination to blame the outside world in general and specific opponents in particular for all shortcomings and dangers.

It is of crucial importance whether and to what extent Senghaas is able to demonstrate the effective presence of these autistic symptoms in the social and political systems of the units in threat or deterrence relationships. In a thorough analysis of deterrence and arms problems of the world after World War II, he has tried, with the help of Deutsch's model of the self-closure of political systems and of pathological, i.e., dysfunctional, learning, to find evidence for his autism model of the politics of deterrence.[19] The case that he makes for his model and the facts and interpretations that he submits are strong. Focusing on the two superpowers since 1945, he sees the following three factors at work. First, they have maintained minimal real exchange relations, e.g., in trade, tourism, etc., and have consistently barred the exchange of "strategically important" goods. Second, the elites have transmitted and received a limited amount of threats which have been communicated to the respective populations. Together with these threats, information is exchanged that causes the increasing similarity of the antagonists in the military-technological competition, as well as in their economic rivalry, and in their behavior toward other actors in the international system. Third, the decisive component of deterrence relations are the quantitatively and qualitatively predominant inner-directed processes and, as a consequence of the deterrence policy, an autistic milieu develops in which this policy keeps reproducing itself. Senghaas proposes that this situation within the closed self-encapsulated systems of the adversaries makes for the fictitious imagery of the projected, yet unreal, external relations with the enemy, the appearance of which is taken for the reality. The reality, however, remains unknown either because the elites withhold it from the public or because they fail to perceive it amidst the noise that they make as the propagate their image of the enemy and of the outside world.

Linking this conception of the interaction and communication patterns between and within the deterrence societies to the arms and strategic development since the Cold War, Senghaas points to the crisis-ridden history of the bilateral relationship, and to the steadily increasing capacity for mutual destruction through more and more sophisticated expensive nuclear weapons, over which neither the military nor the scientists nor the policy-makers exercise effective reliable control. In Senghaas' judgment the introduction of the ABM and the MIRV systems, and the related provisions in SALT I, the current strategic debate about further improvements in the accuracy of the missiles and missile heads and the protection system for the missile sites, are the most recent examples of the lethal folly of nuclear politics and of the "logic" of deterrence.[20]

If this judgment is correct, if peace will come only when the strategy of deterrence has been abandoned,[21] it is clear that the implications of his critical stance are far-reaching. It would indicate that attempts to influence and change the interaction between the deterrence parties are in vain and that arms control measures are inadequate to stop the fatal dynamics of the arms race, because the antagonists inevitably violate or evade the common agreement and engage in another armament round. The cause is said to lie in the pathological condition of the political systems of the adversaries. Hence the remedies must be sought in that direction.

Senghaas has not shied away from the logical conclusions of his critical approach: the social, economic, and political structures and the communication processes in the states must be basically overhauled to abolish the barriers of self-encapsulation, of injustic, of elitism, and of manipulation. In addition, he recommends a wide expansion of international transactions and exchanges. Once these changes are implemented, measures of effective disarmament can be decided upon and enacted.[22] He does not, however, exclude the feasibility of short- and middle-range programs to avert the nuclear cataclysm and to prepare for the tackling of the long-range programs. Among these immediately available devices he names open systematic and consistent efforts by peace researchers to arouse the public and the elites to the dangers inherent in the deterrence system, the pursuit of non- or de-escalation strategies unilaterally as a means to solicit compliance by the other parties, the adoption of extensive linkages among the antagonists and the construction of institutional and organizational patterns of coordination of their actions, and positive feedback processes linking the new strategies of internal and international policies.[23] Senghaas holds that more cooperative modes of interaction would slowly push back the deterrence strategy and thus allow some form of peaceful co-existence.

The provocative nature of Senghaas' conception and analysis has caused a considerable stir in European peace research and among groups whose world-view or vested interest are affected by this perspective. Scholars from the socialist countries have taken exception to his contention that the deterrence strategies of both superpowers and of their allies show autistic symptoms, and that the policy processes on each side suffer from undue pressure and influence of the military-industrial complex.[24] They argue that the decision-making and communications processes in communist society are such as to be immune from these vices that they see rampant in capitalism. Moreover, they evaluate the recent development in détente much more favorably as a sign that peace-promoting interaction is possible between the nuclear antagonists.

The reaction in Western countries has been much more diversified and ranges from a total rejection of Senghaas' thesis to fundamental conceptional critiques, and to arguments about specific theoretical and substantive issues. Many suggest that he erroneously presents the rather unique bipolar U.S.-U.S.S.R. situation as the typical form of deterrence interaction, presumably valid for other regions, eras, and military conditions. Others point out that he has failed to offer conclusive empirical evidence for his set of hypotheses. Taking only the history of U.S.-Soviet relations after 1945, some show that many phases in this interaction sequence do not fit the model of autistic enmity in its pure propositional form. Neither the beginnings of the Cold War until around 1953 nor the developments since 1962 meet the criteria of his conception. Several critics take issue with his totally negative view of the contribution of deterrence to the aboidance of open nuclear war and with his unwillingness to give any credit to measures and proposals for arms control as a preliminary step to disarmament. Others again attack as overly broad and illusionary his proposals for overcoming deterrence and building a stable peace. Many radicals rebuke him for his indictment of Soviet policies along with American ones.[25]

It is a difficult task to evaluate adequately such a comprehensive and tentative analytical scheme in a few words. A crucial limitation has been and still is the lack of sufficiently verified empirical evidence. The research program that Senghaas and his colleagues have undertaken is geared toward that objective, but major findings have not been published.[26] The autism hypothesis, although very provocative and stimulating, is another difficult aspect of the framework, first because it eludes scientific verification, and second because it is presented as a general explanatory concept to unlock many unresolved issues in the competitive threat and conflict behavior of antagonistic elites and societies. In some ways it threatens to become a momocausal explanation for everything political. It also tends to belie an over-whelming load of evidence that bespeaks the large-scale multiple communication and interaction events characteristic for current East-West relations. The Senghaas conclusion that arms control measures are ineffective and unsuited for the central deterrence problem cannot hold up if the major tenets of his theory appear not fully warranted and if arms control is conceived in a more dynamic peace-oriented fashion. Moreover, his suggestions for change are not convincing in that in his understanding the level of pathological autistic hostility is so high that it would take drastic methods to liberate the decision elites from their self-centered obsession and to restore meaningful interaction.

All these critical points are not meant to deny the merits of the principal conception in Senghaas' writings. His approach complements the traditional mode of analysis in that it emphasizes the impact of intrastate factors on the development of global deterrence and arms control politics. Recent research has shown that the attributes of states are more significant determinants of their external behavior than are attributes of the external interrelationship patterns of which they are parties.[27] Though limited, this indication supports research efforts to look at domestic political, social, and economic conditions and processes for a better understanding of what has evolved in the international system since World War II. It is desirable that Senghaas and others continue their serious exploration of his pronounced alternative view, in order to establish as reliably as possible to what extent governments and the public elites behave in a manner that bars even minimal success in reducing international tensions, and in reversing the arms race that rushes the world society ever closer toward the brink of the holocaust. It depends on the outcome of this research whether the peace forces will learn to pay more attention to the structures of internal policy-making. This research renews interest in the complex problems of how images are formed about the global system and about other countries and what affects these images so that popular perceptions change.[28]

The brief discussion of deterrence and of the arms race in its various forms and on various levels has shown that bipolar military interaction still constitutes the most immediate and most destructive threat to the future of peace in the international system. It follows that our efforts to assure peaceful development of the world community require at least a two-pronged action program geared toward global levels of interaction and toward the policy-making level of each state, in particular of those whose policies, actual or intended, weigh most in the determination of the future of the globe. Action is urgently required, but it must be implemented with caution and modesty, as scholarly research is still tentative, and since partisan perception and biased thinking weigh heavily in this political and military policy area.

Dependency Patterns and the Problem of Peace

The structure of the international system is characterized by the dominance of a few state actors and by the significantly weaker role of the large majority of states, many of which find themselves in conditions of dependency from one of the dominant actors. In recent years, students of peace and conflict have turned with renewed interest to the important issues that result from the problem of dependency in its various forms. On the one hand, the question of imperialism has been reopened because of the persistent symptom of the wide disparity between the situation in highly developed countries and in the poor regions of the globe. On the other hand, new forms of international involvement and penetration have emerged which the classical diplomatic analysis is ill-suited to understand and to tackle. Among these we find new economic elements, e.g., the multinational corporations, developments in communication, e.g., satellites and other instruments for global dissemination of news and views, patterns of cultural influence, e.g., signs of the expansion of national or regional cultural traits and habits into areas with indigenous cultural traditions, whereby the latter are weakened and often destroyed. The list of such trends is much longer and much more diversified, but for the purposes of our discussion we need no further general examples. It is more significant to try to connect these indications of dependency with the prospects for peace or violent conflict in the international system as a whole. Recent research on these problems is rich in hypotheses, but tentative in empirical findings and analytical conclusions. However, importance for the central issues of the management and resolution of international conflicts is paramount.

In our introductory remarks we pointed to the two concepts of peace, negative peace and positive peace, and to their meaning for the presence or absence of conflict in global relations. It is easy to see that dependency and conflict are closely related; overt violent conflict has more to do with ruptures in the condition of dependency, while latent conflict is inherent in its undisturbed routinized practice. If these propositions are to hold up, we have to take another look at structural violence and its theoretical and practical link with dependency.

Herman Schmid has argued that peace research, by focusing one-sidedly on the subjectivistic conception of conflict, has neglected to deal adequately with the objectivistic notion of conflict that sees the cause of the conflict in the given structure of the political, social, economic reality and not merely in the minds of men.[29] A case where the conflict is real but latent is the relationship between master and slave in which the latter is exploited by the former without rising against the suppressor; once he does so, the real conflict simply becomes overt. It is the factor of exploitation or deprivation that constitutes the central criterion for the diagnosis of structural violence and dependency in the world system.

The most important recent contribution to the basic theory of imperialism and dependency has come from Galtung, due to the fact that his conceptual work rises beyond the partiality of perspective and the spatial or temporal limitations that characterize most of the writings in the field of imperialism or dependency. He also elaborates clearly the conflict dimension inherent in these deviations from the model of interaction among equal and sovereign states. Taking his cue from the evident asymmetry in the international system, from his concept of structural violence, and from the widening gap in economic well-being and development, he defines imperialism as "a system that splits up collectivities and relates some of the parts to each other in relations of harmony of interest, and other parts in relations of disharmony of interest, or conflict of interest."[30] He conceives of the harmony (disharmony) of interest as follows: if the two parties are linked in such a way that the gap in the living condition between them is decreasing (increasing), then we have a condition of harmony (disharmony).[31] Going beyond much of the classical imperialism and dependency discussion, Galtung points out that in order to determine whether the interaction is symmetric or asymmetric, two factors have to be examined: (1) the value-exchange between the actors–inter-actor effects; and (2) the effects inside the actors–intra-actor effects.[32] Both elements must be considered to establish the profit rates for the parties. These figures reveal the asymmetry in the relations *between* the center and the periphery states as a whole and at the same time the gap between the center (the power elite) and the periphery *within* each state, imperialist as well as dependent. An additional factor, the feudal interaction structure, enables the center state to maintain and reinforce the inequality between the interaction parties; i.e., the dependent states are exclusively linked to the imperialist center without interaction among themselves or with the outside world.[33] Since Galtung puts crucial emphasis on the beneficial connection (the harmony of interest) between the elites in dominant and in dependent states, he is able-at least logically–to extend the phenomenon of imperialism into the future, when the asymmetry between these elites might have disappeared but the inequality between the elites and the underprivileged masses in dependent states will continue or even grow worse. Whatever the value of this future-oriented speculation, the merits of his imperialism conception are evident.[34]

Galtung's theorem encompasses imperialist phenomena of all ages and of many kinds. He moves beyond the overly narrow confines of economic imperialism or beyond the stale proposition that imperialism amounts to the expansion of political power beyond the state boundaries. Although he emphasizes the structure of imperialism, he manages to account for the changes of dominance as a process. His inclusion of the intra-actor consequences, or the spin-off effects, in the definition of imperialism makes the concept comprehensive and versatile for the understanding of many diverse conditions and situations.

The drawbacks in Galtung's conception are not numerous, but they raise difficult questions for which there are no easy answers. It seems arbitrary to assert that the relationship between the elites of the center state and of the dependent peripheral states must be characterized by a harmony of interest, although asymmetrical in payoff. This thesis would rule out a situation in which the imperialistic state establishes total rule over the dependent state, administering its affairs with officials who are recruited and trained in the dominant society, and exploiting the colony more or less indiscriminately. To exclude this pattern means to eliminate a significant part of the history of classical imperialism. Moreover, there is no need for that exclusion in the logic of Galtung's theorem.

Another more serious issue is the charge that his conception is static, an exercise in taxonomy, rather than dynamic.[35] The claim is that Galtung describes the structural properties of various stages of imperialism, but fails to offer a detailed examination of the forces that shape the dynamics of each phase and cause the international system to move into a new stage of imperialism. Although Galtung offers some remarks about causal links between the different stages of imperialism, it is indeed correct to say that he does not pay much attention to the inner dynamics of the imperialistic relationship as a process which in fact must be considered as a major factor for the growth and demise of imperialism.

A principal critical point that has been raised against Galtung's understanding of dependency, but also applies to many other concepts developed by him, is the question of whether the center-periphery model has universal relevance, and whether it is sufficient to posit that structural violence is present in international interaction in order to conclude that the underdog, the dependent community or group, is entitled to overcome that condition of structural violence regardless of the circumstances and of the means employed.[36] More specifically, is it possible to encompass in one definition such widely diverse phenomena as quasi-hegemonial alliances, colonial domination, various patterns and degrees of economic dependence, post-colonial relationships, regional preeminence of particular states, or the penetration of foreign economies by giant multinational corporations? Is it feasible to suggest a unified strategy to overcome and remove these instances of so-called "structural violence?" The criticism implied in these questions is legitimate; but we must point to the significant lacunae in traditional and quantitative research regarding the detailed description and classification of the phenomena of imperialism and dependence compared with the other problems of contemporary international relations, e.g., the superpower rivalry and détente, deterrence, European peace and security, etc. Once the descriptive and classificatory endeavor has been taken up and perfected by the critics of Galtung, and of others who belong in the group of critical peace research, we may hope for a richer and more comprehensive amount of data and policy suggestions with which to tackle the hard questions raised by these critics.

As of now, the critical peace researchers, together with the students of imperialism, have provided us with much material and analytical considerations that enable us to develop a differentiated perspective on the multiple facets of international politics and economics. Of foremost interest here are economic issues such as global production and distribution, control and accumulation, multinational corporations, case studies of dependency, and the political implications of these economic symptoms and developments.[37] What emerges from these studies gives us cause for serious concern about the future of peace in the global system. Even if the balance of deterrence should hold between the two superpowers, it is unlikely that the other factors making for imbalance, dependence, and growing gaps in development can be controlled to avert overt conflict, unless these disparities are seen and removed by the dominant states and groups as soon as possible. Critical investigations have shown that official international development organizations have been misused for partisan purposes to maintain the old pattern of inequality and to slow down the trends toward even development.[38] Others have pointed to the feudal structure of relations in alliances and regional associations and to the negative effects of this type of connection on interaction and mutual perception between actors within and without the various feudal systems.[39] It is plausible to argue that the scheme of feudal dependence and interaction lacks stability in times of conflict. This assumption is strongly supported by the finding that status inconsistency, i.e., wide discrepancies between a nation's ranking on two or more dimensions of its status set, is an important cause of aggressive behavior and internal instability, usually expressed through increases of the armed forces; a somewhat simpler version establishes a positive correlation between rank disequilibrium and aggression in groups of individuals, in societies, and in the international system.[40] The immediate relevance of these findings is obvious, if we consider that the developed states have been engaged in a dangerous competition of selling large amounts of arms to developing areas and poor countries of the globe, where more than two thirds of all local and regional violent conflicts have occurred during the last fifteen years.[41] This condition contributes nothing to a reduction of the development gap or of existing international tensions; it serves rather to incite those who receive these weapons to use them against rival states or against internal opponents, and to exacerbate the dangers of a major, even worldwide conflagration culminating in the use of nuclear forces with results too well-known. Even if the ultimate confrontation can be averted, it is certain that without major efforts by the rich and powerful states to cure the pressing ills of inequity, dependency, and deprivation, the future of the world will bring more violent conflict, great upheavals, and reversals in the international system, and severe destabilization which will affect developed and developing societies alike. The problem is urgent, as recent events during the winter 1973-1974 have proven, and policy-makers should do everything possible to encourage and initiate further research on these complex economic, political, and social issues.[42]

Regional Integration and Peace

In view of the structure of the contemporary international system and in awareness of the continuing probability of the outbreak of major hostilities at and below the global level, the academic community of peace and conflict researchers has maintained, even increased, its search for ways and means of preventing, reducing, and solving international conflict that do not presuppose a working world government or world federation. Major attention has focused on emerging structures and processes of transnational organization and cooperation and in particular on the theory and practice of regional integration. The major underlying assumption in this academic endeavor seems to be that conflict behavior will become less violent the more the states are bound together into patterns of intensive, more or less regularized cooperation and coordination. General systems theorists have proposed that natural and social systems tend to progress from multiplicity and chaos to oneness and order.[43] It is characteristic for the advocates of federalism and for the students of integration to equate oneness and order and gear their thinking to the achievement of a united or federated decision-making machinery to promote peace and stability in and among the human communities.

Under which conditions is integration, broadly conceived,[44] feasible? Which level of integration is necessary to meet the needs of peace and order? The range of answers is broad and shows the unresolved state of the debate that has been going on among policy-makers and scholars. Some assert that states and regions have usually been unified under one ruler through the use of overt force, through warfare.[45] Others insist that for groups of states to coalesce an external threat must be present that fulfills an integrative function.[46] A large group of observers looks at the organization of the world from another angle, i.e., from the acknowledged fact that technologically, economically, and in many other realms of human existence interdependence and interaction have reached such a high level that it mandates supranational (at least regional) mechanisms to control these forces and to provide adequately for their use in the future. This task is of immediate relevance for the decision-maker and for the diplomat, because it is unmistakably clear that especially in the highly developed regions the interrelationships are so close-knit and intensive that a state could break out of this grid only at the risk of damaging itself and the other members of the system.[47] A considerable number of scholars from diverse backgrounds warn against the apparent negative effects of military and economic regional groups and stress the mitigating role of universal organizations and of transnational non-governmental associations and movements that might counter-balance the divisive impact of the regional coalitions.[48]

From these summary remarks it becomes clear that the debate about regionalism as an instrument of peace is inconclusive. Most recognize the necessity to rise beyond the level of national policy to forestall the breakdown of the fragile condition of non-war and to construct the foundations for a stable peace order. But here the consensus ends. Regional integration means for some too much transnational steering abrogating national "sovereignty," while others reject it as far too little since it leaves intact the right of states to pursue independent policies without regard to the common good of mankind. We have to see this fundamental debate as the panorama for the specific discussion among the experts on regional integration. We do not contend that these specialists disagree on the importance of the transnational dimension of a future peace system, but according to their empirical or normative estimate of the feasibility of integration on the global level they conceive of the level and extent of regional integrative schemes quite differently. This conceptual divergence, together with significant methodological divisions, renders difficult any attempt to describe and analyze the contribution of regional integration to world peace.

In order to avoid unnecessary terminological confusion we have to try to distinguish regional "integration" from related but not identical terms, such as regional cooperation, regional organization, or regionalism. Ernst B. Haas, a leading student in this field and a proponent of the neo-functionalist approach, has defined integration as "a process for the creation of political communities defined in institutional and attitudinal terms." He elaborates that "the study of regional integration is concerned with explaining how and why they voluntarily mingle, merge, and mix with their neighbors so as to lose the factual attributes of sovereignty while acquiring new techniques for resolving conflict between themselves."[49] The main features of Haas' understanding are well summarized here. He links regional integration directly with the process of political community formation. The terminal state of that process is narrowly delimited. From his original work on European integration we know that his perspective has been shaped mainly by the West European development, especially by the hopes for political union of leaders like Monnet and many others. More recently, he has circumscribed the direction of the process less exclusively, but the basic tenet is still the goal of political organization in a community transcending the single states. He also suggests that there is a clear linkage between this kind of regional integration and new (better) methods of conflict resolution.

Haas' propositions and scheme of analysis have provoked considerable criticism from a varied group of scholars and policy-makers. The conceptions of "spillover" and automatic politization have tended to dominate the debate. The two notions make up a central element of the neo-functionalist model because they flow from the basic premise that (successful) integration will begin in a technical area, e.g., trade and tariffs, and then extend ("spill over") into the realm of political cooperation and administration. For the political process to develop freely, Haas proposes a pluralist pattern of political and social participation within the individual components of the system of functional integration.[50] The internal pluralism then helps shape the interaction among the units, in that it diversifies the bargaining and enables the participating elites to resolve a crisis and settle on a compromise that may find acceptance among the constituencies of the successful parties and interest groups rather than in rigidly organized national blocs of the member states.

It is clear that these parameters of regional political integration lack the general applicability required for this type of social scientific inquiry and model-building. The stipulation of pluralism and of spillover is ill-suited for the condition of regional integration in developing areas, e.g., in Africa, Latin America, Asia, or in Eastern Europe. Its relevance is in question even in Western Europe, where there are no clear indications that spillover has occurred and where the pluralist characteristic of the community interaction process suffers from severe imbalances and distortions, due to the lack of effective parliamentary involvement and to the over-emphasis on intergovernmental and interadministrative consensus.

Another critique with considerable merit is directed against the teleological nature of the neo-functionalist theorem: Why does it contain the requirement that integration advance toward a new political community in which the citizens transfer their allegiance to and legitimize a transnational decision-making authority, if the researcher is primarily out to engage in adequate empirical analysis of current and evolving integration schemes? Do we have to exclude a regional scheme of functional cooperation and coordination that is not scheduled to extend beyond strictly defined limits of, e.g., specialized economic integration? Moreover, given the search for resulting conflict management and resolution techniques, the limitation to integration as a process leading to the higher political community is an undesirably restrictive conception that excludes many interesting aspects without strengthening the search for a better peace order.

Haas has suggested another limitation which requires some comment on empirical, normative, and methodological grounds. He speaks of regional integration only if the process of unification is non-coercive.[51] How many current efforts of integration fulfill this requirement? If we were to understand coercion in a narrow formal sense of overt subjugation, Haas would be justified in excluding it from the study of regional integration. It seems, however, more realistic to conceive of coercion in various ways including quasi-coercive pressures that arise from the greater strength of some partner in economic, military, technological, or similar terms or from the superior technique of bargaining and deciding that one group wields over the other. More basically, the achievement of an integrated area in which peaceful order prevails through the use of force is an interesting subject for study because it could reveal significant factors applicable for more or less peaceful integration efforts. Despite these drawbacks, Haas' conceptual framework has contributed to a better grasp of the structural and procedural properties of political and semi-political integration, as exemplified by the West European and to some extent the Latin American cases.[52]

While this approach focuses on the policy-making process as such, a second major line of analysis deals with international transactions as they relate to regional integration. Karl Deutsch has been a pioneer in communications and transaction analysis, which studies a range of transaction flows and enables the observer to establish the boundaries of identifiable existing and nascent communities. Deutsch has hypothesized that if a population shares values, common memories, loyalties, identifications, and goals, the members communicate (transact) with one another on a wide range of concerns; the boundaries of a particular community will be marked by noticeable relative discontinuities, i.e., by a marked thinning of the transaction flows. For the study of regional integration, the same set of assumptions is introduced in order to determine whether the formation of security-communities, amalgamated or pluralistic, can be verified in terms of an intensification of the network of communications and transactions. Deutsch distinguishes between amalgamated integrated security-communities, which are formed through the formal merger of two or more previously sovereign units and adopt a common government, and pluralistic integrated security-communities, in which the sense of community is not translated into the abolition of the legal independence of the states, but which constitute an area where conflicts are solved in a peaceful cooperative manner.

To have some reliable measure for the presence or absence of the conditions for integrated security communities, transaction analysts have used foreign trade data to index ranges of economic transactions, international mail deliveries, newspaper and periodical circulation to index information exchange or social communication, educational exchange to index cultural interaction, and diplomatic representation and activity to index political transaction.[53] So far, results of the quantitative measurement of such transaction data have demonstrated the applicability and usefulness of this approach. In terms of basic orientation, the transaction analysts also emphasize the question of how new and larger communities are formed, but they do not restrict their normative and empirical work to the terminal goal of a full-fledged state nor do they assume automatic politization, since they hold that community and a zone of peace may come into existence without the formal insignia of political unity and statehood. On the other hand, it is questionable whether the number of transactions and communications is enough to draw conclusions about the rise or decline of community trends in a particular region. Is it not necessary to break down the data in the broad categories we have mentioned and to examine the substance of the messages and transactions?

To answer such critical questions may be beyond the quantitative method of analysis either because the data are not available or because it is impossible to arrive at relevant reliable sub-categories of, e.g., mail or telephone communications. Trade data, however, can be sub-divided into commodities, the analysis of which could reveal significant details about the exact nature of the interrelationship.[54] This shows that additional data collection and evaluation is required to improve the tool of transaction analysis. Moreover, as many studies by its practitioners prove, its limits are perceived and the approach is enriched by adding the examination of public opinion and of elite attitudes.[55]

Neither the neo-functionalists nor the proponents of the transaction-communications approach have asserted that their conceptual and analytical schemes are mutually exclusive. But only recently have they begun to suggest the overlapping and complementariness of the two modes of viewing regional integration with special reference to the creation and maintenance of peace structures.[56] The benefits of such a marriage are evident, since the concern with the material bases of the interrelationship will support or correct the insights from the analysis of the political decision-making processes that evolve in the regional system. With the help of such a combined approach, the divergence of transaction data and of findings about the community decision-making process that have emerged in the study of West European integration after 1945 (trade among the members of the European Economic Community reached a crest in 1959-1960 and has remained essentially constant since, whereas policy-making in the community has expanded considerably since 1957), may become a central research interest and lead to new methods and concepts to explain the integrative process and to elaborate proposals to speed it up and improve it.[57] In addition, the two-pronged approach will help register new opportunities and incentives from either of the two research areas and their impact on both decision-making and interaction elements of integration.

From the presentation of the two dominant approaches to regional integration, the parameters and variables for its analysis emerge in broad outline. However, it must be noted that recent research along these lines has produced relatively little additional empirical material or major innovative conceptual suggestions. Mostly it adds descriptive accounts or it contains usually valid but minor criticism of the neo-functionalist or transaction paradigms. But the debate has raised the level of problem awareness and opened some perspectives which stimulate further research on a wide range of issues. Several researchers have addressed themselves to the difficult issues regarding the boundaries of integrative systems. It is clear that there is rarely total congruence in the membership of a particular integrative community and in the associations of its member states with other intergovernmental organizations, or of groups within these states with international non-governmental organizations. There exist tensions in the perception of the degree and intensity of the interaction in the integrational unit by the governmental officials or the public elites. The impact of such factors on integration as an ongoing process has been little studied.[58]

Others have taken a closer look at the functionalist assumption that elite social learning and attitudinal change result from involvement in the integrative process: one author reports that socialization of participants in international organizations does generate some attitude change toward the adoption of an internationalist outlook, but that conflict processes within the organization also have a significant effect on the attitudes of participants.[59] Another researcher has found that, in the case of French and German parliamentarians in the European Parliament, the exposure to the integrative process creates cognitive, but not affective, changes; they gain more complex perceptions, better information and greater interest, but they do not change their attitudes on the issues that are involved; he reasons that those who come to the Parliament usually want to come because of their commitment to the European cause.[60] The urgency of the problem of attitudinal change in integrative processes is underlined by the recent finding that the general public in the European Community lacks interest in the effort to achieve unification and that the fringe groups, such as the poor, the radicals, the Communists, and others, are rather dissatisfied with the community that has evolved.[61] These studies reveal that the various dimensions of the process of integration must be viewed and analyzed together, because advances in one direction, e.g., policy-making at the community level, may be impeded or even outweighed by lags in other areas, such as public attitudes or transactions.

An interesting suggestion has recently been made concerning the role of middle powers in integration. We are familiar with the crucial role of the core area in the successful construction of larger integrated communities. But much less is known about the pre- and post-integration role of counter-core units, middle powers that are opposed to the formation of the community. A recent essay posits the following stages of the involvement of the counter-core actor: (1) repeated attempts at obstructing the path to the integrated community without openly breaking with the other units; (2) strong resistance to the document of integration without rejecting it; (3) occupation of leadership positions in the new community once the core power desists from its pivotal role. The author has already found numerous historical cases that prove the general hypothesis.[62] If further research is carried out along these lines, it might become possible to predict the most likely course of integration and to devise strategies to forestall the failure of a community-building effort by accounting for the crucial roles of the leading middle-sized states in ongoing processes of regional integration. This line of research is of particular relevance for a world order based on the expansion and diversification of regional sub-systems and relies on these as guarantors of the maintenance of peace.

Little attention has been paid to the aspect of gains resulting from the integration of previously sovereign states into an evolving integrative structure. Focusing on integration in developing areas, a researcher has proposed to examine five hard questions, the answers to which are crucial for the continuation or cancellation of an integrative process:

(1) the extent to which the leadership perceived a probability of net national gains;

(2) the extent to which there are tangible immediate gains;

(3) the extent to which gains are increasing over time;

(4) the extent to which equity in the distribution of gains is perceived;

(5) the extent to which gains are increasing proportionately faster than losses.[63]

These questions are not only relevant but also researchable. We can see today that they are salient not only for developing areas but also for economic and other functional communities in developed regions. If students of integration fail to take them into account, they will be unable to develop more comprehensive or more predictive models and to link integration schemes to peace strategies in any meaningful manner. To some extent, Nye's revised neo-functionalist model that reflects the lessons of integration experiments in developed as well as developing regions encompasses the basic issues that are raised by this and the preceding criticisms and suggestions.[64] However, much more work in these new directions is required to translate the elements of the model into fully adequate analytical and decisional approaches to present and future integrative efforts in varying functional areas and on different levels.

Up to this moment, we have looked at integration as an answer to the quest for peace in a world which at present cannot turn into a universal community with a centralized governmental structure. For those who reject the notion of a world state or world federation as illusionary or as dangerous, regional integration often becomes *the* remedy for all the ills afflicting mankind. The peace-promoting quality of integration is an assumption held by a large number of social scientists and also of policy-makers.[65] It is to the credit of the critical school of peace research, in particular of Galtung, that the overly positive role of integration has been modified to some extent. We want to emphasize that the result of this revision has not been to condemn integration, but to show that association or disassociation must be employed according to the specific circumstances that characterize the interaction pattern and the parties in the particular situation.

Galtung's conception of negative and positive peace and his theory of structural violence and dependency are the main premises for his evaluation of integration and disintegration as instruments of conflict management and resolution. If it were merely a question of averting or ending war, the choice between associative or dissociative policies would not be crucially significant. But the wider dimension and greater depth of Galtung's approach makes the distinction meaningful. He argues that in conditions of equilibrium or symmetry between the parties the best way toward the achievement and stabilization of peace is a policy of association: the relationship between two topdogs will be less exposed to the danger of violent and bitter conflicts if the partners are linked together in a multiple network of interaction and interdependence leading to fusion. The same applies to underdogs with the additional results that they would gain strength against the topdogs. For situations of actual hostility or mutual violent hatred the strategy of association and integration would be most damaging; here the dissociative approach of separating the opponents seems appropriate. Moreover, if the parties in conflict are unequal—in Galtung's terms, if one is a topdog and the other is an underdog—dissociative measures are the only answer in the first stage of the confrontation, because associative interaction in an asymmetrical condition would merely strengthen the dominant actor, due to its greater capabilities and impact. Once the weaker party has gained enough autonomy and self-respect and is able to maintain itself against the other party, it can initiate steps towards association and integration. This two-stage process can involve conflict-provoking behavior on the part of the underdog(s) in the first phase in order to bring about the collapse of a system of asymmetrical dominance, e.g., colonialism, before cooperative integrative measures are taken. Thus peace-making and peace-keeping might require a whole range of policies from total isolation and separation to total integration and amalgamation, according to the nature of the conflict and the parties. Galtung holds that associative policies are likely to gain in importance due to the general patterns of political development, but he points out that in view of persistent large inequities between many states and regions dissociative strategies, including increased conflict awareness and behavior, will be employed–and have to be employed–to move closer to the goal of positive peace, social justice, and equality within and among states.[66]

The validity of this perspective on peace and integration can be tested in many historical and contemporary cases. On account of the higher level of available information and of West European scholarly concern the European region has been the subject of very intensive research efforts. Full-fledged integration of the blocs into one transnational community is clearly out of the question, although some radical federalists and functionalists might still disagree. Total separation or dissociation of Eastern and Western Europe would also fail as peace strategy. To evaluate the current state of European cooperation and to devise a suitable policy for increased coordination in a system of European security and peace, it seems best to adopt a mixed approach measuring the associative and dissociative elements of the web of interrelationships and formulating action guidelines that help maintain negative peace without weakening the chances for a more equitable structure of positive peace throughout all of Europe.[67] The uncertainty and controversy surrounding the whole issue of the direction, intensity, and objective of European integration through peaceful but far-reaching change proves the conceptual, ideological, and decisional complexity of the coupling of peace and integration. To do justice to the European problems–or for that matter to nearly all remaining issues of regional organization all over the globe–much additional conceptual and empirical research as well as innovative political and economic planning is required. Otherwise, the danger will continue to loom large that governments supported by public elites persist in pursuing outdated policies of national sovereignty or ill-fated visions of transnational fusion.

International Organizations and World Peace

Although students of peace and conflict have not given much attention or credit to the role of the United Nations and other international organizations in safeguarding peace and in reducing tensions, the interest and hope remain alive that the web of international institutional and organizational links will eventually contribute to a better, though still imperfect, system of world peace. Much academic study tries to answer the question: What accounts for the weakness of many international organizations? Some attribute the meager results to constitutional or structural defects in the machinery of the UN system; thus Bouthoul argues that Article 2(7), of the UN Charter constitutes an invitation to genocide, as long as it occurs within the borders of sovereign states, and suggests that major domestic violence be included on the agenda of the General Assembly and of the Security Council.[68] Others complain that many international organizations are mere mirror images of the fragmented, polarized, and hierarchical international system, and they call upon the leaders of these organizations and upon the developing countries who hold a clear majority of votes in most of these bodies to enforce changes and to redress the grave inequities.[69]

Still others, sympathetic to the plight of the United Nations, emphasize that at this point the only hope lies with the United Nations, and that its role in peace-keeping, arms control and disarmament, economic and social development, and other vital areas could grow and expand by incremental reforms, additional functions and by emerging circumstances (needs, constraints).[70] They share the apprehension about the lagging performance of the world organization; but they believe—and rightly so—that the likelihood of swift and far-reaching changes in its functioning is very slim under the present condition of the international system, while the shakeup of the international order would probably result in the collapse of the UN system without guaranteeing the construction of a more powerful and more effective substitute organization.

An important prerequisite for a crucial involvement of the United Nations in the maintenance and strengthening of international peace is the parliamentary behavior of the member states in the central organs of the United Nations. Researchers have given considerable attention to the voting patterns and to the preparation, deliberation, and implementation of resolutions in the General Assembly and the Security Council. Their intention has been to ascertain the behavioral characteristics of states and groups in the world organization.[71] Other researchers have focused on the participation and interaction of delegates in the Assembly and its committees in order to determine whether and to what extent private exchanges and public speeches are indicative of the reputation of the delegate and of his mission and for his negotiating skills; results confirm that national background and diplomatic reputation are important predictors for the scope and success of the active involvement of the delegates.[72] A study of the cooperative behavior of members of regional organizations as expressed in UN votes has brought out that regional cohesion is highest among groups of developing countries on such issues as economic development, global economic redistribution, and to a lesser extent on military and diplomatic non-alignment, regardless of the degree of functional specificity, institutional and power homogeneity, and integrative commitment of the regional organizations to which they belong. Western countries, however, show a deterioration in their regional organizational unity in UN roll-call voting. In general, most governments pursue divergent policies in their regional organizations and at the United Nations; this means that there is little commitment to supranational behavior in the United Nations, but also little effort to use the world organization for narrow regional organizational objectives.[73]

Despite these rather unmistakable indications that the development of the United Nations as a whole is dependent on the lackluster support of the member states who find themselves in disagreement on most issues, the vital role of the United Nations in the field of peace and conflict control is nevertheless generally acknowledged. This affirmative judgment is based on the record of peace-keeping and peace-making under UN auspices, the most recent examples being Cyprus and the Middle East after October 1973. The arrangements in the Middle East and the decision of the UN Security Council leading to them have upset some predictions that the Cyprus operation would become the ceiling of the operational freedom of UN measures.[74] They also help reduce the widespread pessimism that under the surface of diplomatic decorum and oratory the governments and their spokesmen at the UN view international crises solely in terms of "Realpolitik," partisanship, and confrontation, and act in disregard of the common good, i.e., fail to assure the maintenance of overall peace.[75] If we keep in mind that the Cyprus operation prior to the recent crisis had surpassed the expectations of many skeptics not only in that it had been accepted by the population, but also in that it offered hope for a satisfactory solution of that bitter conflict,[76] we could argue that there are endogenous factors in the mechanism and in the environment of the UN system which have contributed to the partial success of the United Nations in fulfilling its first and foremost statutory obligation to maintain international peace and security.

Some scholars have examined the achievement of the world organization in international conflict management and compared its record with that of major regional organizations. They have found that the United Nations excels in dealing with high-intensity conflicts, with disputes that escalate to include neighboring states, with disputes among smaller and middle powers, and with disputes among non-aligned states or even with one party being non-aligned and one belonging to a bloc. The success of the United Nations has somewhat declined over the years, especially after 1963, and it has never been able to manage conflicts between parties from opposing Cold War blocs. The role of the Secretary-General has always been crucial in cases where the United Nations got involved officially, as well as in disputes that never reached the agenda of the Security Council. The higher the conflict intensity, the more dynamic has been the UN involvement; once the United Nations has decided to establish and supervise a truce, it has nearly always been successful. The regional organizations have in all not been markedly more successful in resolving disputes within their own domain. On the basis of their examination the scholars concluded that the UN peace-keeping machinery and operations should be strengthened and expanded for conflicts below the threshold of active superpower hostility and involvement.[77]

It emerges from our brief review of the systemic dimension of the preservation of peace and of the control and resolution of conflicts that the United Nations organization has played a more significant role than its critics perceive and concede. The other instruments of peace which we have surveyed are quite defective and unreliable. This insight should not lead us into exaggerating the uses of the world organization as it is currently constituted. But it might encourage researchers and decision-makers to explore feasible ways and means to fulfill the potential of the charter provisions, with renewed commitment to the ideals of the UN Charter, and to go beyond those ideals to promote a new structure of negative and positive peace. Among major avenues for future research that would deal directly with a peace order as a continuous challenge for the United Nations, we mention here such neglected issues as the decision-making process of the UN Security Council as peace-keeper and peace-builder and ways of improving its operations,[78] or the emerging and potential role of the General Assembly as a universal deliberative body that helps reveal the major trends and problems of global politics and set broad guidelines for law-making and political action at the global, regional, and state levels. These lacunae of current peace and international relations research must be filled if researchers and policy-makers want to contribute fully to their common task of building a better and more stable international system.

Peaceful Co-existence

Much has been written about the theory of peaceful co-existence and about its relevance for the creation of peaceful relations between different political and social systems.[79] In many ways the elaborate definition of peaceful co-existence, proposed by the socialist countries and by many developing countries, is similar to the world order concepts that are based on the continued sovereign independence of all states, except for the explicit prohibition of the use of force in international conflicts. Such disputes must be settled peacefully; interference in internal affairs by outside states or other outside organs is also ruled out.[80] What is distinctly different for peaceful co-existence is the expressed intent of its advocates to wage the ideological struggle against the adversaries with all the means that are compatible with the code of principles of co-existence.[81] While the essentially status quo models, to which we have alluded, are built on the expectation that very little will change in the nature of the international system and its state actors, peaceful co-existence in its original understanding hinges on the evolution of the whole world toward a full-fledged socialist community in which the tensions and disagreements of state interaction are to disappear. This underlying expectation relates the concept of peaceful co-existence closely to the ideas of world order to which we have referred.

Due to its fundamental antagonistic quality the socialist view of the future structure of global interaction has suffered much misunderstanding and willful distortion in the West. Recently West European social scientists have made efforts to clear up some of the misconceptions, and to develop conceptual lines that reflect socialist thinking accurately and at the same time adjust it to the new conditions of global economic, social, and political exchanges which necessitate significantly increased collaboration among the different groups in the international system. One of the crucial irritants in the East-West dialogue has been the Western thesis of a convergence of the two systems. Regardless of how much the two sociopolitical systems show similarities, the convergence hypothesis runs counter to the whole socialist world-view and it harmonizes little, if at all, with the basic ideas in Western thinking.[82] As an alternative, some authors have suggested to speak of co-operation or commutation, i.e., of joing endeavors that either do not affect the essence of their political and social foundations or affect them equally in changing them towards the ideal of a just and democratic society.[83] In this manner, they try to avoid the static connotation of the practice of peaceful co-existence without implying violence as a motor for system change. Moreover, these various notions of peaceful co-existence as cooperation protect the weaker states against the factual predominance of the powerful states in asymmetrical relations, in that they do not have to commit themselves in a formal binding manner to anything beyond the basic norms of co-existence, while they benefit from the security umbrella that is erected with these principles.

These short remarks show that peaceful co-existence can be a significant tool for the strengthening of the peace system on the global as well as on the regional levels. Moreover, its change potential suggests its use in the global process, at the end of which we hope to see emerge a structure of peaceful interaction providing not only for the absence of war, but also for social justice and equality on a worldwide scale. In the immediate future we can expect a further expansion of the policies of peaceful co-existence on the condition that its overly narrow ideological connotation and polemical quality continue to be reduced.

NOTES

1. This general perspective underlies to some extent *Disarmament and Arms Control* ed. by Frank Barnaby and Carlo Schaerf, a volume of proceedings of the Third Course given by the International Seminar School on Disarmament and Arms Control of the Italian Pugwash Movement (New York: Gordon and Breach Science Publishers, 1972), which contains lectures on (1) technology of weapons or mass destruction; (2) disarmament: history and future prospects; (3) dynamics of arms trade; (4) European security; and (5) gaming and simulation aspects of conflicts.

2. Cf. here N. Z. Alcock and Keith Love, "The Vietnam war as a Richardson process," Journal of Peace Research 1969, No. 2, pp. 105-112, in which casualties are measured rather than arms expenditures. On the basis of these data the authors propose that meaningful peace negotiations would start only after the withdrawal of substantial numbers of American combat troops. This forecast was verified in the subsequent Vietnam development. Cf. also Paul Smoker, "Nation State Escalation and International Integration" *Social Processes in International Relations* ed. Kriesberg, esp. pp. 493, 496f. In this essay Smoker finds that at a certain level of the arms race international cooperative structures, e.g., international non-governmental organizations, of the sub-system in which the arms race takes place, collapse, decline or at least stagnate. This finding applies for pre-nuclear and nuclear conditions. It is to some extent supported by the measurement of trade/defense ratios: the more a country prepares for war, the less it trades with a potential opponent. The connection of the two findings is not spelled out by the author. For a fine example of a historical quantitative arms race analysis see John C. Lambelet, "The Anglo-German dreadnought race, 1905-1914," Peace Science Society (International), Papers, XXII, 1974, pp. 1-45.

3. For some evaluating remarks about the uses of arms race data and studies cf. Albert Wohlstetter, "Theory and Opposed-Systems Design," *New Approaches to International Relations* ed. Kaplan, pp. 47f., and Raymond Tanter, "The policy relevance of models in world politics," Journal of Conflict Resolution Vol. 16, No. 4, December 1972, esp. pp. 572f. and 580 (Table 3). The conflict interaction issue will be fully discussed below.

4. Two views that deviate from American strategic thinking support this suggestion. Cf. Gallois, *Paradoxes de la Paix,* esp. p. 271, and d'Oliveira e Souce "Métamorpheses de la guerre," Science et Paix 1973, No. 203, pp. 10ff., where he draws a parallel between nuclear warfare and feudal warfare with regard to alliance dependency patterns.

5. See in particular Rapoport, "Critique of Strategic Thinking," *International Conflict and Behavioral Science* ed. Fisher, pp. 211-237. Cf. also his remarks in his "Directions in Peace Research" *Conflict Control and Conflict Resolution* ed. Höglund and Ulrich, pp. 232f., and in his "Various conceptions of peace research," Peace Research

Society (International), Papers, Vol. XIX, 1972, pp. 91-106 (French: "Les différentes conceptions d'une science de la paix," Science et Paix 1973, No. 1, pp. 16ff). The Rapoport thesis that strategic thinking tends to simplify and to misinterpret the situation is to some extent strengthened by the main finding in John R. Raser and Wayman J. Crow, "A Simulation Study of Deterrence Theories," *Social Processes in International Relations* ed. Kriesberg, pp. 372-389; the authors found that strategic thinking has failed to examine the effect of invulnerability and of the consequent capacity-to-delay-response on the actor's sense of the strength of the state, on its aggressiveness, and on its willingness to engage in war to achieve its major objectives. While the literature denies a correlation between the capacity to delay the response and the incurred magnitude of war, their simulation showed a strong correlation.

6. See P. Terrence Hopmann, "Internal and External Influences on Bargaining in Arms Control Negotiations. The Partial Test Ban," *Peace, War, and Numbers* ed. Russett, pp. 213-237. Other related findings will be discussed in another chapter.

7. See here Richard E. Gift, "Trading in a threat system: The U.S.-Soviet case," Journal of Conflict Resolution Vol. 13, No. 4, December 1969, pp. 418-437.

8. See Steven Rosen, "War Power and the Willingness to Suffer," *Peace, War, and Numbers* ed. Russett, pp. 167-183.

9. For these results see Carl Friedrich von Weizsäcker (ed.), *Kriegsfolgen und Kriegsverhütung,* op. cit., especially his introduction and the essential contribution by Horst Afheldt, "Analyse der Sicherheitspolitik durch Untersuchung der Kritischen Parameter," pp. 25-74, and by Afheldt and Philipp Sonntag, "Stabilität und Abschreckung durch strategische Kernwaffen-eine Systemanalyse," pp. 303-415. For English summaries of the major findings from these studies see Afheldt, "Political conclusions," Journal of Peace Research 1973, No. 3, pp. 259-264, and Afheldt and Sonntag, "Stability and deterrence through strategic nuclear arms," ibid., pp. 245-250. Cf. also Weizsäcker, "Bedrohungsvorstellungen als Faktor der internationalen Politik," Jahrbuch für Friedens- und Konfliktforschung I, 1971, pp. 15-29. For a similar judgment about the destabilizing effects of ABM and MIRV programs cf. K. Tsipis, "U.S. Strategic Weapons–Offensive and Defensive," *Disarmament and Arms Control* ed. Barnaby and Schaerf, pp. 23-40. The American debate about ABM and more recently about MIRV has brought out significant evidence to the same effect.

10. For this very interesting argument supported by data, see Wohlstetter, "Is there a strategic arms race?" Foreign Policy, No. 15, Summer 1974, pp. 3-20, No. 16, Fall 1974, pp. 48-81. For more details and many other references from the field of strategy and arms control see the excellent paper by Pierre Hassner, "Paix et Guerre Entre les Théories: Combats, Jeux et Débats sur la Maîtrise des Armements," paper prepared for the Ninth World Congress of the International Political Science Association, Montreal, August 1973.

11. Cf. here Charles Iklé, *Every War Must End* (New York: Columbia University Press, 1971), especially the conclusion in which he points to the deterrence strategy as the culmination of the failure to study the other questions adequately.

12. Cf. here Igor Glagolev and Makar Goryainov, "Some Problems of Disarmament Research," Journal of Peace Research I, No. 2, 1964, pp. 150-154; also Goryainov and Glagolev, "Concerning research on peace and disarmament conducted in the USSR," International Social Science Journal Vol. 17, No. 3, 1965, pp. 417-419. For detailed information cf. Newcombe, H. and A., *Peace Research Around the World,* p. 19. For a recent Soviet contribution cf. Barsegov and Khairov, "A Study of the Problems and Peace," Journal of Peace Research 1973, No. 1-2, esp. pp. 71f. and 78f.

13. This view is held for instance by Alan Newcombe, "Initiatives and responses

in foreign policy," Peace Research Reviews III (3), June 1969, p. 80. Newcombe is a Quaker and World Federalist. Scandinavians have been leading in disarmament research. Cf. here, e.g., Pertti Joenniemi, "An analysis of the economic consequences of disarmament in Finland," Peace Research Society (International), Papers, XIII, 1970, pp. 29-46; also Unto Vesa, "The development of Chinese thinking on disarmament," Instant Research on Peace and Violence IV (2), 1974, pp. 53-78, and Malvern Lumsden, "New military technology and the erosion of international law: The case of the dum-dum bullet today," ibid., IV (1), 1974, pp. 15-20.

14. John C. Polanyi, "First step: Sealed records caches?" Disarmament and Arms Control I (1), Summer 1963, pp. 3-19. For further details see also H. and A. Newcombe, *Peace Research Around the World,* p. 168.

15. For the full argument and the detailed exposition of the scheme see Erland Brun Hansen and Jörgen Wilian Ulrich, "A Weapons Transfer System for Inter-Nation Conflict Regulation: A Proposal," *Conflict Control and Conflict Resolution* ed. Höglund and Ulrich, pp. 156-173; esp. pp. 162f.

16. Senghaas is part of a rather large group of scholars who focus on society and on its reform to bring about a positive change in the process of international politics, especially in the arms and deterrence field. Cf. Karl W. Deutsch, "Abschreckungspolitik und gesellschaftliche Ordnung. Zum Problem der sich wandelnden Gesellvchaft," Jahrbuch für Friedens- und Konfliktforschung I, 1971, pp. 41-53 for a moderate example of this thinking. A much sharper radical view is expressed by Krippendorff, Introduction to *Friedensforschung,* edited by him, esp. pp. 14f., his "Peace research and the Industrial Revolution," Journal of Peace Research 1973, No. 3, pp. 185-202, and his "The state as a focus of peace research," Peace Research Society (International), Papers, XVI, 1971, pp. 47-60. Senghaas is strongly influenced by Deutsch as well as by the critical sociology of the Frankfurt school (Adorno, Horkheimer).

17. This definition is taken from *Webster's Third New International Dictionary.* According to the *Grand Larousse Encyclopedique,* Vol. I (1960), autism is defined as "état mental caracterisé par un repliement du sujet sur lui-même, avec perte plus ou moins importante des contacts avec le monde extérieur. Dans ses formes les plus bénignes, l'autisme est seulement une prédominance de la vie intérieure sur la vie de relations. . . . Dans les formes plus intenses, le sujet souffre de l'isolement auquel il se constraint lui-même et rejette sur le monde extérieur la responsabilité de tous ses ennuis. . . ." See Senghaas, *Abschreckung und Frieden,* pp. 178f. In his "Zur Analyse von Drohpolitik in den internationalen Beziehungen," Jahrbuch für Friedens- und Konfliktforschung I, 1971, pp. 89-132; pp. 105ff. Senghaas gives the most complete account of the autism hypothesis. He quotes from the work of a German physician and psychologist, E. Bleuler, *Das autistisch- undisziplinierte Denken in der Medizin und seine Uberwindung* (Berlin, 1927), in which Bleuler described autistic thinking in individual patients and in medical research and analysis; with regard to the latter he claimed that there was a trend in modern science to seek the fulfillment of wishes and the confirmation of affective needs rather than objective truth and logical realistic explanations of experience. This thrust in Bleuler's argumentation is already an important approximation of what Senghaas suggests.

18. Senghaas, "Zur Analyse von Drohpolitik in den internationalen Beziehungen," pp. 105ff., refers to and briefly summarizes the following two essays: Theodore M. Newcombe, "Autistic Hostility and Social Reality," Human Relations I, 1947, pp. 69-86, and Erich Lindemann, "Individual Hostility and Group Integration," *Man and International Relations* ed. J. K. Zawodny, (San Francisco, 1966), Vol. I, pp. 62-75.

19. For Deutsch's model see his *Nerves of Government. Models of Political Commu-*

nication and Control (New York: Free Press, 1966 Pb), chapter 13, especially pp. 219-228. Senghaas' most elaborate presentation of the autism model of deterrence is found in his *Abschreckung und Frieden,* pp. 170-188. See also his "Zur Analyse von Drohpolitik in den internationalen Beziehungen," pp. 107-113. Further, see his more recent study, *Rüstung und Militarismus* (Frankfurt: Suhrkamp, 1972), especially the theoretical part, pp. 11-93.

20. Senghaas has presented his viewpoint in a number of different publications. He has also developed a graph to depict the elements and linkages of his model of autism in deterrence systems:

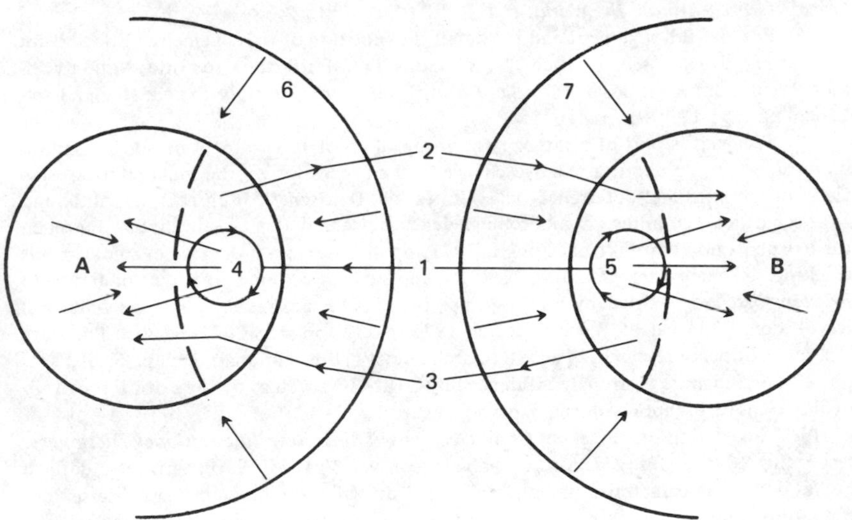

A and B are the two deterrence societies. On transaction path 1 actual, measurable exchange processes take place such as trade, tourism, etc. On transaction paths 2 and 3 the respective elites transmit those threats which are recognized by the corresponding elites and passed on to the public. The majority of deterrence processes takes place within the respective elites (4 and 5). The threats engendered there impress above all the public and circulate around the focal point of the elite. Threats directed at the enemy reflect more back to one's own society (6 and 7) than they affect the enemy.

From: Dieter Senghaas, "Zur Analyse von Drohpolitik in den internationalen Beziehunger," Jahrbuch für Friedens- und Konfliktforschung, I, 1971, p. 108.

Figure 2.1: THE AUTISM MODEL OF DETERRENCE POLICY

See also Senghaas, *Abschreckung und Frieden,* p. 188. For the full presentation of the conceptual framework and of its applications to current problems of deterrence and détente see the following studies by Senghaas: Ibid., part II; his "Zur Pathologie organisierter Friedlosigkeit," *Friedensforschung* ed. Krippendorff, pp. 217-259; his *Rüstung und Militarismus,* pp. 11-93; cf. for European aspects of the armaments complex Senghaas, Volker Rittberger and Burkhard Luber, "MFBR: Aufrüstung durch Rüstungskontrolle," Aus politik und zeitgeschichte Beilage zu Das Parlament, March 31, 1973, pp. 26-54, and Albrecht, Galtung, Joenniemi, Senghaas, and Verona, "Is Europe to demilitarize?" Instant Research on Peace and Violence, 1972(4), especially pp. 187-196; also Senghaas, "Armement par une politique de maîtrise des armements? Réflexions sur les négociations MBFR," Science et Paix, 1973, No. 2-3, pp. 20-48. See also his "The Impact of Domestic Interests and National Decision Systems in the Post-1945 Arms Race: Some Reflections on Armament Dynamics," paper prepared for the Ninth World Congress of the International Political Science Association in Montreal, August 1973, his *Aufrüstung durch Rüstungskontrolle* (Stuttgart: Kohlhammer, 1972), his short unpublished manuscript "Diverse Ammerkungen zur forschungsstrategischen Diskussion über Rüstungsdynamik" (1974), and several pertinent essays in his *Gewalt, Konflikt, Frieden* (Hamburg: Hoffman and Campe, 1973). Cf. also Carola Bielfeldt and Senghaas, "Kann die BRD abrüsten?" *Leviathan,* 3, 1973, pp. 291-309, and Klaus Jürgen Gantzel, "Armament dynamics in the East-West conflict: An arms race?" Peace Science Society (International), Papers, XX, 1973, pp. 1-24. Gantzel uses Senghaas' approach. For the broader setting of his thinking cf. Senghaas (ed.), *Zur Pathologie des Rüstungswettlaufs. Beiträge zur Friedens- und Konfliktforschung* (Freiburg: Rombach, 1970), his "Conflict formations in contemporary international society," Journal of Peace Research 1973, No. 3, pp. 163-184; his "Kompositionsprobleme in der Friedensforschung," *Kritische Friedensforschung* ed. Senghaas pp. 313-361; and his "Friedensforschung–Theoretische Fragestellungen und praktische Probleme," Jahrbuch für Friedens- und Konfliktforschung II, 1972, pp. 10-22.

21. See Senghaas, *Abschreckung und Frieden,* p. 294.

22. See here Senghaas, "Zur Analyse von Drohpolitik in den internationalen Beziehungen," esp. pp. 126ff. and 131f., and his *Abschreckung und Frieden,* pp. 253ff.

23. See here Senghaas, "Zur Analyse von Drohpolitik in den internationalen Beziehungen," pp. 131f.

24. Cf. here the statements by several spokesmen, in particular, Prof. A. L. Narochnitsky from the Soviet Union, at the scientific symposium "Principles, Possible Structures and Perspectives for a System of Collective Security and Cooperation in Europe," Vienna, October 14-15, 1972, reported in Peace and the Sciences, March 1973, No. 1, pp. 35ff. et passim. Senghaas presented a paper on "Armament Dynamics as a Restrictive Condition in the Attempt to Overcome the East-West Conflict" at the congress.

25. For detailed critical remarks see Josef Joffe, "Abschreckung und Abschreckungspolitik. Kritische Bemerkungen zu Dieter Senghaas' Beitrag," Jahrbuch für Friedens- und Konfliktforschung I, 1971, pp. 133-158. For the full range of critical views cf. also the discussion of Senghaas' and Joffe's papers, ibid., pp. 195-212. For a moderate critique from the viewpoint of an arms control and disarmament student cf. Erhard Forndran, *Abrüstung und Friedensforschung* (Düsseldorf: Bertelsmann Universitätsverlag, 1971), pp. 25-56 and pp. 119ff. Cf. also Pierre Hassner, "Paix et guerre entre les théories: Combats, jeux et débats sur la maîtrise des armements," esp. pp. 15ff. et passim, and Hervé Savon, "Une recherche sur la pathologie des relations internationales," Etudes Polémologiques 5, July 1973, pp. 35-44. For a few specific comments, cf. Ernst-Otto Czempiel, *Schwerpunkte und Ziele der Friedensforschung* (Munich: Kaiser, Mainz: Matthias-Grünewald, 1972), pp. 25ff. et passim.

26. The most elaborate description of the research program "Armament Dynamics in the East-West conflict and possibilities of affecting it," *Mitteilungen* der Hessischen Stiftung Friedens- und Konfliktforschung (HSFK), 4, April 1972.

27. See here James N. Rosenau and George H. Ramsey, Jr., "External versus Internal Sources of Foreign Policy Behavior: Testing the Stability of an Intriguing Set of Find-

ings," a paper prepared for presentation at the Ninth World Congress of the International Political Science Association, Montreal, August 1973. The main finding in this paper is especially important since Rosenau has been a major representative of the action-reaction hypothesis focusing strongly on interaction factors.

28. Although there has been considerable research in the general area of public opinion and images, it seems that much more specific study and information is necessary to answer the difficult questions raised by Senghaas' hypotheses. For some earlier material see part I: National and International Images, especially the papers by W. A. Scott and by Karl W. Deutsch and R. L. Merritt, *International Behavior, A Social-Psychological Analysis* ed. by Herbert C. Kelman (New York: Holt, Rinehart and Winston, 1965).

29. See Herman Schmid, "Politics and Peace Research," Journal of Peace Research, 1968, pp. 217-232.

30. Galtung, "A structural theory of imperialism," 1971, No. 2, pp. 81-117; p. 81. While emphasizing Galtung's contribution, we certainly do not underestimate the earlier research on problems of underdevelopment and the North-South gap, for which Gunnar Myrdal's numerous works, including his monumental *Asian Drama, An Inquiry into the Poverty of Nations* (New York: Twentieth Century Fund and Pantheon, 1968), are outstanding examples. What sets Galtung's approach apart from these earlier studies of developing countries is his concern with the conflictual element in conditions of socioeconomic disparity.

31. See op. cit., p. 82. "Living condition" is to be measured by indicators such as income, standard of living, quality of life, autonomy, etc.

32. See ibid., p. 85ff., for his excellent discussion of the significance of these factors for political, military, economic, cultural, and social aspects of the status and development of the states.

33. See for the elaboration of this argument ibid., pp. 89ff.

34. For the full argumentation see ibid., esp. pp. 94ff., 103ff. and 107ff. (for strategies for structural change in both interstate and intrastate dominance systems). For the broader theoretical dimension cf. Galtung, "Violence, Peace, and Peace Research," Journal of Peace Research 1969, No. 3, pp. 167-192, his "A Structural Theory of Aggression," *Anger, Violence, and Politics* ed. by Ivo K. and Rosalind L. Feieraband and Ted R. Gurr (Englewood Cliffs, N.J.: Prentice-Hall, 1972) pp. 85-97, also his "Peace Thinking," *The Search for World Order* ed. Lepawsky et al., pp. 120-153, his "Theorien des Friedens," *Kritische Friedensforschung* ed. Senghaas, pp. 235-246, also Galtung, Manuel Mora y Araujo, and Simon Schwartzmann, "The Latin American System of Nations: A Structural Analysis," *Conflict Control and Conflict Resolution,* ed. Höglund and Ulrich, pp. 86-113, and Galtung, "East-West Interaction Patterns," *Social Processes in International Relations,* ed. Kriesberg, pp. 272-307.

35. For this charge see Gottfried van Benthem van den Berg, "Theory or taxonomy? Some critical notes on Johan Galtung's "A structural theory of imperialism," Journal of Peace Research 1972, No. 1, pp. 77-86. Also Galtung, "A rejoinder," ibid., pp. 87-90.

36. See here the remarks by Hassner, "Paix et Guerre Entre les Théories," pp. 32, 34 et passim.

37. We refer here only to a few exemplary studies from a fast-growing body of literature, e.g., Helge Hveem, "The global dominance system," Journal of Peace Research, 1973, No. 4, pp. 319-340; Sivert Langholm, "On the concepts of center and periphery," ibid., 1971, No. 3-4, pp. 273-278, Per Olav Reinton, "Inequality in international systems of nations," Peace Research Society (International), Papers, XI, 1969, pp. 47-55, Skjelsbaek, *Peace and the Systems of International Organizations.* (Magister's Thesis, Oslo University, 1970); Klaus Jürgen Gantzel, "Zu herrschaftssoziologischen Problembereichen

von Abhängigkeitsbeziehungen in der gegenwärtigen Weltgesselschaft," *Imperialismus und strukturelle Gewalt. Analysen über abhängige Reproduktion.* Ed. Dieter Senghaas (Frankfurt: Suhrkamp, 1972), pp. 105-120, and Gantzel, "Dependency structures as the dominant pattern in world society," Journal of Peace Research, 1973, No. 3, pp. 203-216; Theotonio dos Santos, "The structure of dependency," American Economic Review, Vol. 60, No. 3, May 1970, pp. 231-236; Osvaldo Sunkel, "Intégration capitaliste transnationale et désintégration nationale en Amérique latine," Politique Entrangére, Vol. 35, No. 6, 1970, pp. 641-700; Sunkel, "Big business and 'dependencia': A Latin-American view," Foreign Affairs, Vol. 50, No. 3, April 1972, pp. 517-531; Stephen Hymer, "The Multinational Corporation and the Law of Uneven Development," *Economics and World Order* ed. by Jagdish L. Bhagwati (New York: Macmillan, 1972), pp. 113-140; also Krippendorff, "Peace research and the Industrial Revolution," Journal of Peace Research, 1973, No. 3, pp. 185-202. For a discussion of the international conflict dimension in current dependency patterns see Senghaas, "Conflict formations in contemporary international society," ibid., pp. 163-184. See also his "Peace research and the Third World," Bulletin of Peace Proposals, 5, 1974, pp. 158-172, his "Die Dritte Welt als Gegenstand der Friedensforschung," DGFK-Hefte, No. 5, November 1974, esp. pp. 3-23, also his introductory essays to *Imperialismus und strukturelle Gewalt,* ed. Senghaas, op. cit., pp. 7-25, and to *Peripherer Kapitalismus. Analysen über Abhängigkeit und Unterentwicklung,* ed. Senghaas, (Frankfurt: Suhrkamp, 1974), pp. 7-36. For a discussion of the new international economic world, see his "Der alte Friedrich List und die neue internationale ökonomische Ordnung," *Leviathan,* 1975 (forthcoming). In this connection reference should be made to "Konflikte zwischen westeuropäischen Industriestaaten und Entwicklungsländern und deren friedliche Uberwindung," DGFK-Informationen, Sonderheft Schwerpunkt II (special issue, no date) in which Senghaas and others present basic research theorems on underdevelopment and dependency as they affect the relations between West European and developing countries.

For a short essay taking issue with the critical understanding of dependency and underdevelopment see Marion Mushkat, "Genèse et avenir du sous-développement," Etudes Polémologiques, 11, January 1974, pp. 30-35.

38. Cf. here Volker Rittberger, "International organization and violence," Journal of Peace Research, 1973, No. 3, pp. 217-226 (a summary of his Ph.D. thesis), and statistics and analyses by Norman Z. Alcock, *The Emperor's New Clothes* (Oakville, Ont.: CPRI Press, 1971). The attacks are directed against the grant and loan policies of such agencies as the World Bank, the IMF, and a few more, which are charged with having pursued a policy of favoring those states that are not antagonistic to financial sponsors of these bodies.

39. Most significant here is Galtung, "East-West Interaction Patterns," *Social Processes in International Relations* ed. Kriesberg, pp. 272-307, where he shows the feudal structure of the Eastern and Western camps and the striking lack of separate ties between the low-ranking members of the two groups. Cf. also the argumentation by d'Oliveira e Sousa, "Les métamorphoses de la guerre," Science et Paid, 1973, No. 2-3, pp. 3-19. However, we should refer here once again to the surprising finding by Milstein, "American and Soviet Influence, Balance of Power, and Arab-Israeli Violence," *Peace, War, and Numbers* ed. Russett, pp. 139-166, who warns that the outside superpower influence on Arab and Israeli violence has been very limited. This indicates that the feudal premise needs some revision and further specification to be generally applicable.

40. See Michael D. Wallance, "Status, Formal Organization and Arms Levels as Factors Leading to the Onset of War, 1820-1964," in ibid., pp. 49-69. For the full argument, including data and caveats, see his *War and Rank Among Nations* (Lexington,

Mass.: D. C. Heath, 1973). cf. also Maurice A. East, "Rank-Dependent Interaction and Mobility: Two Aspects of International Stratification," Peace Research Society (International), Papers, XIV, 1970, pp. 113-127, also James Bennett and H. R. Alker, Jr., "Restructuring Processes in the Global Stratification System: An Outline of a Simulation Model," paper prepared for the Annual Meeting of the International Studies Association, New York, March 1973, and Galtung, "A Structural Theory of Aggression," *Anger, Violence and Politics,* ed. I. K. and R. S. Feierabend and T. R. Gurr, esp. p. 87, and his "East-West Interaction Patterns," esp. pp. 298f. and 304f.

41. See the contributions by W. Guthridge "Arms Control and Developing Countries" and "Arms to Developing Countries" and by Kaldor, "Factors governing the supply and demand of major weapons," *Disarmament and Arms Control* ed. Barnaby and Schaerf. Also Bruno Fritsch, "The Problem of a Global Social Order," *Worldsociety* ed. Landheer et al., p. 154. For extensive studies about arms trade with developing countries cf. Ulrich Albrecht, *Der Handel mit Waffen* (Munich: Hanser, 1971) and Albrecht and Birgit A. Sommer, *Deutsche Waffen für die Dritte Welt. Militärhilfe und Entwicklungspolitik* (Reinbek: Rowohlt, 1972)

42. It goes without saying that the recent changes in the international economic system have brought about a sharp increase in special research on issues relating to the world economy. The study of interdependence has evolved from an essentially political to a global economic-political perspective and is pursued most intensively in the United States. Cf. here Edward L. Morse, "The politics of interdependence," International Organization, Vol. 23, No. 2, Spring 1969, pp. 311-326, and his "Transnational economic processes," ibid., Vol. 25, No. 3, Summer 1971, pp. 23-47; also Richard N. Rosencrance and Arthur A. Stein, "Interdependence: Myth of reality?" World Politics, XXVI, No. 1, October 1973, pp. 1-27, and Donald J. Puchala and Stuart I. Fagan, "International politics in the 1970's: The search for a perspective," International Organization, Vol. 28, No. 2, Spring 1974, pp. 247-266. Cf. also Herbert J. Spiro, "Interdependence: A Third Option Between National Sovereignty and Supra-national Integration," paper prepared for the Ninth World Congress of the International Political Science Association in Montreal, August 1973. For a thorough inquiry into the foundations of the interdependence discussion see Hayward R. Alker, Jr., "Methodological Implications of Interdependence Controversies," paper prepared for the Annual Meeting of the International Studies Association in St. Louis, March 1974.

For reasons that we have given at the beginning of the brief discussion, we refrain from a longer report about detailed data and tentative findings that are still little more than hypotheses. For opposite reasons, the problem of the multinational corporations has merely been alluded to, because the current debate is so rich and intensive that it is impossible in this survey to review and evaluate its present state adequately. Needless to say, the role of these giant companies can hardly be overestimated in the international economic and political system. For two significant essays on the consequences of multinational corporations for the international system see Chadwick F. Alger, "The multinational corporation and the future international system," Annals of the American Academy of Political and Social Science 403, September 1972, pp. 104-115, and Joseph S. Nye, "Multinational enterprises and prospects for regional and global political integration," ibid., pp. 116-126.

43. See here Laszlo, *The Systems View of the World,* pp. 50ff. et passim for the general thesis and its various aspects and implications.

44. The definition of integration will be considered, when we turn to the specialized scholarly discussion of the conception of regional integration.

45. For this rather widespread conviction see Bouthoul, *Traité de Polémologie,* p.

469. Bouthoul, however, makes reference to the occasional merger of peoples with their free consent.

46. For the general argument and some examples from postwar Europe see Gould and Barkun, *International Law and the Social Sciences,* p. 106.

47. For this widespread observation and estimate cf. here Karl Kaiser "Transnational politics: Toward a theory of multinational politics," International Organization, Vol. 25, No. 4, Autumn 1971, pp. 790-817; also Gould and Barkun, *International Law and the Social Sciences,* pp. 307ff. and Krippendorff, Introduction to *Friedensforschung,* p. 21. Krippendorff emphasizes the elaborate legál linkages.

48. For the skeptical critique of regional organizations, cf. Quincy Wright, "Building a Social System for Mankind," *Worldsociety* ed. Landheer et al., p. 183 et passim. Cf. also the remarks by C. F. von Weizsäcker in the introduction to *Kriegsfolgen und Kriegsverhütung,* p. 20. Cf. also Robert C. Angell, *Peace on the March. Transnational Participation* (New York: Van Nostrand Reinhold, 1969) for a strong argument in support of transnational participation by international officials and non-governmental groups and organizations. From a legal viewpoint Verwey, *Economic Development, Peace, and International Law,* warns explicitly against a regional approach to economic development, since it would maintain a fragmented world and threaten international peace.

49. For these definitions see Ernst B. Haas, "The Study of Regional Integration: Reflections on the Joy and Anguish of Pretheorizing," *Regional Integration: Theory and Research.* Ed. Leon N. Lindberg and Stuart A. Scheingold (Cambridge, Mass.: Harvard University Press, 1971), pp. 3-42, pp. 6f. This essay represents Haas' thinking, as it has evolved over more than fifteen years, in a clear and comprehensive manner. Moreover, it offers an interesting evaluation of other conceptions of integration.

50. For the recent development of the "spill-over" and pluralism theses see ibid., esp. pp. 32ff.

51. See ibid., pp. 3f.

52. For criticism and extension of the neo-functionalist model of integration see Leon N. Lindberg, "Political Integration as a Multidimensional Phenomenon Requiring Multivariate Measurement," ibid., pp. 45-127; Joseph S. Nye, "Comparing Common Markets: A Revised Neo-Functionalist Model," ibid., pp. 192-231; and Philippe C. Schmitter, "A Revised Theory of Regional Integraiton," ibid., pp. 232-264. For an examination of the East European integration process in the light of Haas' neo-functionalism cf. Andrzej Korbonski., "Theory and Practice of Regional Integration: The Case of Comecon," ibid., pp. 338-373. For earlier essays on integration and neo-functionalism cf. the informative anthology *International Political Communities* (Garden City: Doubleday Anchor, 1966), especially the articles by Haas, Lindberg, Haas and Schmitter, Nye, Korbonski, and Wionczek.

53. From the large body of relevant transaction and communications literature see for the approach as a whole and major conceptual and technical issues Karl W. Deutsch et al., *Political Community and the North Atlantic Area* (Princeton, N.J.: Princeton University Press, 1957), pp. 3-7. 23ff. and Deutsch, *Nationalism and Social Communication: An Inquiry into the Foundations of Nationality* (Cambridge, Mass.: MIT Press, 2nd ed. 1966 Pb), pp. 86-106; cf. also Deutsch et al., *France, Germany, and the Western Alliance: A Study of Elite Attitudes on European Integration and World Politics* (New York: Scribner's Sons, 1967); see further Deutsch, "The Propensity to International Interactions," *Social Processes in International Relations* ed. Kriesberg, pp. 246-254, and Richard Savage and Deutsch, "A statistical model of the gross analysis of transaction flows," Econometrica, Vol. 28, No. 3, July 1960, pp. 551-572. For an excellent summary of the transaction approach, of its recent developments and of its application to

West European integration see Donald J. Puchala, "International Transactions and Regional Integration," *Regional Integration* ed. Lindberg and Scheingold, pp. 128-159. See also Puchala, "Patterns in West European Integration," revision of a paper prepared for the Annual Convention of the American Political Science Association, 1970.

54. Cf. here the critical remarks by Haas, "The Study of Regional Integration . . . ," pp. 22f. For an interesting preliminary evaluation of the main premises of neo-functionalism and of the transaction approach see Michael B. Dolan, "A Quantitative Analysis of the Neo-Functionalist and Systemic Approaches to the study of Regional Integration," paper prepared for the Annual Convention of the International Studies Association, St. Louis, March 1974.

55. Cf. here for many examples Deutsch et al., *France, Germany and the Western Alliance,* and Puchala, "International Transactions and Regional Integration," *Regional Integration,* pp. 140ff. Puchala is able to demonstrate in the French-German relationship that the attitudinal and transaction data have essentially the same results.

56. Haas, Puchala, Nye, and Stuart Scheingold ("Domestic and International Consequences of Regional Integration"), ibid. All indicate in varying degrees their interest or commitment to the research methods and goals of both approaches.

57. For the analysis of trade data see Hayward Alker, Jr., and Donald Puchala, "Trends in Economic Partnership: The North Atlantic Area, 1928-1963," *Quantitative International Politics* ed. Singer, pp. 287-316. The policy-making process in the European community has gained in intensity and complexity and fits Haas' understanding of cumulative, though incremental, bargaining on the transnational level. For a more recent argument focusing on integration, leadership, and the external role of EEC see Puchala, "Internal Order and Peace: An Integrated Europe in World Affair," paper prepared for the Ninth World Congress of the International Political Science Association in Montreal, August 1973. Cf. also Henri Etienne, "L'Emergence d'une Souveraineté Européenne," paper prepared for the same Congress in Montreal.

58. Cf. here three exploratory suggestive articles: William R. Thompson, "The regional subsystem. A conceptual explication and a propositional inventory," International Studies Quarterly, Vol. 17, No. 1, March 1973, pp. 89-117, further John D. Mitchell, "Cross-cutting memberships, integration, and the international system," Journal of Conflict Resolution, Vol. 14, No. 1, March 1970, pp. 49-55; also Louis J. Cantori and Steven L. Spiegel, "The analysis of regional international politics: The integration versus the empirical systems approach," International Organization, Vol. 27, No. 4, Autumn 1973, pp. 465-494. The last article argues against the teleological orientation of the integration approach, which is said to have caused the neglect of important empirical variables, but the two authors fail to develop convincingly their alternative scheme of analysis.

59. See Peter Wolf, "International organization and attitude change: A re-examination of the functionalist approach," International Organization, Vol. 27, No. 3, Summer 1973, pp. 347-371. The author criticizes the inadequacy of original functionalist thinking, but the neo-functionalism of Haas, Lindberg, Nye, and others cannot be charged with the same omission.

60. See Henry H. Kerr, Jr., "Changing attitudes through international participation: European parliamentarians and integration," ibid., Vol. 27, No. 1, Winter 1973, pp. 45-83. It is surprising that the author rates the cognitive changes so low in terms of social learning. In view of the very weak position of the European Parliament this change is actually quite significant. To validate his findings about French and German parliamentarians, it would be necessary to compare them with the Dutch or British members; moreover, it would be desirable to compare the changes among the various parliamentary groups along ideological rather than national lines.

61. See Puchala, "Europeans and Europeanism in 1970," ibid., Vol. 27, No. 3, Summer 1973, pp. 387-392, where he reviews the report by the Commission des Communeautés Européennes, *Les Européens et l' Unification de l' Europe* (Brussels: General Directorate for Press and Information of the European Communities, 1972). Puchala calls this report the first study of sophisticated opinion patterns in Europe about unification that proves standard judgments to be wrong.

62. See the brief article by Jean Barrea, "The counter-core role of middle powers in processes of external political integration," World Politics, Vol. 25, No. 2, January 1973, pp. 274-287. The historical cases are (1) Nova Scotia in emerging Canada; (2) New South Wales and Queensland in emerging Australia; (3) South Africa; and (4) Bavaria in nineteenth century Germany. The author also lists New York in the thirteen colonies, and Tuscany in Italy as further examples that merit research. It is clear that this paradigm could be applied to contemporary instances of integration.

63. See Lynn K. Mytelka, "The salience of gains in Third-World integrative systems," World Politics, Vol. 25, No. 2, January 1973, pp. 236-250. She suggests also some important factors and remedies for these problems.

64. See Nye, "Comparing Common Markets; A Revised Neo-Functionalist Model," *Regional Integration* ed. Lindberg and Scheingold, esp. pp. 208ff. See also Nye, *Peace in Parts* (Boston: Little, Brown, 1971) in which he discusses specifically conceptual and empirical aspects of the "peace through integration" thesis. Cf. further his "Regional Institutions," The Structure of the International Environment, Vol. IV of *The Future of the International Legal Order,* eds. Cyril E. Black and Richard A. Falk (Princeton: Princeton University Press, 1972), pp. 425-447.

65. For an equation of associative policies, e.g., regionalism and functionalism, with the progress of peace cf. John W. Burton, *Peace Theory. Preconditions of Disarmament* (New York: Knopf, 1962). We refer to his book because it presents the traditional image of peace through association, violent conflict through dissociation so succinctly and without any modification or qualification.

66. For the elaboration of this basic theory see Galtung, "Peace Thinking," *The Search For World Order,* ed. Lepawsky et al., pp. 120-153, especially the typologies on pp. 138 and 141, and his "Theorien des Friedens," *Kritische Friedensforschung* ed. Senghaas, pp. 235-246. For the application of the conceptual framework to major regions (Europe, Latin America, the Middle East, and the Far East), cf. his "Europe–bipolar, bicentric, cooperative?" Journal of Peace Research, 1972, No. 1, pp. 1-26; Galtung, Mora y Araujo, and Schwartzman, "The Latin American System of Nations: A Structural Analysis," *Conflict Control and Conflict Resolution* ed. Höglund and Ulrich, pp. 86-113; Galtung, "Middle East and the theory of conflict," Journal of Peace Research, 1971, No. 3-4, pp. 173-206; and his "Japan and future world politics," ibid., 1973, No. 4, pp. 355-385. Other West European critical peace researchers essentially follow Galtung's analytical framework. See, e.g., Senghaas, "Conflict formations in contemporary international society," ibid., 1973, No. 3, pp. 163-184 and his "Kompositionsprobleme in der Friedensforschung," *Kritische Friedensforschung* ed. Senghaas, pp. 313-361; also his "Friedensforschung–Theoretische Fragestellungen und politische Problems," *Jahrbuch für Friedens- und Konfliktforschung* II, 1972, pp. 10-22. Further, his "Zur Analyse von Drohpolitik in den internationalen Beziehungen," ibid., I, 1971, pp. 126-132. Cf. also Vilmar, "Systematischer Entwurf zur Kritik der Friedensforschung," *Kritische Friedensforschung,* especially pp. 364f., 369 et passim, and Volker Rittberger "Organized multinational cooperation within regional settings: A preliminary analysis," Peace Research Society, (International), Papers, XVII, 1971, pp. 95-118. Rittberger argues that regional institutions are mainly an instrument for the old elites to maintain their predominance in a multinational setting.

67. From the West German literature that contains a particularly vivid and varied discussion of the many issues involved in the quest for a European peace and security system, cf. a few additional essays by Jost Delbrück, "Modelle eines gesamteuropäischen Sicherheitssystems," Jahrbuch für Friedens- und Konfliktforschung II, 1972, pp. 87-102; also Heinz Kramer, "Transaktion zwischen Ost- und Westeuropa als Mittel kooperationsfördernder Systemveränderung" ibid., pp. 117-143; further Vilmar, "Kommutation–Friedenspolitische und friedenspäda-gogische Bedeutung produktiver Lernprozesse zwischen Ost und West," ibid., pp. 103-116; and by a leading specialist in European questions, Gerda Zellentin, "Europäische Friedensordnung, Zielvorstellungen, Strategien und Handlungspotentiale," ibid., pp. 72-86. See also her "Intersystemic regionalism and peace in Europe," Journal of Peace Research 1973, No. 3, pp. 235-244. Cf. also the various pertinent essays by Galtung, Senghaas, and others that have been referred to above.

68. See Bouthoul, *L'Infanticide Différé,* p. 244. Many others share this view with Bouthoul, but they put it in less blunt terms.

69. Cf. e.g., the critical notes and the suggestions for change by Alcock, *The Emperor's New Clothes,* who indicts the foreign aid policies of the major developed countries and urges complete disarmament and peace-keeping under the UN auspices, where the veto should be abolished and the voting should be weighed according to the level of social development, with the U.S. and the USSR holding most votes. Cf. here also Rittberger, "International organization and violence," Journal of Peace Research, 1973, No. 3, pp. 217-226. For extensive data indicating the gross disequilibrium in international organizations see Skjelsbaek, *Peace and the Systems of International Organizations,* and the recent essay by Chadwick F. Alger and David Hoovler, "Regional Participation in International Organizations (Governmental, Non-governmental, Corporations and Banks)," paper prepared for the Ninth World Congress, International Political Science Association, August 19-25, 1973, Montreal. Alger and Hoovler deal with organizations outside the UN system.

70. This attitude is well represented by Quincy Wright, "Building a Social System for Mankind," *Worldsociety* ed. Landheer et al., pp. 178-196 in particular pp. 194ff., and by Verwey, *Economic Development, Peace, and International Law,* especially the concluding chapters, and by Ulrich Duchrow, " 'Gerechte Gewalt,' Gewalttätigkeit und Gewaltlosigkeit im B-Waffen-Zeitalter," *BC-Waffen und Friedenspolitik* ed. E. V. Weizsäcker, p. 133, where he endorses a suggestion by Häfele and Seetzen that the non-nuclear member states "subpoena" the superpowers before the UN to explain every single armament measure. The underlying assumption is that this would increase the pressure on the leading military powers to search for new ways toward world security and would create worldwide public awareness of the urgent need for such a development. For a careful estimate of the future role of the United Nations see Alker and William J. Greenberg, "The UN Charter: Alternate Pasts and Alternate Futures," in E. H. Fedder (ed.), *The United Nations: Problems and Prospects* (St. Louis: University of Missouri Press, 1971), pp. 113-142.

71. The number of roll-call voting studies is very large. The best study, although by now outdated, is still by Hayward R. Alker, Jr., and Bruce M. Russett, *World Politics in the General Assembly* (New Haven: Yale University Press, 1965). Hanna Newcombe from the Canadian Peace Research Institute has been very active analyzing UN voting patterns. See, e.g., her *Patterns of Nations: Interactions in the UN 1946-1971* (Oakville, Ont.: CPRI Press, 1973). Considering the unique constellation of UN voting in terms of its very limited effect on international policy-making, I still doubt that these votes in the General Assembly are at all representative for a state's ideological or material political attitudes.

72. For exemplary work by a leading specialist see, e.g., Alger, "Interaction and negotiation in a committee of the United Nations General Assembly," Peace Research Society (International) Papers 5 (1966), pp. 141-159, and his "Interaction in a Committee of the United Nations General Assembly," *Quantitative International Politics* ed. Singer, pp. 51-84. His research findings indicate the possibilities and the rather severe constraints in this kind of empirical study.

73. See the very interesting essay by Haas and Edward Thomas Rowe, "Regional organization in the United Nations: Is there externalization?" International Studies Quarterly, Vol. 17, No. 1, March 1973, pp. 3-54. For the deplorable fact that most states show little commitment to the universal goals and tasks of the United Nations and measure their commitment primarily in the narrow terms of their national advantage, cf. Alger, "The United States in the United Nations," International Organization, Vol. 27, No. 1, Winter 1973, pp. 1-23, and Ernst-Otto Czempiel, *Macht und Kompromiss. Die Beziehungen der Bundesrepublic Deutschland zu den Vereinten Nationen, 1956-1970.* (Düsseldorf: Bertelsmann, 1971). These two references could easily be complemented by studies about other UN members.

74. This prediction was offered by James A. Stagenga in his very good review article "Peacekeeping: Post-mortems or previews," International Organization, Vol. 27, No. 3, Summer 1973, pp. 373-385.

75. Cf. here the ambivalent findings that implicitly endorse the pessimistic view, in Doris A. Graber, "Perceptions of Middle East conflict in the UN, 1953-1965," Journal of Conflict Resolution, Vol. 13, No. 4, December 1969, pp. 454-484; and Randolph M. Siverson, "Role and perception in international crises: The case of Israeli and Egyptian decision makers in national capitals and the United Nations," International Organization, Vol. 27, No. 3, Summer 1973, pp. 329-345. Both essays are methodologically dubious and weaken the findings and suggestions considerably.

76. For a detailed and revealing analysis of the Cyprus operation see the excellent article by Malvern Lumsden, "Some Factors Affecting Local Acceptance of a UN Force: A Pilot Report from Cyprus," *Conflict Control and Conflict Resolution* ed. Höglund and Ulrich, pp. 117-142.

77. See Ernst B. Haas, Robert L. Butterworth, and Joseph S. Nye, *Conflict Management by International Organizations* (Morristown, N.J.: General Learning Press, 1972), esp. pp. 26f., 43f. and 60f. The study contains many other important findings that remain unreported here, but that cast new light on the widely divergent performance characteristics of various regional organizations. For a viewpoint favoring regional over global security provisions see Lynn H. Miller, "The Prospects for Order Through Regional Security," *Regional Politics and World Order,* ed. Falk and Mendlovitz, op. cit., pp. 50-74. Cf. also Tanter, "The policy relevance of models in world politics," Journal of Conflict Resolution, Vol. 16, No. 4, December 1972, p. 575, where he briefly describes an intricate computer simulation of UN peace-making, its success and failure, according to five major characteristics of disputes. This model developed by Alker and Christensen could be used to reconstruct histories of UN peace-keeping and to forecast future developments and possibilities.

78. Cf. here Sydney Bailey, "The veto in the Security Council," International Conciliation, No. 566, January 1968, for one of the few serious efforts to study the decision-making process of the Security Council.

79. For an older collection of East European contributions to the understanding of peaceful coexistence cf. E. Weichelt and J. Kirsten (eds.), *Zu den völherrechtlichen Prinzipien der friedlichen Koexistenz.* Aktuelle Beiträge zur Staats- und Rechtswissenschaft aus den sozialistischen Ländern, Heft 7 (Postdam-Babelsberg, 1964). An excellent

up-to-date account, essentially descriptive, is that of Philippe Bretton and Jean-Pierre Chaudet, *La Coexistence Pacifique,* Collection U (Paris: Librairie Armand Colin, 1971).

80. For the UN declaration of the principles of peaceful coexistence (Res. 1815 XXVIII) and 2625 (XXV) and for detailed comments see ibid., pp. 40f.

81. See ibid., p. 31.

82. For a thorough review of the convergence theory see Wilfried von Bredow, *Vom Antagonismus zur Konvergenz.* Studien zum Ost-West-Problem (Frankfurt; Main: Metzner, 1972). The author goes so far as to call the convergence thesis a tool in the Western strategy; this is the way the Socialist countries perceive it. For our purposes, this question need not be resolved.

83. The notion of cooperation in a rather practical sense underlies the suggestions by Galtung, "Europe–bipolar, bicentric, cooperative." Journal of Peace Research, 1972, No. 1, pp. 1-26, and Albrecht, Galtung, Joenniemi, Senghaas, and Verona, "Is Europe to demilitarize?" Instant Research on Peace and Violence 1972(4), pp. 181-246. Cf. also Zellentin, "Intersystemic regionalism and peace in Europe," Journal of Peace Research, 1973, No. 3, pp. 235-244. Interesting material is also in "Principles, possible structures and perspectives for a system of collective security and cooperation in Europe," Scientific Symposium, Vienna, October 14-15, 1972, Peace and the Sciences, March 1973, No. 1. Bredow, *Vom Antagonismus zur Konvergenz,* proposes the term "antagonistic cooperation" to capture the dialectical nature of East-West interaction. Fritz Vilmar, "Kommutation–Friedenspolitische und friedenspädagogische Bedeutung produktiver Lernprozesse swischen Ost und West," Jahrbuch für Friedens- und Konfliktforschung, Vol. II, 1972, pp. 103-116, recommends the concept of "commutation," which implies that both East and West should change together toward a socialist democratic order that rests on equality, justice, and freedom.

PART TWO

IN SEARCH OF CONFLICT RESOLUTION

Chapter 3

CONFLICT–PREMISES AND MODELS

Human conflicts, on all levels of interaction, have always occupied the minds of observers and scholars because it is widely believed that the causes of human discontent and violence lie primarily in man's nature and in his attitudinal and affective make-up. This statement, though far too general, indicates the diversity of scholarly concerns, and it shows the tentative quality of hypotheses and findings in this field of research. Actually, we should speak of *fields* of research, since individual psychology, anthropology, social psychology, sociology, political science, ethology (the scientific study of animal behavior), and many special interdisciplinary endeavors deal with the complex aspects of conflict behavior among individuals, within and among social groups, between governments, states, and regions. A much debated question at present is whether and to what extent the study of animal behavior can contribute to a better understanding of man. We also face the more difficult problem of how we can apply insights and experimental findings from laboratory studies involving individuals and groups of two or three to the analysis of perception and interaction patterns that are typical for large social units or for governmental leaders and the political decision-making bodies. The answers to these questions remain elusive. If we are aware of the formidable barriers to conceptual clarification and scientific experimentation in the crucial area of interaction as it relates to peace and conflict, we are able to judge to some degree the merits of current scholarly efforts and to acknowledge the difficulties, the advances, and the lacunae in what they are trying to achieve. There is a considerable amount of basic theorizing about conflict in general and international conflicts in particular.[1] Some of these conceptions must be familiar to us, if we want to grasp the underpinnings and the inadequacies of the many laboratory experiments and games that have been going on for more than a decade, primarily in the United States.

General Aspects of Conflict and Conflict Resolution

In approaching conflict, we have to establish the degree of permissible abstraction and the adequate level of analysis: Can we draw firm conclusions pertaining to conflictual interaction between states from general conceptualizations and from empirical evidence about conflict patterns between individuals, small groups or social classes? The propositions and findings in the scholarly literature do not allow an unequivocal answer to this crucial query. Tentatively, we assume that inference from the other levels of conflictual interaction is necessary and feasible.

CONFLICT–SUBJECTIVE OR OBJECTIVE?

At this point we must briefly return to a principal question that has already received some attention in the introduction. Students of conflict are not in agreement about the relative importance of structural and predispositional factors as determinants of conflict.[2] There cannot be a clear answer to this whole question because the two conflict parameters are intertwined, in that the participants shape their actions according to their perception of the structural properties on the conflict. Does this mean that in the final analysis perception is all that counts, because the real conditions and events matter only if and how far they are picked up perceptually in the decision-making of the parties involved? Or are we to argue that what is perceived is merely a reflection, an image, though probably distorted, of the structure, the "objective reality," of the conflict situation? We could also juxtapose "personality" (defined as a configuration of behavior potentials or internal programs within the individual) and "situation" (here seen as the physical environment, including other people, external to the individual) and thus express the contended issue concisely.[3]

As indicated previously, there are indeed quite a few students of conflict and of conflict settlement who look at the problem in this dichotomized fashion and emphasize one aspect at the expense of the other as the key to the achievement of peace. John Burton and his associates in London are proponents of the "conflict resolution through changed perception" approach.

They maintain that in conflict situations the prime task and opportunity is to bring about changes in the perception of the antagonists; this is to be achieved through "controlled communication," i.e., a procedure in which messages, as they are transmitted, are checked for their veracity, accuracy, and seriousness. This examination requires the presence of a third party–in Burton's scheme academic specialists–who thereby contributes to correcting misperceptions and to transforming predispositional ill will into new values that enhance mutual understanding and cooperation, thus improving the prospects for a settlement of the conflict. Burton shows an overriding concern with perception for the past by rigidly claiming that the mediator should never suggest solutions and that the parties should never be asked to accept a compromise; he holds instead that the parties must arrive at the solution by themselves in finding alternate goals rather than compromises.[4] It is obvious that such a lopsided representation of the qualities of the technique of "controlled communication" stresses its basic defects and neglects its merits. The view is untenable that conflicts are primarily "subjective"; but this correction does not entail the opposite conclusion that there are no subjective conflicts. The best way of seeing it is to assume and search for the subjective and the objective, the predispositional and the structural, aspects of a conflictual interaction situation. According to the presence and relative strength of these two characteristics, we can devise our tools for the challenging tasks of rectifying misperceptions and of laying the foundations for a new set of values and objectives that can be shared by the parties in conflict.[5]

Only a few scholars and practitioners see the nature of human conflict, in particular that of international conflict, the way Burton does. Most tend to assume that disputes in varying degrees contain incompatible interests, the resolutions of which require far more than changed perceptions. However, the exact quality of the adverse goals, and the degree to which they are at all open to modification, is greatly contested. Some hold the view that the essential targets in most conflicts are pursued rigidly, but that they can be modified or satisfied by complex compromises. Others emphasize the principal adversity and irreconcilability inherent in serious conflict.

For the latter perspective, in which conflictual interaction is seen as flowing from an objective, structural dichotomy, let us briefly consider Galtung's conception. He defines conflict as a situation with incompatible goal states. These goals may be either subjectively defined values or objectively defined interests.[6] In terms of structural thinking, it is clear that the clash of antagonistic objective interests is the most severe and most intractable conflict type. While Galtung perceives the range of difficulties that arise in an effort to control and resolve subjective conflicts–he is less optimistic than Burton about the chances for long-lasting and thorough removal of the conflict issues–he is aware of the immense impediments to the management and resolution of objective conflicts. In the case of a dispute that involves incompatible objective interests, Galtung holds that the conventional methods of peace-making (negotiations leading to a compromise) are unlikely to bring about a successful termination of the conflict. Here he often sees a need for structural changes whereby the interests are altered, even at the expense of one or the other party to the conflict. In a socioeconomic conflict, it might involve the abolition of the ownership of a large production facility and the establishment of a process of self-management that would shift the benefits to the previously dependent salaried workers. In an international structural conflict situation, e.g., an imperial or colonial relationship, it necessitates the rupture of the old asymmetric links to produce a change in the nature of the interests and to open possibilities for an effective resolution of the conflict. The severity of the requirements and issues involved needs no further elaboration at this point.[7]

A TENTATIVE CONCEPTION OF CONFLICT

The short exposition of the two extreme trends in the study of conflictual interaction and of conflict resolution is far from complete and is not meant to be comprehensive; it serves to show that the question is wide open as to whether we should approach the problem from the perspective of the personality or of the structure. It is probably impossible to divide real conflicts into subjective and objective, perceptual and structural ones. In our judgment, it is more prudent and realistic to posit that most conflict situations contain elements of both and that therefore the best strategy for research and for practical application is a mixed approach, whereby we trace the different strands and components of a particular conflictual interaction, regardless of whether it is interpersonal, intergroup, interclass, or international.[8]

Except for basic differentiation, the terms "personality" and "structure" are still too broad to be useful for a full-fledged, detailed examination and description of a conflict situation. If we depict the two dimensions of conflict as clusters of personality and structural variables, we are able to list the major components of this multivariate phenomenon along the two main conceptual lines. Thus the study of the structure of conflict entails:

(1) The basic preconditions of interaction between the parties in conflict;

(2) The specific conflict situation;

(3) The wider environment (third parties, the particular global and regional system past and present, the military, economic, and geographic circumstances); and

(4) The dynamics of the conflict process (the development of the conflict, major factors, e.g., military and political alliances, informal alignments, the ideological dimension, involvement of regional and global organizations).

In the examination of the role of personality for conflict we would consider such issues as:

(1) Motives;
(2) The cognitive structure;
(3) A value-orientation ranging from trust to mistruct; and
(4) More specifically, the perceptions held by the decision-makers, the public elites, or the general publics of the parties to the conflict and of involved outside forces.[9]

The division that is suggested here is still deficient in that it excludes some dimensions of conflict interaction and conflict resolution that are of central importance. Some answer is needed as to the functions of conflict.[10] The customary view is to consider conflict to be an evil or a nuisance. Yet there are numerous occasions in which conflict is the only method to defeat a growing danger or to eliminate a long-festering source of hatred, unrest, or deprivation. If these valuable effects of overt conflict arc known and accepted, it becomes more difficult to analyze a conflict situation, but it also enriches the outcome of the examination. Here is a large lacuna in peace and conflict research.

Another issue that has also received only scant attention, although it is truly crucial, is the problem of how conflicts end.[11] To be able to propose a better normative scheme of conflict termination, scholars and decision-makers need to know in full detail, on the basis of empirical analysis, how social, economic, political, or military disputes are ended: by mutual agreement, by the cessation of overt hostilities without any formal agreement, by the decisive outcome of a limited battle in the confrontation without overall victory or defeat, by a concession of inferiority by the weaker party, by a mutual decision to follow the suggestions for termination from outside states or organizations. There are other types of conflict termination, the relationship of which to conflict resolution is not at all clear. Moreover, we should know how the end of a dispute in one sphere of interaction, e.g., in the military or economic realms, affects the situation in another, e.g., the political one. Only if we have clearer ideas about the range and level of interrelationships between the various spheres of interaction, cooperative or conflictual, we will be able to recognize the long-range implications of instances of conflict termination for the nature of international peace. This set of problems is surely a new frontier for peace and conflict research.

A Note on Aggression and Non-violence

So far we have not dealt with a particular issue that has given rise to a fundamental debate among scientists from many disciplines in the natural and social sciences, and which seems to be of great significance for the understanding of conflict: Is man a born aggressor and killer, or does he learn such behavior? This question is not only complicated, but in the final analysis is also unanswerable, a fact that well explains the steady flow of books and articles on this subject. The whole discussion of aggression is not of primary relevance in the context of this study; this is why we restrict ourselves to a brief consideration of some of the major recent developments in this great debate.

The thesis of man's innate instinctual aggressive drive is argued by the famous ethologist Konrad Lorenz and it has been popularized by such authors as Ardrey, Storr, and Morris, to name just the leading proponents of this viewpoint.[12] They assert that this natural aggression is part and parcel of man's genetic endowment and plays a vital role in human functioning if it is controlled adequately, that is, neither too much nor too little. This kind of theorizing rests on very shaky scientific foundations. It is also tantamount to a denial of the search for ways to order human relations in conditions of peace, justice, and freedom. If we accept their reasoning we must give up the hope that human interaction, e.g., diplomatic negotiations, will result in a cooperative solution agreeable and satisfactory to all parties involved.

Despite the popular appeal of the proponents of the thesis of instinctive aggression, we have no reason to succumb to the pessimistic gloom that flows from it. Leading students of animal and human behavior have responded virogously and have shown convincingly that there is a lot of evidence to counter the views of Lorenz and his followers. Ethologists, anthropologists, psychologists, and other social scientists are among them.[13] They deny the direct transferability of findings from the animal world to the humans, and they express severe reservations about the relevance of the underlying conception and the asserted empirical verification of the aggression hypothesis. They do not deny the presence of aggressive trends in human behavior, but they argue that they originate in social learning rather than in the genes. Some also hold that there may be a broad pattern of behavioral potentials implanted in human nature, *including* the propensity for aggressive attitudes, but that their development and expression depends on the general cultural environment of the social group in which the individual is brought up.

Another important group of scholars links aggression to frustration in that the experience of the latter is likely to cause the former. In this theory the question of innate or learned behavior does not arise. In revised form, the frustration hypothesis could include the element of anxiety or fear as the intermediate link between the experience of frustration and the aggressive response. Aggression in this understanding would always presume frustration and anxiety, but there is no automatic progression ending in aggressive behavior because man is capable of adapting to the adverse experience through rational thought and action.[14]

From the various views on aggression it becomes clear that the stipulation of an irresistible instinctive drive toward aggressive behavior lacks empirical proof and is therefore untenable. The causes of human aggression are by no means established, and recent developments fail to provide any decisive clarifications as to whether we are born with some kind of natural energy that moves the individual to assert himself and might of course be perverted into aggressive behavior, or whether such conduct is exclusively the fruit of early social learning. Conclusive evidence for one or the other hypothesis would have important consequences for the conception of human conflict and for the strategy of peace within and among human communities. Unfortunately, this evidence is not likely to become available in the foreseeable future. Therefore, we must content ourselves with the refutation of Lorenz' thesis by most serious researchers in the field.[15]

It seems appropriate to add a few remarks about a major trend in research which is a strong antidote against the aggression theorem and strives actively to offer theoretical and practical suggestions to overcome aggression and violence in human relations. The study of non-violence has its origins first and foremost in the working and writing of Gandhi, whose example inspired millions of human beings to disavow the use of naked force and to defy repressive unwielding regimes through peaceful, non-violent resistence, trying to promote their just cause by means of superior reasoning and moral persuasion. The whole concept would be unthinkable if man were aggressive by nature. Gandhi challenged his oppressors and their crass belief in the absolute superiority or armed power, and he proved to the world the strength of his spiritual and philosophical principles.

Ever since Gandhi gained prominence in India, members of the peace movement and sympathizers in the scholarly community have studied his writings and his action programs which contributed so decisively to the awakening of the Indian people and to the peaceful liberation from British colonial rule. Gandhi himself considered the essential elements of his strategy to be universally valid and, true to his belief in the power of reason and morality, he further asserted that non-violent resistance could be initiated against all regimes and rulers without risking brutal suppression and the killing of large numbers of resisters. Thus he advised the Jews in Nazi Germany to resist the persecution by the regime peacefully, because he did not realize or did not wish to realize the exceptionally ruthless character of the antisemitic campaign in this modern totalitarian state. Still the emergence of totalitarian rule does not prove the pessimistic axiom of ubiquity of aggression and violence, nor does it disprove Gandhi's belief in the efficacy of human reason and ethics.

We need not describe in detail the procedure of Gandhi's numerous campaigns of disobedience and non-violent resistance. The general facts are widely known, and much of his strategy has been integrated into the conceptions of non-violent resistance and civilian defense that have been developed in recent years. The most notable change involves the emphasis on non-violent *action* whereby the scope of non-violence has been shifted away from passive resistance. This development is logical in that it fulfills the fundamental idea of Gandhi's peaceful change.

It is symptomatic that the turn toward a more action-oriented conception of non-violence has set in in several countries at about the same time, without essential prior communication among the researchers. As briefly mentioned in the introduction, the leading proponents of this activist approach are the American Gene Sharp, the British Adam Roberts, and the German Theodor Ebert. In the following we present a few major aspects of their research results and of their programmatic conclusions for peace action. This is fitting at this juncture of our survey since the new schemes of non-violent action are designed for both intra- and interstate conflict situations. Moreover, they are clearly distinguishable from abstract conceptual reflection, model-building, and painstaking empirical work characteristic of most of the other peace research evaluated here.

Explicitly separating non-violence from pacifism,[16] the modern Gandhians base their conception on the premise that no regime can maintain itself in the long run without support or at least compliance from its subjects. Political power in that sense depends on the participation of the general public even if the regime is tyrannical or totalitarian.[17] Therefore, non-violent action is principally always feasible whenever people feel that something must be done to protest and eventually to overcome the exercise of illegitimate power, be it political, economic, or military. The American civil rights movement and the campaign against American involvement in Vietnam are two recent examples in a long history of non-violent action dating back to early labor strikes and to numerous protest movements against oppressive rule or the suppression of minorities.[18]

By refraining from the use of violence in the conflict with the powerful opponent, non-violent actionists either ensure that the non-use of violence will be reciprocated or they demonstrate that the violence employed by the opponent fails against their determination, organization, and willingness to suffer, and that it will be terminated as soon as the opponent realizes that nothing short of mass murder or mass detention will break the resistance movement. In most cases, the argument goes, the oppressor will shy away from the ultimate measure to overwhelm the non-violent movement or, if he does opt for brutal force, he will concede his inability to meet the challenge in a fitting manner and to maintain public order and security, and will contribute to his own demise. This means that the non-violent actionists calculate the risks of their involvement without blindly trusting the moral attitudes of those whom they oppose; they are convinced that this rational calculation of costs and benefits will in most cases convince the wielder of power that it is more opportune for himself and for the community to seek a compromise in the conflict.

This key element of the strategy of non-violent action is highly controversial. Even if the participants in a non-violent campaign are thoroughly educated and trained in the underlying philosophy and in its practical implementation, it is neither certain that all of them will be able to withstand the counterforce of suppression nor can it be taken for granted that the rulers who nowadays dispose of an enormous array of means of control and manipulation must give in to the demands of the protestors or resort to naked violence. Such means as spying, sabotage, betrayal, rumors, and clandestine operations are not the prerogatives of the resisters. Their opponents can deploy them, too, and they are in the advantageous position of being able to control the huge appartus of government, including the military, the economy, and the centers of communication and information. Nevertheless, the overriding factor speaking for the adherence to the principle of non-violence even under the most trying circumstances is the certainty of bloodshed, protracted battle, and probable defeat if the protesters use force to advance their cause.

The same argument underlies the evolution of a non-violent alternative to traditional instruments and agencies of national defense. The scheme of "civilian defense" or "social defense"[19] has developed out of concern that the potential repercussions of military conflict between states are no longer bearable. The threat of a nuclear holocaust is too familiar to need any further explanation and, in addition, the uses of a military establishment are by now limited for most countries in the world, considering its financial and social costs as well as its inefficacy against nuclear blackmail or against superior atomic or conventional weapons. Civilian defense might even be substituted for the deterrence strategies of the superpowers because they cost enormous sums of the national budgets, seem to serve no military purpose short of all-out global destruction, and provide little if any security.

How are civilian defense programs to be organized and for which situations? If an external aggressor invades and occupies a state and deposes the legitimate government, the proponents of civilian defense argue that the invading power can best be resisted and ultimately worn out by a general strategy of non-cooperation, boycott, and disobedience carried out by a highly motivated and disciplined population. Historical precedents, successful and unsuccessful, are numerous, especially from countries under Nazi rule. The students of civilian resistance contend that failure is frequently due to lack of adequate general training and mobilization and to the mistake of adding violent measures to non-violent ones. If the resisters use violence, the main barrier against violent retaliation is removed and the campaign of active resistance is bound to fail.

It becomes absolutely clear that a serious effort to implement a program of civilian defense requires thorough permanent involvement of the total population, independent initiative and intensive participation and cooperation, and a sincere commitment to the values underlying their political and social system. Moreover, it depends on the large-scale enlistment of all mature citizens and even of the students in elementary and secondary schools in recurrent training and refresher exercise, surpassing military service in scope, duration, and intensity. Briefly, civilian defense requires the ideal citizenry that will maintain maximum cohesion, sincerity, and intelligence even under severe pressure and grave hardship administered by the foreign occupying power. Still the advocates of civilian defense claim that their action program for non-military protection is viable.

A detailed description and analysis of the elaborate provisions for a comprehensive civilian defense scheme would go beyond the scope and purpose of this study, but we should briefly consider a more normative dimension developed mainly by Ebert and his associates and in which certain extensive social, political, and economic changes are postulated: in order to be fully effective, the civilian defense program must be carried out in a fully egalitarian fashion combining participation, democracy, and socialism. This political ideal is seen as both a prerequisite and a result of the adoption of civilian defense. The intimate connection between the implementation of the program and equal participation is plausible, since it is unlikely that the citizens would be sufficiently motivated if traditional hierarchies and privileges were to be preserved in this effort. However, the postulated evolution toward democratic socialism need by no means follow from the character of the non-military defense program. Wishful thinking and speculation apparently triumph here over the sober spirit of scholarly normative thinking.

Far more serious reservations have been raised against the conception, primarily on foreign policy grounds. Can a state afford to leave the alliance of which it is a member, to forfeit the nuclear guarantee of a superpower, to disarm totally and then expect to deter potential enemies with its civilian defense strategy? Why should one prepare oneself only against invasion and occupation at a time when international conflicts can be fought with nuclear threats, intercontinental missiles, and many other instruments that have made territorial aggression to a large extent obsolete? If invasion and occupation take place, why should one be confident that civilian defense will overcome the aggressor who wields all the tools of modern totalitarian control?

What can be concluded in favor of non-violent action and civilian defense? The internal use of such schemes of resistance and action is of undeniable significance. Except for unusual circumstances, there is normally room for non-violent involvement to remedy domestic ills. Considering the pervasiveness of violence in most modern societies, we urgently need far wider knowledge and application of non-violent techniques of conflict management in many walks of life. Basic research and practice-related work has progressed rapidly during the last decade, and the only question now is how to spread the non-violent techniques quickly so that violent conflict will eventually disappear.

The potential of civilian defense is far more difficult to estimate. Its application as the only scheme of national defense is still highly improbable. Most military experts consider it somewhat useful as a fallback provision if major military or political strategies fail. Nevertheless, it should be accorded more serious attention. As a first step it could be adopted in those situations where there is little evidence of potential major conflict among the neighboring states and in the region as a whole and where full-fledged military establishments are far too costly in terms of their defense function. A developing country might save considerable sums and enlarge its developmental budget, thereby strengthening its socioeconomic infrastructure and its international position. Once it proves the viability of its non-military defense it might sponsor a regional agreement banning military establishments and arms from the area, just as steps have been taken to declare certain zones non-nuclear. The case of highly armed states in volatile regions is far more complex, but we hope that a major neutral country in Europe or elsewhere might initiate its civilian defense program and eventually abolish its armies and discard its arms. It sounds utopian, but it is a relevant utopia toward which we should direct our efforts. The proponents of non-violence and of civilian defense are convinced that human aggression and violence can and must be overcome and that their reflections and action programs will bear fruit. Their suggestions pose a great challenge for mankind. They may offer the only alternative to communal violence and to nuclear annihilation.[20]

As we return to the discussion of conflict concepts and models, we must bear in mind that the brief excursus on aggression and non-violence is not a disgression from the overall focus of this peace research survey. Both issues to which we addressed ourselves are atypical but nevertheless of great importance. In the following we shall not refer to them explicitly, but it is hoped that our brief analysis will add a meta-empirical dimension to whatever we report of conceptual and experimental research relating to the perception of and interaction in conflicts. Mindful of the aggression hypothesis, we should be wary of overly optimistic proposals for conflict resolution; and being aware of the philosophy and practice of non-violence, we should be suspicious of those voices that deny any prospect for successful management and resolution of interpersonal or interstate conflicts.

Models of International Conflict

The availability of data-processing methods and machines has enabled the scholar to construct complex models of conflict and conflict resolution, and to analyze many cases of conflict interaction. Of course, one question plagues all such research: Are the most important data available, and if so, are they quantifiable in a way that all data are compatible and bring out meaningful results? Looking at the few items we have listed above, we notice that this methodological and heuristic question is difficult.[21] We must keep these pre-analytical considerations and conditions in mind as we approach some of the recent examples of model-building in the social scientific study of conflict behavior.

A main premise in approaching conflict models is the constant awareness that we deal here with an utterly complex phenomenon, the analysis of which, whether it is done abstractly or empirically, makes for diverse findings and conclusions. In the following sections we must try to reflect as adequately as possible the wide array of general conceptions and specific insights. Conflict, a multi-causal, dynamic process in which the actors are subject to a wide variety of learning and feedback mechanisms, allows for many different questions and answers. The situational inputs, the structuring of the important actors and their arenas of interaction, their policy perspectives, their problem-solving or decision-making rules, the changing sequences according to which certain of these rules are involved, or the decreasing availability of non-violent decisional alternatives, all these factors are conceivable factors making for war or peace.[22]

In the study of conflictual interaction at the international level, it is particularly important to account for the presence of certain causes and effects and for their relative weight in each case. The need for such specification is a further constraint, in that it is scientifically impossible to give a fully reliable account of a particular case of international conflictual interaction. This limitation is due to the fact that each decision and each development in the history of the case may be connected with an at best wide, at worst infinite, number of causes, at least from the viewpoint of the observer-analyst. His choice of parameters and variables is crucial for his conclusions. A common simplifying step has been to abstract in the interaction model from all real circumstances and to speak in terms of two equal parties in a bilateral relationship. Others focus on individual cases of interaction in order to find typical patterns of conflict behavior.[23] More recently, very complex models have been constructed based on massive data from a multitude of structures and cases.

A major example for the last type of model at a high level of abstraction and organization is, as we have already mentioned, the "Correlates of War" study by Singer and his associates, who have brought out that diplomatic standing, status, alliance membership, capability distribution, and membership in international organizations affect in varying degrees the occurrence of warfare among state actors.[24]

MODELLING INTERNATIONAL CRISES

Another comprehensive approach to interaction is the study of international crises, in which the event itself or rather the interrelated sequence of events is the analytical focus. The particular merit of this recently developed framework for analysis is its exclusive concern with conflictual interactions, so that the possibility diminishes significantly that the researchers seek information and insights from non-comparable types of human interaction. For the development of a general crisis model, Charles F. Hermann's work has been most important. He has insisted on a rigorous definition of crisis that diverges somewhat from the vague common sense understanding; a situation is said to be a crisis "if it (1) threatens one or more important goals of a state, that is, the group of authoritative policy makers who constitute the state, (2) allows only a short time for decision before the situation is significantly transformed, and (3) occurs as a surprise to the policy makers."[25]

The three dimensions of threat, decision time, and awareness can be depicted as scales along which we seek to establish the precise properties of a crisis situation as it appears to the decision-maker. Threat may range from low to high; time from short to extended; and awareness from surprise to anticipated. Eight basic decision situations derive from the possible relations between the three ranges:

(1) Crisis situation (high threat/short time/surprise);
(2) Innovative situation (high threat/extended time/surprise);
(3) Inertia situation (low threat/extended time/surprise);
(4) Circumstantial situation (low threat/short time/surprise);
(5) Reflexive situation (high threat/short time/anticipated);
(6) Deliberative situation (high threat/extended time/anticipated);
(7) Routinized situation (low threat/extended time/anticipated);
(8) Administrative situation (low threat/short time/anticipated).[26]

This scheme is not merely useful to attach labels to a lot of international situations which require attention from the policy-makers. It also sketches the criteria for the determination of the nature of the conflictual interaction and of likely possibilities for its peaceful settlement.

We notice, of course, that before we can take up this last aspect of the analysis we need to expand the framework so that it encompasses the interaction of two or more parties. This requires that we differentiate the situational properties in terms of the perceptual characteristics of the various parties involved. Such a complicating expansion of the questions and data is indispensable because the actors in the conflict will most likely have divergent estimates as to the threat, time, and surprise components of the situation facing them. In the case of sharp dichotomies in their respective perception the crisis situation will probably worsen and a solution will become more elusive. The researcher faces enormous difficulties in performing the various analytical and evaluate operations, on the basis of which he can make suggestions as to how to handle a concrete conflict.

It would be unwarranted if we focused exclusively on this crisis model, because other scholars have developed independently their own frameworks and hypotheses from which they have derived additional propositions that help to explain the processes of crisis interaction. Hermann has listed four basic models which group the numerous propositions into different theoretical perspectives that might explain apparent contradictions between the competing hypotheses about crisis; the four models are (1) the individual stress model; (2) the organizational response model; (3) the hostile interaction model; and (4) the cost calculation model. The first one comprises all the hypotheses which stipulate that stress affects the ability of the individual decision-maker to cope with the crisis. The second model rests on the axiom that crisis decisions are concentrated in the hands of a small number of top foreign policy decision-makers. The third conception summarizes those views that consider the actions of a state in crisis as a function of the hostility its leaders perceive to have previously been received from the other side. The fourth model sees the policy-makers calculating the benefits of a decision against the costs its implementation is likely to involve.[27]

The four models are not necessarily mutually exclusive. If an individual researcher principally adheres to the perspective of the stress model, but also sees evidence for the salience of aspects of the cost calculation model, his working hypotheses will deviate from those of both frameworks. Others again embrace different propositions and combinations, so that striking divergences and contradictions in their premises and findings are inevitable. What counts here is not so much that such contradictions arise, but that the four models give at least a semblance of order to a mass of seemingly unconnected facts and guesses. These theoretical perspectives, separate or integrated into one model,[28] should prove immensely helpful for specific issues in perception and interaction. All indications speak for the great relevance of crises as analytical forms in the empirical and policy-related study of international conflict.[29] The biggest hurdle to be overcome in the application of the crisis concepts and hypotheses to a wide range of concrete conflict situations is the difficulty of extracting and verifying relevant data that are mostly unrecorded or not accessible to the researcher until long after the termination of the conflict. Most students of society and politics face this impediment in their research, but it is exacerbated in the study of crises.

A slightly less abstract framework has been elaborated by Oran Young, who emphasizes the implications of crises for the stability of the international system as a whole or of some sub-system. Together with the elements of Hermann's crisis definition he lists some alternate factors that reflect more on the basic processes and dynamics of crises. Here he distinguishes between positive feedback crises, overload crises, starvation crises, steering crises, and adaptation crises; among these, the most common are the positive feedback and the adaptation crises.[30] To document these types of conflictive situations requires less secret, as well as less quantifiable, data and, if investigated carefully, their occurrence can be explained not only for the past or present, but there is a good chance that they can be forecast over the short and middle range. Moreover, this classificatory scheme is directly applicable in the foreign policy decision-making process.

NOVEL PERSPECTIVES FOR CONFLICT MODELS

For the measurement and short-term prediction of international conflict Edward Azar has formulated a model which he has tested with data from Egyptian-Israeli conflict behavior. His basic assumption is that during relatively short periods of time certain factors, e.g., capabilities and perception, remain stable, and that the interaction behavior of A and B at Time 1 is a function of their behavior at Time t-1 and a determinant of the interaction at t + 1. He emphasizes that the model must be simple and that its predictive range is limited to one year. Relevant information is scaled and computer-stored as to (1) time; (2) actor; (3) target; (4) source; (5) activity; and (6) issue-area. The interaction events can range from the merger of states A and B into a new sovereign state to all-out war between A and B. Azar distinguishes thirteen interaction points and divides them into two regions, one of friendliness and the other of hostility, and assigns each of them a numerical value, in rising sequence, with a positive (+) symbol for friendliness and a negative (–) one for hostility. Out of these data Azar has developed a quantitative measure which makes available the DI's, the dimensions of interaction. If the measures for friendly and hostile interaction are added up, we get a cumulative single figure for the overall level of friendliness or hostility. If the measures for t-1 and for t are known, Azar argues we are able to predict the comprehensive figure for t + 1. His projections for the conflict between Israel and Egypt have been correct over a period of four years. He indicates, however, that the model is satisfactory only in situations of high levels of hostility and of symmetry in military capability.[31]

The advantages of this kind of model are strong; the analyst is able to work with relevant aggregate data that comprise the full range of the interaction pattern without making its understanding overly difficult. The fact that real data are used strengthens measurably the applicability of the model without sacrificing the basic features of abstraction and simplification. The forecasting aspect is of immediate usefulness for those involved in specific instances of decision-making in conflicts. On the other hand, there are some limiting elements that weaken the general validity of the analytical framework. For one, it is immensely difficult to arrive at any measure of interaction for conflict situations involving more than two parties, or those situations in which the parties are blatantly unequal or the level of hostility low. Moreover, as the model is presented, it does not help in explaining the conflict behavior of the disputants. Last, the question must be raised of whether the data that have been collected and processed are complete and clear enough to allow the inferences and numerical values attached to them. This last issue is, of course, a basic question, but it appears to be especially crucial in this instance. Attempts to expand and refine the basic model are currently underway. But we must realize that the step beyond the level of bilateral symmetrical interaction is complicated.

Most models of international conflict interaction contain general abstract hypotheses that are drawn from, and relate to, all spheres and levels of human interaction, primarily in conditions of bilateral symmetry. An excellent example of this type of modelling is a set of axioms and hypotheses by Robert North. They deal with perception, communication, stimulus-response (s-r), reward, deprival, and punishment, to mention a few major items. Typically, most of the hypotheses lack empirical verification so far, but ongoing research is trying to remedy that. To illustrate the range and precision of this kind of model, we summarize a few major assumptions: the higher the tension in the international system, the stronger the probability that an incident will be perceived by an involved actor as injurious, threatening, or provocative. Once a reaction process has set in, the higher the tension, the stronger is the probability that the issues of earlier competition will be obscured, that the actors will look for threats and respond with counter-threats, and that acts of violence or potential violence will increase. The higher the tension generated by a reaction process, the greater the probability of violence, no matter what the consequences. As tension increases in the interaction process, time will be perceived by the leaders involved as an increasingly salient factor in decision-making, and they will become increasingly concerned with the immediate future rather than with long-range considerations and outcomes. As tension increases, the leaders involved in an interaction process will perceive their own range of alternatives and that of their allies as becoming more restricted than those available to their adversaries.[32] The utility of these and other hypotheses lies in their guiding role in primary research as well in their applicability in laboratory and simulation exercises. The total set of axioms and hypotheses covers international conflictual interaction, as it affects the decision-making machinery, and the minds of the leading representatives of the main state actors. The broad dimension of the international system does not weigh heavily in this analytical scheme, except as it is perceived by the policy-makers. But we clearly notice the indirect importance of such propositions for the behavior in acute international conflicts, in which they may restrain decision-makers from acting rashly or irresponsibly, so that they at least mitigate the pressures of time and decisional alternatives.

Other models are designed to cast light on aspects of conflict interaction, which so far have received too little attention and where a maze of implicit assumptions about structural and personality characteristics has co-existed in a confused fashion. Thus the general problem of conflicting goals and values has been analyzed more systematically; a distinction between the actual value position, the desired value position, and the minimal level of acceptable value is suggested. According to the precise constellation of these varying measures on the value scale and to the presence and degree of overlapping of one or more of these value ranges in a situation of goal competition between two interacting parties, quite a few conflict processes and outcomes may result. It is clear that the bitterness of the conflict and the possibilities for a mutually agreeable solution will differ markedly if the parties pursue only incompatible desired goals but do not clash in their actual or minimal values, or if they clash on all three fronts of goal incompatibility. Without giving a set of concrete examples, we have a clear indication that the statement that a conflict involves a clash of objectives or values needs considerable explication and differentiation to become concise and meaningful.[33]

Focusing on the role of communication in conflictual situations, two researchers have argued that we have to reconsider the general belief that the ability to communicate is an important pre-condition for satisfactory resolutions of conflict. They point out that while the opportunity to communicate might have beneficial effects when the parties operate with reward potentials, it may be detrimental when a coercive base of power predominates. Only under conditions of reward power are communications likely to enhance the prospects for a mutually satisfactory agreement, because they probably consist of promises and exchanges of information regarding the consequences of a favorable solution to the conflict.[34]

In this context, it is apparent that conflicts often are conflicts of understanding, the sources of which could lie in the differences between the cognitive structures of the parties; moreover, these divergences could also constitute an important factor in the search for a successful termination of the conflict. A group of authors has suggested classifying societies and political communities according to their positions on two cognitive-cultural dimensions: (1) associative-abstractive and (2) case-oriented and universal-oriented, and to evaluate conflicts according to the relative significance of these paramaters of sociopolitical behavior.[35] This research approach is promising, but it requires much more work before more reliable hypotheses can be formulated. It adds a novel component to the more conventional abstract conflict models based on major psychological axioms.[36] But due to its preliminary quality, it would serve no relevant purpose to include here a detailed description of the underlying ideas and the major conceptual and analytical characteristics.

Conflict is preceded and accompanied by tension between the parties. This truism covers a major difficulty in approaching conflict, namely the development of a general measure of tension that would help detect the severity of tension in an actual conflict and predict the likely outbreak of conflicts in the future. The scarcity of serious work on this issue speaks for the dilemma which the researcher confronts. We can, however, report that Alan Newcombe and his associates in the Canadian peace research institute have constructed a general "tensiometer" using GNP and military expenditure data, both of which are easily available. With the tensiometer they establish an empirical criterion for the probability that certain states ranking high in terms of tension ratio and defense burden will engage in war or warlike conflict. They have applied this general measure to past events as well as to current cases and, most important, to future developments. They have found out that beyond a certain critical value on the tensiometer the probability of involvement in war increases five times and that in those instances war was not averted. The measure is still rather crude, and it has not yet been tested in a sufficient number of empirical cases. Despite this limitation, the tensiometer promises to become a major tool in the general as well as specific analysis of international conflict.[37]

The various models and approaches which we have briefly described give an indication of the breadth, the gains, and the lacunae of basic research on conflictual interaction. We should keep the major directions of scholarly models in mind as we consider the more specific theoretical propositions, empirical findings, and policy suggestions concerning perception and interaction in interstate conflict.

NOTES

1. See Kenneth Boulding, "A Pure Theory of Conflict Applied to Organizations," *Conflict Management in Organizations* ed. Elise Boulding (Ann Arbor: Foundation for Research on Human Behavior, 1961) pp. 43-51; esp. p. 44 et passim. Cf. for his theory in much greater detail his *Conflict and Defense. A General Theory* (New York: Harper and Row, 1962,1963).

2. Cf., e.g., the contributions in Paul Swingle (ed.) *The Structure of Conflict* (New York: Academic Press, 1970), esp. Single's introductory remarks.

3. For these definitions see Kenneth W. Terhune, "The Effects of Personality in Cooperation and Conflict," ibid., pp. 193-234; esp. p. 229.

4. See here John W. Burton, *Conflict and Communication. The Use of Controlled Communication in International Relations* (New York: Free Press, 1968) and pertinent chapters in his *World Society* (London: Cambridge University Press, 1972), esp. pp 153ff.

5. For an interesting debate between a critic and a cautious associate of Burton, cf. Ronald J. Yalem, "Controlled communication and conflict resolution," Journal of Peace Research, 1971, No. 3-4, pp. 263-272, and C. R. Mitchell, "Conflict resolution and controlled communication," ibid., 1973, No. 1-2, pp. 123-132. Mitchell's account and defense of Burton's position is more convincing than any of Burton's own descriptions. In a personal communication to this author, Mitchell has offered a highly refined defense of the Burton position and argued that recent developments in their thinking do full justice to both the subjective and objective components of conflict and that their position avoids the normative angle that is inherent in the objectivist-structuralist conflict hypothesis. Despite these clarifications the main criticism of the subjectivist conflict hypothesis remains valid.

6. See here Galtung, "Peace Thinking," *The Search for World Order* ed. Lepawsky et al., pp. 123f. His other writings, as previously cited, follow the same basic model of conflict.

7. For an even more outspoken representation of this viewpoint cf. Lars Dencik, "Peace research: Pacification or revolution?" Proceedings of IPRA Third General Conference, I, pp. 80f. et passim. For some fresh and unorthodox ideas geared toward small- as well as large-scale structural changes cf. Deutsch, "Abschreckungspolitik und gesellschaftspolitische Ordnung. Zum Problem der sich wandelnden Gesellschaft," Jahrbuch für Friedens- und Konfliktforschung I, 1971, pp. 45 et passim.

8. A fine example of this mixed approach is Adam Curle, *Making Peace,* op. cit.

9. For the personality-related points a through c see Terhune, "The Effects of Personality in Cooperation and Conflict," *The Structure of Conflict* ed. Swingle, pp. 229f.

10. For a classic theoretical study from a purely sociological viewpoint cf. Lewis Coser, *The Functions of Social Conflict* (New York: Free Press, 1964).

11. A stimulating general essay about this problem is Coser, "The Termination of Conflict," *Social Processes in International Relations* ed. Kriesberg, pp. 37-44. There are hardly any recent studies of this complex issue area, except for some works on peace treaties and cease-fire agreements.

12. Konrad Lorenz, *Das Sogenannte Böse. Zur Naturgeschichte der Aggression* (Vienna, 1963) English: *On Aggression* (New York: Harcourt, Brace and World, 1966); Robert Ardrey, *African Genesis* (New York: Athenaeum, 1961), and his *Territorial Imperative* (New York: Athenaeum, 1966). Anthony Storr, *Human Aggression* (New York: Athenaeum, 1968). Desmond Morris, *The Naked Ape* (New York: McGraw Hill, 1968). For a scholarly affirmation of the aggression hypotheses from a social psycho-

logical perspective cf. Bouthoul, "Sociologie de l'aggressivité," Etudes Polémologiques, 7, January 1973, pp. 29-36, and Victor Werner, "Pourrait-on maîtriser la violence?", ibid., 11, January 1974, pp. 5-15.

13. From the huge body of literature cf. here Ashley Montagu (ed.) *Man and Agression* (London: Oxford University Press, 1973), especially the contributions by Montagu, Berkowitz, Barnett, Dubos, Hellmuth, Scott, Schneirla, Boulding, Holloway, and Groote. All these essays are critical discussions of the writings of Lorenz, Ardrey, Morris, and Storr. Cf. also *Aggressionstrieb und Krieg.* Symposium des Internationalen Instituts für den Frieden, Wien. Ed. Walter Hollitscher with an introduction by Rolf Denker (Stuttgart: Deutsche Verlags-Anstalt, 1973). The symposium was held to evaluate the aggression thesis, especially emphasizing its relationship to war and conflict. For an up-to-date survey of aggression research cf. Rolf Denker, "Zum gegenwärtigen Stand der Aggressionsforschung: Versuch einer Synthese," pp. 7-33. For an interesting Soviet Russian view cf. Wladimir Pawlowitsch Efroimson, "Die Genealogie des Altruismus," pp. 129-164. Among the active participants in the symposium were Walter Hollitscher, Montagu, Kortland, Fuchs, E. Moore, Mushakoji, Poljanov, Schönfeld, Wiatr, Roede. The discussion brought a strong majority agreement that Lorenz' arguments are untenable on empirical and logical grounds.

14. For a detailed examination of the conception of aggression in Freud's, Lorenz', and Follard's writings see Klaus Horn, "Menschliche Aggressivität and internationale Politik. Vorklärungen" Senghaas (ed.), *Friedensforschung und Gesellschaftskritik,* op. cit., pp. 116-151. Cf. also the brief observations by Senghaas, *Aggressivität und Kollektive Gewalt* (Stuttgart: Kohlhammer, 1971), esp. pp. 28-40.

15. These brief remarks are drawn from the two collections quoted above. We know that our short evaluation is far from adequate for such a big and important issue, but we feel justified in giving it so little attention because the scholarly debate so far has not only been inconclusive, but it has not really focused on the control and resolution of human conflicts.

16. See, e.g., Gene Sharp, "The Technique of Non-violent Action," Adam Roberts (ed.), *Civilian Resistance as a National Defense. Non-violent Action Against Aggression* (Baltimore, Md.: Penguin, 1969), pp. 107-127, p. 109.

17. See here ibid., esp. pp. 107ff, and Sharp, *The Politics of Non-violent Action,* esp. part I as well as his *Exploring Non-violent Alternatives* (Boston: Porter-Sargent, 1970) and his many papers and essays in which he develops this basic conception. Similar axioms are also spelled out in the writings of Ebert and Roberts.

18. For case listings and case histories see Sharp, *The Politics of Non-violent Action,* and the various contributions in Roberts (ed.), *Civilian Resistance as a National Defense.* See also A. P. Hare and H. Blumberg (eds.), *Non-violent Direct Action* (Washington, D.C.: Corpus Books, 1968) for specific American cases.

19. The term "civilian defense" is predominant in the English-speaking countries, whereas "social defense" ("Sozialverteidigung") has been introduced by Ebert and is widely used in Central Europe.

20. The best introduction to the various trends and groups in the study of non-violence and civilian defense is still Roberts (ed.), *Civilian Resistance as a National Defense,* which contains a few contributions by military experts who take a rather dim view of the exclusive use of civilian defense; it also offers six essays on past experiences and articles by Sharp, Ebert and Roberts as well as two other authors on the conception of civilian defense. The collection *Soziale Verteidigung. Friedens- und Sicherheitspolitik in den 80er Jahren,* ed. by the Studiengruppe "Soziale Verteidigung" der Vereinigung deutscher Wissenschaflter e.V. (Gelnhausen/Berlin: Burckhardthaus-Verlag, 1972) emphasizes the

German trend in civilian defense thinking mainly represented by Ebert. But it also contains an outstanding short essay by Galtung, "Nichtmilitärische Verteidigungsmassnahmen," ibid., pp. 84-94, where he outlines his catalogue of measures for non-military defense without postulating the end of certain political or economic features of Western societies. Ebert's "Vermutungen über den dialektischen Prozess zur Sozialen Verteidigung," ibid., pp. 2-17, is rather ideological. The same applies to Egbert Jahn's "Soziohistorische Voraussetzungen der Sozialen Verteidigung," ibid., pp. 28-36. See also Ebert, "Von aggressiver Drohung zu defensiver Warnung. Das Konzept der sozialen Verteidigung," Senghaas (ed.), *Friedensforschung und Gesellschaftskritik,* pp. 152-200, his "Verteidigung ohne Drohung. Praxeologien der gradualistischen Abrüstung und gewaltfreien Verteidigung," Jahrbuch für Friedens- und Konfliktforschung, I, 1971, pp. 213-246 and pp. 247-256 for the subsequent critical discussion of his paper; also his "Friedensbewegung und Friedensforschung–Historische und aktuelle Wechselwirkungen," ibid., II, 1972, pp. 156-172. Cf. further Egbert Jahn, "Civilian defense and civilian offensive," Journal of Peace Research, 1973 (3), pp. 285-294. Adam Roberts has spelled out his more functional civilian defense strategy in his long essay "Civilian Defense Strategy," Roberts (ed.), *Civilian Resistance as a National Defence,* pp. 249-294. For a specific legal aspect see Pertti Joenniemi and Roberts, "Civil Resistance and the law of military occupation," Instant Research on Peace and Violence, IV (1), 1974, pp. 38-46. For critical voices questioning the whole strategy or aspects of it see the contributions by Jones, Goodspeed, Bramsted, and Schelling in Roberts (ed.), *Civilian Resistance as a National Defence,* also the extensive critique of Ebert's conception by Forndran, *Abrüstung und Friedensforschung,* op. cit., pp. 57-98, and a few pertinent remarks by Weizsäcker, "Bedrohungsverstellungen als Faktor der internationalen Politik," Jahrbuch für Friedens- und Konfliktforschung, I, 1971, pp. 28f. A comprehensive guide to problems of non-violence and conflict management with special emphasis on community involvement and educational exercises is Paul Wehr, Conflict Regulation. AAAS Study Guides on Contemporary Problems (Washington, D.C.: American Association for the Advancement of Science, 1975).

21. For a general examination of the problems of the construction of relevant conflict models cf. Tanter, "The policy relevance of models in world politics," Journal of Conflict Resolution, Vol. 16, No. 4, December 1972, pp. 555-583. See esp. Tables 1 and 4 for illustration of the stakes and problems involved.

22. See Hayward R. Alker, Jr., and Ronald D. Brunner, "Simulating international conflict: A comparison of three approaches," International Studies Quarterly, Vol. 13, No. 1, March 1969, pp. 70-110; esp. pp. 96f., 105 et passim for this list of causal elements of war and peace.

23. One such effort is John H. Sigler, "Cooperation and conflict in United States-Soviet-Chinese relations, 1966-1971: A quantitative analysis," Peace Research Society (International), Papers, XIX, 1972, pp. 107-128.

24. We refrain from any further elaboration of Singer's premises and findings. Cf. in particular Singer, "The 'Correlates of War' project: Interim report and rationale," World Politics, Vol. 24, No. 2, January 1972, esp. pp. 265ff., where he gives some preliminary findings and a full bibliography of the project.

25. See Charles F. Hermann, "Threat, Time, and Surprise: A Simulation of International Crisis," *International Crises* ed. Hermann, pp. 187-211; p. 187. See also his "International Crisis as a Situational Variable," *International Politics and Foreign Policy,* ed. Rosenau, pp. 409-421; esp. p. 414 for a similar definition. For a critical, but sympathetic discussion of the three elements of crisis and for a comparison with some other current conceptions of decision-making in critical situations see James A. Robinson,

"Crisis: An Appraisal of Concepts and Theories," *International Crises* ed. Hermann, pp. 20-35; esp. pp. 23ff.

26. For these concepts and terms see Hermann, "International Crisis as a Situational Variable," pp. 415f. Of particular interest is the three-dimensional situational cube into which he has placed a number of U.S. crisis situations for illustration.

27. These models are presented and elaborated in Hermann and Linda B. Brady, "Alternative Models of International Crisis Behavior," *International Crisis,* pp. 281-303. Their evaluation is based on thirty-one propositions concerning crisis that they abstracted from the ten research papers reprinted in Chapters 2-11 of that volume.

28. Hermann and Brady, ibid., p. 302, give a simple flow chart putting together main features from the four basic models. It should be pointed out that this integrated framework deals only with one actor in the interaction structure. To incorporate two or more actors in an international conflict situation would complicate the model immensely, but it is feasible due to the available data-processing techniques, and it is necessary for direct policy relevance of such a comprehensive model.

29. In the following sections we shall return to specific findings from the crisis literature. Cf. here for the merits and diversity of the crisis approach Hermann, "Threat, Time, and Surprise: A Simulation of International Crisis," ibid., David C. Schwartz, "Decision-Making in Historical and Simulated Crises," ibid., pp. 167-184; Glenn D. Paige, "Comparative Case Analysis of Crisis Decisions: Korea and Cuba," ibid., pp. 41-55; and Thomas W. Milburn, "The Management of Crisis," ibid., pp. 259-277.

30. See Oran Young, *The Politics of Force,* pp. 15ff., esp. p. 23. A positive feedback crisis is defined as a pattern of interaction which constitutes a sequence of mutual amplifying responses. Typical examples of this kind of crisis are most escalation processes, arms races, and the like. An *overload crisis* is a situation in which too many demands are placed on a given system in too short a period, leading either to a complete breakdown or to serious malfunctioning. The *starvation crisis* results from an inadequate supply of inputs, e.g., disintegration of relationship patterns following a decline in political or economic support. He speaks of a *steering crisis,* if the actors in the system receive distorted, inaccurate, or inadequate information, if they fail to process the received information in useful ways, or if they fail to make connections between received data and memory traces. The steering pathologies that are the consequence of these negative feedback processes cause distortion, rigidity and in general impede the ability of the policy-makers to arrive at and to implement decisions. *Adaptation crises* can occur when marked changes in some aspects of the international system are not accompanied by proportionate changes in other parts of the system. Thus it is an open question whether the global political system has been adapted to contemporary arms technology or to recent economic transformations. Cf. for these distinctions also Young, *The Intermediaries. Third Parties in International Crises* (Princeton, N.J.: Princeton University Press, 1967), esp. pp. 11-16.

31. See Edward E. Azar, Towards the Development of an Early Warning Model of International Violence. Studies of Conflict and Peace, Report No. 13, Department of Political Science, University of North Carolina, Chapel Hill, 1973. This paper is representative for the good use of events data in the study of acute interstate conflict. Cf. also his earlier paper. "The dimensionality of violent conflict: A quantitative analysis," Peace Research Society (International), Papers, XV, 1970, pp. 122-167.

32. Robert C. North, "Axioms and Hypotheses Concerning Active and Passive Defense Systems and the Types of Responses They Seem Likely to Evoke," *Weapons System Decisions* ed. Davis B. Bobrow (New York: Praeger, 1969), pp. 39-91; p. 57. For additional information about the various conflict hypotheses cf. North, "The Behav-

ior of Nation-States: Problems of Conflict and Integration," *New Approaches to International Relations,* ed. Kaplan, pp. 320ff., 346ff., and Nazli Choucri and North, "The determinants of international violence," Peace Research Society (International), Papers, XII, 1969, pp. 33-63. Choucri and North, *Nations in Conflict: Population, Expansion, and War* (San Francisco: Freeman, 1974) contains the full description and analysis of their conflict model and of its empirical merits. They emphasize here general factors as causes of inter-State conflict, such as differences in military capability, wealth, domestic, pressure, and their impact on tension and threat perception.

33. For this viewpoint and its systematic elaboration see Bengt Höglund and Jörgen Wilian Ulrich, "Peace Research and the Concepts of Conflict–Summary and Criticism," *Conflict Control and Conflict Resolution,* ed. Höglund and Ulrich, esp. pp. 18ff. They also show that a fully symmetrical conflict relationship is a rather unusual situation. They give nine conditions of symmetry: (1) same level of organization; (2) same order of magnitude; (3) same power potential; (4) same intensity of interaction; (5) same spheres of interaction; (6) same value system; (7) having mutually exclusive goals with the same degree of offensivity; (8) on the same value dimensions; and (9) with the same norms regulating their conflict behavior (p. 24).

34. This interesting argument has been submitted by Bertram H. Raven and Arie W. Kruglanski, "Conflict and Power," *The Structure of Conflict* ed. Swingle, pp. 69-109; esp. pp. 89ff. They point out, however, that threats (i.e., coercive power) may also promote conflict resolution when they are issued in a cause that is accepted as legitimate by the other party.

35. For a presentation, though not always convincing, of this sound idea see Edmund S. Glenn, Robert H. Johnson, Paul R. Kimmel and Bryant Wedge, "A cognitive interaction model to analyse culture conflict in international relations," Journal of Conflict Resolution, Vol. 14, No. 1, March 1970), pp. 35-48. They classify the U.S. as a case-oriented abstractionist society, while the USSR is seen as a universal-oriented abstractionist community. See esp. pp. 41ff.

36. A fine example of a model of psychological intergroup conflict is Bengt Abrahamsson, "A Model for the Analysis of Inter-Group Conflict," *Conflict Control and Conflict Resolution,* ed. Höglund and Ulrich, pp. 72-85. He bases his analysis on the role of dissatisfaction and satisfaction in individual and social behavior. See esp. pp. 80f. et passim for the full model.

37. From numerous papers we refer here only to a few. See Alan Newcombe, "Toward the development of an inter-nation tensiometer," Peace Research Society (International), Papers, XIII, 1970, pp. 11-27, and Newcombe and James Wert, "The use of an inter-nation tensiometer for the Prediction of war," ibid., XXI, 1973, pp. 73-83. See further Newcombe, John D. Barber, James Wert, Mark Haven, and Cathy Hiebert, "An improved inter-nation tensiometer for the prediction of war," Peace Research Reviews, V, No. 4, 1974, Newcombe, Nora S. Newcombe, and Gary D. Landrus, "The development of an inter-nation tensiometer," International interactions, I(1), 1974, pp. 3-18 and Newcombe's short paper "The Inter-Nation Tensiometer and the Middle East," paper prepared for the Annual Meeting of the International Studies Association in St. Louis, Mo., March 1974. Cf. also Norman Z. Alcock, "An empirical measure of inter-nation threat: Some preliminary implications for the Middle East conflict," Peace Research Society (International), Papers, XV, 1970, 51-72; esp. p. 66, where he confirms Newcombe's basic premise concerning the link between arms expenditure and the probability of foreign war.

Chapter 4

PERCEPTUAL DETERMINANTS OF CONFLICT BEHAVIOR

Theoretical Aspects

The study of perception as an important variable of international conflict behavior has recent antecedents, although individual and social psychological theory and research began in the early decades of the twentieth century. These precursors of current perception research are still significant because their initiation and expansion shaped the whole discipline of psychology. Among these approaches and conceptions are the stimulus-response theory, the Gestalt psychology, the notion of perception as the result of interaction between individual and his environment, the theory of stereotypes, perception as learning, the theorem of cognitive dissonance, and transactional psychology.[1] In the light of these conceptual and analytical background factors it is not surprising that we still face a wide variety of recent approaches to the general problem of perception. Moreover, we have to deal with a large number of phenomena relating to personality structure and perceptual processes.

One way to get access to the complex problem is to ask what determines and shapes perceptions. One author suggests three main elements: (1) functional factors (predispositions, needs, values, attitudes, etc.); (2) structural factors or stimulus factors (e.g., the organization of stimuli); and (3) learning.[2] Looking at the same problem from the angle of personality structure and behavior potentials, another scholar distinguishes between: (1) motives; (2) cognitive structure; and (3) a value-orientation of general trust/mistrust.[3] Although these listings contribute little to simplifying the problem, they help at least to group the issues into a few clusters, around which we can organize our discussion.

Does perception count? Is it a foregone conclusion that how we perceive the environment and a particular situation determines (or co-determines) our subsequent action? If scientific work, primarily experimental psychology, had failed to support this presumption, there would be no point in discussing perception in international conflict behavior. It can be stated, however, that according to the present state of knowledge in perceptual psychology, "assumptions which influence the selection of observed data also provide a guide to action."[4] This general formulation avoids the many uncertainties and difficulties that are involved with regard to the exact nature of observation, perception, and decision.

TRADITIONAL THEORIES OF PERCEPTION

Before we enter into the discussion of current perceptual research, let us take a brief look at the major inputs from older schools of psychology.

(1) The initial stimulus-response theorem centered on the axiom that the perceptions of reality result from actual stimuli from the environment and that they make up a set of images congruous with the external reality. This rigid view of perception precludes the possibility that different experiences may be due to varying predispositions and preconceptions of individuals and of groups.

(2) Gestalt psychology showed that inherent unifying factors determine how reality is perceived, and also largely whether new events are perceived at all. The human mind creates a coherent image of the world and perceives events as patterned wholes to fulfill the need for coherence and to conform to past experiences.

(3) Another traditional psychological school proved that people form images under the influence of values, emotions, purposes, and social groups, contrary to the theses of the "stimulus-response" and Gestalt psychologists. The theory of stereotypes brought out that humans have a strong tendency to seek support for already adopted views in selecting new evidence. Group beliefs are the most rigid type of stereotypes.

(4) Past experience and learning have more recently been recognized as important determinants of perception. This accounts for the marked differences that separate cultures, societies, and groups.

(5) A last influential conception should be briefly described, the theory

of cognitive dissonance. Every individual acquires an ordered set of images and expectations. If this cognitive pattern is upset by conflicting images, a "dissonance" is most likely to occur which might negatively affect the behavior of the individual.

(6) Neurophysiological research by Livingston has contributed an interesting finding. Some perceptual selection occurs already at the receptor points of the nervous system, which eliminate certain percepts even before they reach the brain.[5] This empirical finding renders the whole perceptual process much more elusive and forces the observer to accept a basic irreparable uncertainty about this crucial aspect of decision-making and -implementing.

Most of the approaches we have just described, in their original shape or in some revised form, figure prominently in the study of perception in international relations. It is probably not too risky to take a catholic view and to argue that all those analytical modes are still relevant, best symbolized in the vigor of current models of "stimulus-response." Even Gestalt psychology, which originated in the early twentieth century, holds considerable interest and its hypotheses have not been proven false, although most psychologists tend to see the formation of images and attitudes somewhat differently. Hence the whole field as it relates to international affairs is still wide open, especially with regard to new conceptual advances, as most research has stayed within the premises of the classical theories. What is new and frequently highly important is the large and detailed concern with foreign policy decision-making and interaction processes in individual and social-psychological perspectives.[6]

IMAGES AND PERCEPTION

A central issue in perception is the formation and content of the images which individuals and social groups hold. The role of images in foreign policy is evident for the policy-makers and for the general public inasmuch as they exert direct and indirect influence on the process of political action. In order to be able to describe in policy-related terms what impact the images have, we must adopt some comprehensive operational conception. As mentioned, images are the composites of cognitive, affective, and behavioral elements. The cognitive dimension of our view of an individual or of a country contains those attributes which we see as "objective" "inherent" characteristics independent of our own subjective judgment about them. The affective component of an image includes our liking or disliking for the person or for the community. The behavioral or action component consists of a set of responses that we formulate in light of the perceived characteristics of the object. On the basis of public opinion studies Scott has argued that there is usually a tendency toward correspondence among the three components of images.[7] This conforms to the views of several classical psychological approaches. Yet we must emphasize that a trend toward harmony is stipulated not merely for incoming perceptions in one of the three dimensions but also primarily for the interrelationship among these components themselves. Moreover, it does not mean that the harmonization occurs as a unidirectional sequence from the cognitive to the affective to the behavioral spheres; if a change, e.g., in the affective segment, is powerful enough, it is possible that it will bring about a modification in the cognitive and behavioral realms.

Some other preliminary assumptions are in order here. Images are subjective conjectures; they comprise what we think (and feel) the world around us is like.[8] Much of the perceptual horizon is formed in childhood and family, also through social learning and interaction with the fellow members of society. This multiple input creates an idiosyncratic perceptual structure for the individual, which results from the confluence of the outside forces and of the inner mental dispositions and abilities. Our beliefs, ideas, preconceptions, and stereotypes are thus constantly involved in our actions. They *are* for us the world in which we have to act, and we derive from them our priorities and our specific objectives, which as a rule are clustered as equivalent compatible options.

It is difficult to change perceptions in individuals and groups once they have gone through the decisive stages of the growth and socialization processes. However, learning is the only way to bring about such changes. Psychologists have found that hostility is normally associated with simple cognitive structures, whereas a more complex knowledge and differentiated viewpoints restrain individuals and groups so that they are much less inclined to develop strong and action-oriented feelings of hostility or of uncritical friendliness. Due to the link between the cognitive and affective sectors of perception, learning can be initiated and sustained by the stimulation and steering of emotional attitudes and symbols. The promise of a reward or the threat of punishment, the appeal to love and hatred, are typical examples of the instruments available in this admittedly tenuous technique of perception change. We can assume that similar interdimensional strategies are available for changing the cognitive angle through the example of behavior that reflects a higher level of knowledge and feeling than that held by the individual or the community. To restate it in more concrete terms: if we are drawn into patterns of cooperative behavior over some time and at high levels of interaction, it is possible that we adjust our cognitive and affective attitudes to that experience. The reversed process is also conceivable, although at a lower degree of probability.

The praxeology of perceptual change through learning is still rather underdeveloped, although its urgency has been highlighted by a recent study showing that cognitive differences significantly impede the understanding between parties in a social situation, increase conflictual behavior, and thus reduce the chance for mutually agreeable compromises.[9] In the light of all these tentative linkages and probabilities, it is apparently not enough to study the incidence of similar educational experience, travel, and acquaintances among the foreign policy elite, although such inquiries are necessary and welcome.[10] What is even more urgently needed is a series of in-depth analyses of the belief systems and images of the major decision-makers, of their supporting agencies, and of their constituencies.[11] Only if we increase our knowledge significantly along these lines shall we be able to ascertain the cognitive, affective, and motivational bases of foreign policy behavior and its conflictual and cooperative dimensions.

PERCEPTION AND RATIONALITY

At this point it seems appropriate to return once again to an issue which we touched upon from another perspective in our discussion of the arms race. Traditional diplomatic theory and modern strategic thinking operate on the basis of the premise that states and their representatives behave rationally in formulating and implementing their foreign policies.[12] How does this axiom hold up in view of what we have argued about the characteristics of human perception, in particular the non-logical elements in cognition and in the affective sector? If we talk about rationality, we must clarify what we mean. The customary conception sees rational behavior in the choice of adequate means for the pursuit of given ends, whatever those ends may be. A broader understanding includes the choice of the values and objectives within the realm of rational action. In terms of analytical thinking we also apeak of rationality as causality, i.e., we determine causes and affects as rational sequences. The act of perception, how ever we depict the role and impact of its various dimensions, is never in conformity with the intrinsic qualities of either ends-means or value rationality, although we keep striving—and ought to strive—to approach the levels of pure rationality. For this and other less principal reasons the rationality hypothesis as such cannot be maintained unless it is significantly qualified.[13]

As an alternative to this misleading proposition and in line with Freudian principles and insights about human psychology, Deutsch and Senghaas have proposed a conceptual framework which covers the dimensions of individual and collective conflict behavior. They contend that, as the individual ego finds itself dependent upon and confronted with the "Id" (the human drives), the "Super-Ego" (his conscience), and outside reality, and can develop widely different cognitive and affective, rational and emotional responses ranging from acceptance to rejection, overt conflict or autistic inversion and seclusion, so the political community is faced with analogous communication and control agents (the outside reality = the global system; the "super-ego" = ethical values and traditions; the ego itself = the political system of the community; the "id" = the interest and pressure groups) with which to interact. It must formulate its behavioral responses, such as international war, imperialistic domination and exploitation, hostility and suspicion, cooperation of integration, domestic unrest, social change, civil war, etc.[14] More systematically, the ego or the community must be strong to meet the expectations and needs of the various forces impinging on its behavioral situation. If it fails—and failure is just as frequent and serious for the collective as for the individual, possibly even more so—certain defense mechanisms are used, among them suppression, projection (transfer of the own drive and desire upon another actor), denial, autism, etc. Without psychologizing unduly, Deutsch and Senghaas trace these defense mechanisms in the world of states.

On the basis of these psychological behavior characteristics, combined with the distinctions between energy-related and information-oriented processes and between autonomous and dependent systems, drawn from modern information and communication theory, the two authors propose a typology of approaches that are valid for individual and collective behavior. They list:

(1) Elimination or destruction;

(2) Exploitation and compellence;

(3) Information acquisition;

(4) Assistance to autonomy;

(5) Demand for response; and

(6) Information imposition.[15]

While the first two types of behavior are self-explanatory and more than adequately represented in the accounts of international and internal politics, the remaining four are equally important. To seek information, knowledge, and expertise from another actor (information acquisition), to try to impose the own ideas and convictions on others (information imposition), and to demand recognition of the own status and importance from fellow actors and uninvolved spectators (demand for response) constitute real impairments of interactor harmony and may become the origin of deep hostility and even overt conflict. Assistance to autonomy, as exemplified in the ideal of unselfish development assistance, is a rare commodity in international behavior, but nobody would deny its crucial relevance for the present and future world peace.

Though tentative, this framework and typology accounts for aspects of the perceptual and behavioral dimension of foreign policy that have been largely neglected. Even preliminary checks of the historical and contemporary international systems reveal the presence of the structures and processes suggested by Deutsch and Senghaas. Moreover, we notice that the criterion of means rationality, the most commonly used standard, is met in fewer and fewer instances of international involvement. By now, warfare and economic exploitation have lost most of their old rationale, what ever there was of it in the past. Rather, we see a highly complex set of response patterns deriving from various rational and non-rational motivational sources.[16]

Let us say a brief word in this context about Senghaas' autism thesis. The applicability of that conception to problems of the nuclear arms race is debatable, but there is no denying the fact that in the history of international relations there are notable incidents of autistic behavior as total seclusion of states from the outside world, as hatred and paranoid fear toward other states and communities, as self-engendered and self-sustained misperception and lack of information. The systematic study of these trends and episodes in history has just begun. Until the completion of that huge research endeavor we have to rely on our fragmentary knowledge of history and on our often random guesses.[17] The main issues to be considered in the pending research are: (1) whether and to what degree we can draw a parallel between individual and collective behavior; (2) to what extent the external policy of a state can be explained in terms of the personality and perception characteristics of the individual decision-maker; and (3) what kind of empirical evidence is available to verify or falsify the highly specific autism hypothesis. These are three large and complex issue areas in which we have currently only preliminary suggestions and tentative findings.

Nevertheless, a few points can be stated firmly. The rationality model is insufficient on both empirical and normative grounds. Perception is not a purely cognitive process. The sequence from perception to action is less direct and exclusive than is stipulated in the traditional viewpoint of the rationality of foreign policy. For policy reasons, it would be most desirable to test attitudinal and perceptual profiles of policy-makers and governmental top officials before they enter office. Such tests could help prevent the influx of individuals into the foreign policy machinery who show abnormal behavioral patterns, and at the same time they would improve our knowledge about the general significance of psychological characteristics for the external conduct of states.

IN SEARCH OF A BASIC PERCEPTION MODEL

It is a difficult enterprise to formalize and schematize the perceptual process, and we must not expect anything comprehensive, due to the unresolved question of the relative weight of cognitive, affective, and behavioral

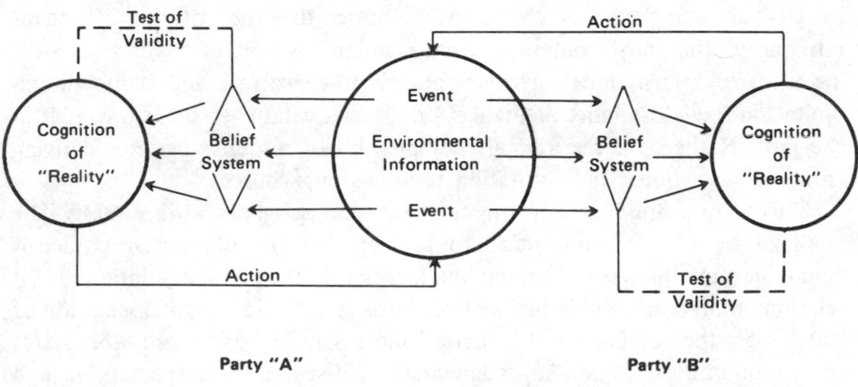

Figure 4.1: THE INDIRECT RELATIONSHIP BETWEEN BELIEF SYSTEM AND ACTION

components and of their interrelationships. Despite all these limitations and uncertainties, we introduce at least one relatively simple, yet adequate model of perception that underlines the major features of the analytical scheme. Starting from the basic stimulus-response (s-r) conception, Ole Holsti has depicted the perceptual step as shown in Figure 4.1.[18]

The flow of information about the environment and about specific events enters the perception and decision-making systems of each actor, not directly, but through the belief system, whereby the information is filtered and inevitably distorted. The actor arrives at the cognition of "reality" in two ways: he may adopt as final the specific information transmitted through the belief system, or he may subject that information to a test of validity which measures the incoming messages once more independently from the images of the belief system. It is noteworthy that he distinguishes between "belief system" and the "cognition of 'reality'." From what we have reported, it seems preferable to speak of perceptual system rather than "belief system" and of the "image of reality" rather than "cognition of reality." In this way we would pull together first the structure and second the outcome of perception, connected by the "test of validity" as the process. Holsti has detailed the components of what he calls the "belief system" within the overall context of perception and decision-making.[19]

Two remarks seem warranted with regard to Figure 4.2. The distinction between images of fact and those of value as segments of the belief system is useful, but we may ask whether it really comprehends the more elaborate and intertwined scheme of cognition and perception. Would it not be better to

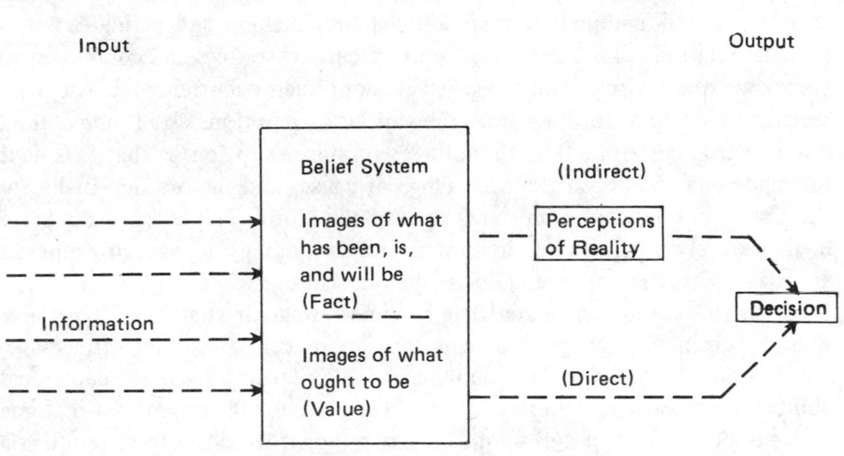

Figure 4.2: THE DUAL RELATIONSHIP BETWEEN BELIEF SYSTEM AND DECISION-MAKING

add an affective component to the belief system and to attempt to indicate how and to what extent the three components influence each other? It is not difficult to assume an impact of the affective and the normative (value) elements on the factual dimension, but it is also perfectly conceivable that the images of the facts contribute to altering the normative and even the affective images, though to a lesser degree.

Our second concern is with Holsti's proposition that the images of the facts go through an additional perceptual screen (the perceptions of reality), while the value images affect the decisional outcome directly. Again, this is a worthwhile argument, but is it the only or the best conception? We hold that *the images of "what is"* influence and are influenced by the perception of this specific situation more directly and powerfully than normative and affective images. It is a matter of degree, that should be spelled out even in a scheme like Holsti's. The assumption of a direct link between the normative (and affective) dimension and the decisional outcome therefore needs to be revised, in the sense that the perception of the specific situation may have noticeable repercussions for the make-up of the value and affect dimensions of the given perceptual or image structure, and that the latter may be a significant factor in the shaping of the former. Any attempt to verify empirically these assumptions poses great difficulties; nevertheless, we should not allow the sacrifice of important analytical aspects for the sake of simplicity.

Mention should be made of the important hypotheses on misperception that were summarized and evaluated by Jervis, who took a predominantly reality-oriented approach to the question and did not try to propose a formal theory of his own of the perceptual process.[20] If we agree that misperception is indeed a major impediment to sound policy-making and acting in international relations, it is imperative for us to learn its sources and consequences before we can devise remedies against its continued occurrence.[21] The main conclusion we have to draw from the various assumptions about perception, but in particular from these hypotheses on misperception, is that it is next to impossible to abolish the wide range of causes and factors that make for the distortions and errors in our images of the world. This is especially grave in the severely complicated circumstances surrounding the way governments and states view each other and devise their measures accordingly.

From the theoretical material it becomes apparent that highest priority must be given to a program in which policy-makers and other officials become aware of the inherent and intrinsic limitations to their perceptual abilities, and learn to adjust their political behavior in recognition of these built-in sources of self-deception. Such a program would at least result in a higher level of skepticism and self-criticism toward their own beliefs, assumptions and intentions. In this process of self-enlightenment a more cautious attitude in viewing the outside world and in preparing the decisions might develop. This hope is based on the empirical proof that more and diversified knowledge reduces the incidence of misconceptions and misjudgments. We must realize, however, that there is no way of completely removing those defects. The search for better modes of conflict resolution and conflict control must be based on this regrettable condition.

Empirical Aspects

The division between theoretical and empirical aspects of perception in conflict behavior is purely a matter of convenience, since it can hardly be maintained in the academic literature. We make this distinction in order to show more clearly the diversity of research findings, frequently contradictory or otherwise incompatible, and to emphasize the policy potential of many of these empirical results. In all these cases, we must keep in mind that the materials and the methodology of the particular inquiry have a clear consequence for the outcome; therefore, what may appear as a substantive contradiction may be due to a difference in approach or data.

To demonstrate the large scope of policy variations relating to the perceptual angle of international conflict, we introduce here a few recommendations, abstract and general in character, but intrinsic to the problem, that have been proposed by Robert North, one of the most experienced students of war and peace among states. He urges the policy-maker to pay great attention to the perceptual, evaluative, and affective processes and to the habit strengths of the own country as well as of the other parties to the conflict. The general tendency is to focus more or less exclusively on the latter. North also points out that any state tends to view the "reward, deprival, or punishment capacity" of others in terms of its overall attitudes, strategy, and posture. Hence perception and communication must always be put into the general context of the relationship. This interlocking quality of the action environment emerges clearly in the following policy recommendation: "If an increase in deprival capacity is intended by Country A to carry a message to and influence Country B, such an increase in deprival capacity must be part of a context that Country B can see, understand, and distinguish from whatever punishment capacities Country B is maintaining and developing."[22] This defense- and deterrence-oriented policy principle can easily be turned into a peace-promoting one. What is significant at this point is the recognition that the practice of perception and communication is indeed inseparably connected with the interaction in the broadest sense.

CASE STUDIES OF PERCEPTION: 1914 AND 1962

North's general propositions warrant our critical attention, since their validity can be checked and verified only by comparing them with specific empirical findings taken from various situational backgrounds. North and his associates, foremost among them Ole Holsti and Dina Zinnes, have given much time and thought to the analysis of the outbreak of World War I and a few more recent crisis situations, and have arrived at some findings of considerable interest. Zinnes has found that for 1914 in particular a relationship exists between a state's perception of itself as a target of hostility and its subsequent expression of hostility and that if it feels persecuted by a particular state it will express hostility toward that state.[23] In a more recent study she checked the data of 1914 as to whether the decision-maker's perception at a given point in time is a result of both the hostile messages he receives at that time and his previous perception, and whether the decision-maker's expression of hostility on a given day is a consequence of both his perception on that day and his previous expression of hostility. She concluded that in general the decision-makers in 1914 were not paranoid in the crisis and reacted "rationally" in that they perceived hostility when hostile messages were received, with an exception for the Dual Alliance (Germany-Austria), whose leaders continued not to perceive any hostility if they received a hostile message and had no prior perception of hostility. Zinnes calls this a symptom of "day-dreaming"; this is quite the opposite of paranoid hysteria, which was alleged in contemporary descriptions and in more recent historical writings. Moreover, she also concluded that in general the previous expression of hostility does not affect the current one, whereas incoming hostile messages usually lead to expressions of hostility.[24]

Holsti, Brody and North compared the crisis of 1914 and the Cuban Missile Crisis of 1962 in terms of the way the leaders defined the situation and perceived and expressed their options. In 1914, the Dual Alliance consistently reacted at higher levels of violence, overperceived the level of violence in the actions of the Triple Alliance, and underperceived the level of violence in their own actions. In the Cuban crisis, however, both sides tended to perceive accurately the nature of the actions of the adversary and then proceeded to act at an appropriate level.[25] Holsti looked at the 1914 situation to find out whether and to what extent individual or national differences or the nature of the situation made for the variation in the perceptions of the decision-makers. On the basis of a content analysis of a large amount of statements by foreign policy-makers during the crisis, which he divided into two periods of different length according to the level of tensions and crisis behavior, Holsti suggested that the particular situation explained most of the perceptions of hostility, especially in periods of great stress.[26]

He also examined the 1914 crisis, and less stringently the Cuban crisis, with regard to the time factor, the perception of alternatives, and the quality of communications. The following results are valid for 1914, whereas the lack of access to the 1962 documents allows only preliminary verification for that latter crisis:

(1) As stress increases in a crisis situation, time will be perceived as an increasingly salient factor in decision-making;

(2) As stress increases in a crisis situation, decision-makers will become increasingly concerned with the immediate rather than the distant future;

(3) In a crisis situation, decision-makers tend to perceive their own range of alternatives to be more restricted than those of their adversaries;

(4) In a crisis situation, decision-makers tend to perceive their allies' range of alternatives to be more restricted than those of their adversaries;

(5) As stress increases, decision-makers will perceive the range of alternatives open to themselves to become narrower;

(6) The hypothesis that as stress increases, decision-makers will perceive the range of alternatives open to adversaries or potential adversaries to expand, was only partly confirmed;

(7) The higher the stress in a crisis situation, the heavier the load of channels of communication;

(8) The higher the stress in a crisis situation, the greater the tendency to rely upon extraordinary or improvised channels of communication;

(9) The higher the stress in a crisis situation, the higher the proportion of intracoalition—as against intercoalition—communication.[27]

Compared with the elaborate and detailed suggestions and recommendations in traditional diplomatic-historical literature, the hypotheses and findings in empirical research appear minimal and occasionally even trivial. That discrepancy is, of course, the result of the well-known difficulties germane to quantitative data analysis, e.g., lack of usable data or overabundance of material, and the standards for selection, measurement, and evaluation. In the 1914 case, there is by now much material, not all of it quantifiable. In the Cuban missile crisis, to take the best-known and well-researched contemporary case, the analyst faces a considerable shortage of quantifiable facts and figures. In the light of these and other difficulties, we must acknowledge that the findings just reported constitute a remarkable advance over the mostly intuitive narrative and causal analysis of traditional studies in diplomacy and international politics.

Yet the methodology and the results submitted by Holsti, North, Zinnes, and others have been contested by other researchers using the quantitative approach. To cite one such case, Gordon Hilton looked at the same 1914 data as those authors, except that he did not include the coding from the Serbian documents. He found that, different from their results, there was no significant relationship between the perception of hostility and the expression of hostility for either the Dual Alliance or the Triple Entente. When he reexamined this counter-intuitive finding, he introduced a lag time of one, two, or three days between perception and expression of hostility and came to the conclusion that there was a significant relationship for the Triple Entente under lag conditions of two or three days, whereas the evidence in the case of the Dual Alliance was inadequate to support such a relationship.[28] In a parallel study he investigated the perceptual aspect of the hostility patterns in 1914, focusing on Zinnes' findings. He found that in general previous perceptions of hostility affected subsequent perceptions. In addition, he concluded that, in the case of the Dual Alliance, incoming hostile messages had no effect on the perception of the decision-makers who perceived hostility throughout the whole prewar crisis period, whereas such messages affected the perception of the leaders of the Triple Entente.[29] This result differs from both Zinnes' and Holsti's findings in that it stipulates a constantly high level of perceived hostility on the part of the top decision-makers of Germany and Austria. The discrepancies in the findings are not easily explained. The difference in methodology—North, Holsti, Brody, and Zinnes have used multivariate analyses, whereas Hilton has employed markov analyses—is certainly one factor. Multivariate analyses test for co-variance of variables; markov analyses focus on whether and how a variable changes through time. Moreover, Hilton has claimed that North and his associates made many statistical mistakes and that they were far from fully exploiting their carefully collected data.[30] His own work has helped to correct some of these errors and omissions and to contribute further insights into this complex area of perception and decision-making. More research and analysis is needed to clear up such divergences with regard to research methodology and findings.[31]

PERCEPTION AND PERSONALITY

The foregoing uncertainty points to another principal explanation of perceptual differences that has received considerable attention in research, and that reflects a widely held belief that the personality of the decision-maker determines to an important degree what his perceptions are going to be like. The situation and the policy-making and interaction processes as such do not become irrelevant, if we assign some weight to the role of the individuals involved in them. The researcher faces, of course, an unknown risk as he tries to gain an insight into the effect of personality characteristics, but as Ole Holsti himself and many others have shown, this research angle must be examined, even more so since the traditional literature and contemporary journalistic and scholarly accounts are full of psychological assumptions and interpretations that demand more systematic and more informed reexamining.

In his analysis of John Foster Dulles' speeches and statements before and during his tenure as Secretary of State, Holsti was able to depict the perceptual range and the major images held by Dulles; the outcome of the examination has explanatory value for Dulles as an individual and as a high official in the decision-making system of the United States. He brought out that Dulles maintained his rigid view of the Soviet Union as the major international rival regardless of changes in its leadership or in its policies. He established a close nexus between the images and beliefs and the policies pursued while in office.[32] The inquiry into the perceptions of individual officials at high levels of governmental authority therefore inform us about three perceptual levels relevant to the understanding of foreign policy as a process: the level of the individual, the level of the governmental elite of which he is a member, and the level of the community as a whole, the thinking of which he represents in that he is one of its citizens. On all three levels, the information that is collected and analyzed is useful in varying degrees.

A study of the perceptual base of non-alignment examined in the speeches of Nehru, Sukarno, and Nasser demonstrated that the differences in the images of these three statesmen were insignificant and that their surprising cohesion was due to a positive assessment of the unity of the Afro-Asian group and not to negative evaluations of the major powers.[33] Two recent papers focusing on the images of the decision-makers of the parties to the conflict in the Middle East, and the images of the delegates to the UN General

Assembly debating the conflict, have shown that antagonistic conflictual views prevail in which the contest is hardened into a confrontation of two major blocs; under such circumstances the opening for conflict resolution measures is extremely narrow.[34] If we hold that officials on lower levels do influence and shape decisions in foreign matters, it is of interest to learn that considerable differences exist among members of a special crisis operations unit in the U.S. Department of State in how they perceive the scope, urgency, time dimension, resolution potential, etc., of crises that affect American foreign policy.[35]

The question arises of whether we can indeed rely on speeches, interviews, and writings of public officials to figure out how they might act in various international situations. The correspondence or correlation between perception and policy-making, "theory and practice," is difficult to establish, but our general premise that such self-expressions help locate to some degree the perceptual dimensions of the potential action range deserves cautious approval, based on the relevance of the findings we have considered so far. Additional information becomes available as we turn to insights derived from other psychological modes of examining perceptions and attitudes.

Two Scandinavian researchers have examined the role of personality in strategic thinking, i.e., in less or more cooperative behavior, under conditions of a laboratory experiment. The attitudes of the participants were measured according to the Social Rigidity Index. This index is constructed from three attitude scales: (1) the California F-Scale (developed by Adorno and others), measuring the general political-social attitude; (2) the Rokeach Dogmatism Scale, measuring open or closed ideological attitude; and (3) the Himmelstrand Political L-Scale, measuring affective versus rational considerations of political and similar questions. The student participants in the experiments were divided into two groups, socially rigid and socially open-minded individuals. In the following Prisoner's Dilemma game the results showed clearly that socially rigid attitudes make for less cooperative behavior, whereas a high degree of open-mindedness, flexibility, and related characteristics strengthens the tendency to cooperate and to be more sensitive to the opponent's behavior, especially if the opponent also acts in a cooperative vein.[36]

In the light of these results, political and social leaders should weigh the proposition that those candidates who want to enter a country's foreign service or other agencies actively involved in external affairs should be subjected to central attitudinal tests in addition to the customary entrance tests, in order to exclude from recruitment those whose personality characteristics portend conflictive rather than cooperative behavior. Such a general test requirement could also be applied to individuals who ascend to responsible political offices, since they more than the career official shape the decisive policies for their community.[37]

Other significant personality characteristics and their consequences for human perception have been described by Bronfenbrenner as they have affected the tensions between the two superpowers. As we have mentioned above, humans are eager to maintain consistent perceptions, especially if they share them with their fellow humans. Research has revealed the so-called "Asch phenomenon": when an individual, after initial unanimity with his six or seven peers, suddenly finds himself as a lone dissenter against their solid majority, he usually adheres to his correct judgment for a while, but at the end, after going through a period of puzzlement and bewilderment, he joins the others in espousing the distorted view. Together with his fear of social deviance, other elements shape the perception of the individual: (1) exposure to pressure for achieving high or unattainable standards of performance; (2) situations in which deviation or failure implies moral weakness or guilt and entails public disapproval; (3) situations in which criteria for objective comparison are minimal or absent; (4) identification with a social group that is striving for upward mobility from a relatively inferior status. When distorted perceptions are directly challenged, humans tend to defend them as forcefully as possible. The same is true when irrational fears and expectations are confirmed by reality. It is interesting—and is also a strong ray of hope—that one confederate is enough to enable the individual to stick to his correct perception of the situation, even against the unanimous disagreement of an overwhelming majority.[38]

The practical relevance of these findings about the human personality in its psychological and social dimensions is urgently demonstrated in a crisis simulation in which the participating military officers reacted violently and irrationally, and acted out of rage on the basis of a sharply reduced range of calculated available alternatives. In addition, reports have shown that initially sane and healthy personnel in nuclear and missile installations began suffering from increasingly frequent psychiatric illness, countering the belief of the reliability of these human beings.[39] To assume that these ominous indications are purely accidental, inasmuch as the participants in the crisis exercise happened to be very aggressive or that the personnel in those installations happened to be ill-suited for their strenuous work assignment, would mean to be careless and negligent in matters that are of grave importance for our survival in peace. It is equally fallacious to ascribe the violent and irrational inclinations in those groups to a lower level of education and knowledge. Raw forms of violence tend to be mitigated to some degree in the course of more and better education, but attitudinal dispositions will never disappear completely nor change into something totally new. Hence we have to take these symptoms into account and to devise intermediate strategies that start from the givens of human nature and enhance the predisposition, however weak it is, for more rational, friendlier, and more cooperative behavior.

PERCEPTUAL CHANGE AND ROLE REVERSAL

How is effective social perception and communication possible in the relationship between states and governments? This question may initially sound rather easy or even naive, but considering the difficulties we encounter as individuals on our private interaction level, we soon acknowledge the immediate complexity of that issue, particularly under conditions of the nuclear arms race. Bronfenbrenner has argued that effective communication is most likely to occur if it is carried out in a context in which there has been prior recognition and, where possible, acceptance of some values cherished by the other party.[40] The barriers that impede or prevent the realization of these conditions in international relations are huge, regardless of whether we consider the contacts between the great powers or the relations between neighboring small states or between ethnic and religious groups within states.

One idea that has recurrently been proposed and examined as a tool for softening hostile postures and for strengthening cooperative feeling and mutual understanding between individuals and collectives is the technique of role-reversal, i.e., a discussion method in which parties A and B present each other's viewpoints. This would involve a serious and sympathetic effort to describe in a rational fashion the values, goals, and even the means of the opponent or the other party. The underlying premise is that through such meaningful role-reversing exchanges, one step in the perceptual and interaction process, both sides will gain a more correct image of what the other party believes and desires, and will better appreciate the motives and objectives. Although the idea has frequently been suggested, relatively little experimental research has been done to check its practical validity.

Recently the well-known psychologist Morton Deutsch, himself an advocate of the technique, and a colleague reported a pertinent experiment, in which they used teachers, enrolled at the Teachers College of Columbia University in New York, to compare the relative merits of self-presentation and role-reversal in seeking an agreement on such controversial issues as the legalization of euthanasia and the illegality of teachers' strikes. In evaluating an elaborate experiment and questionnaire they found strong evidence that role-reversal was not better suited than self-presentation for promoting agreement between the disputants and, in the case of the euthanasia issue, actually impeded the chance for a mutually acceptable agreement. In the issue of teachers' strikes, role reversal was slightly more effective in terms of the final consensus and more satisfying to the participants than direct self-presentation.

The authors have suggested that the preference for one or the other of the two techniques of argumentation may have to do with the thrust of the two issues; to take the opposite stand from the own ethical and sociolegal view of euthanasia, as role-reversal requires, may cause considerable discomfort or a feeling of guilt, and as a consequence the individual may be reluctant to abandon his personal attitude and join in a common agreement. Compared with that sensitive issue, the question of teachers' strikes is much less principal and it is easier to argue both sides of a well-known public dispute. The two authors also point out that role-reversal may require some training and that facilities for such training do not exist. Despite the negative results of their comparison, they conclude that role-reversal still remains a useful instrument for the control and resolution of various types of conflicts.[41]

In our judgment, the results of the Muney/Deutsch experiment justify the following cautious recommendations. To detect perceptual distortion and mistrust between parties in international conflict situations, the parties to a dispute should be invited to begin the process of negotiation or even of communication with a written or oral statement in which they present the case of the opponent as if it were their own, i.e., they should try to set out openly and without exaggeration what the motives and intentions of the other side are, and avoid propaganda for their own cause as well as self-serving maligning of the adversary. Undoubtedly such an exercise would not result in immediate and automatic understanding and peace. But what seems feasible is a larger awareness on both sides and on the part of the international community of where the major misperceptions and distortions lie, and what possibilities exist to remedy these erroneous conceptions and begin bridging the gaps in perception and intention. Such statements of the opponent's intent would be particularly helpful in crisis situations where direct contact between the parties appears to be out of the question due to an emotionally overcharged atmosphere of hostility and hatred. In those cases, a face-to-face meeting of the diplomatic representatives, speaking each for the own cause, might well excerbate the tensions and postpone the beginning of meaningful communication. In general, the technique of role-reversal could be tried in practice as well as in diplomatic simulation experiments and, if even marginally helpful, could be adopted as an instrument of diplomacy. Its tentative adoption would certainly not damage the current diplomatic practice, but it might enrich the choice of available approaches to the amelioration of the perceptual and interaction processes in contemporary international relations.

With the discussion of role-reversal we have come to the dividing line between the problem areas of perception and interaction. It has become clear that the conceptions and findings about perception in international conflicts are still tentative. They are a testimony to the immense complexity and uncertainty surrounding the facets of perception, and they emphasize the great need for further expanded work in this field. In the meantime, the practitioner should be receptive to what the researchers have made available. Remarkable advances have occurred in conceptualizing the problem in the international context and in clarifying some historical and simulated research results. If the community of foreign policy-makers actively collaborated in research efforts through interviews, games, simulations and attentive criticism, far beyond current levels, the academic specialists could progress faster. We hope that the next few years will bring a rapid increase of scholarly attention and pertinent research findings that will enhance the diplomat's ability to avoid the pitfalls of misperception and distortion.

NOTES

1. For a brief summary review of the antecedents of current perception theory see Vivian J. Rohrl-Wedge and Bryant Wedge, "The role of perception in international politics," International Studies Newsletter, preliminary issue A, Fall 1973, pp. 32-50, pp. 34ff.

2. See Abrahamsson, "A Model for the Analysis of Inter-Group Conflict," *Conflict Control and Conflict Resolution,* op. cit., p. 72.

3. See here Terhune, "The Effects of Personality in Cooperation and Conflict," *The Structure of Conflict* ed. Swingle, pp. 229f.

4. See Rohrl-Wedge and Wedge, "The Role of Perception in International Politics," p. 34. This statement is fully justified in view of recent findings in perceptual research.

5. This brief descriptive account follows ibid., pp. 35f.

6. One of the best examples of this specific interest in psychological aspects of international relations is the volume of essays edited by Kelman, *International Behavior. A Social-Psychological Analysis,* which is divided into two parts, one on national and international images, the other on interaction processes. A more recent critical review and suggestive essay along normative lines focusing on psychological aspects of conflict resolution is Alan G. Newcombe, "Initiatives and responses in foreign policy," Peace Research Reviews, Vol. 3, No. 3, June 1969. Grant Hugo, *Appearance and Reality in International Relations* (New York: Columbia University Press, 1970) is a knowledgeable and imaginative study, but it clearly shows the limits of intuitive psychologizing by the layman who discounts the contributions of individual and social psychology and reaffirms quite strongly the old-fashioned tenets of realism and power.

7. For this conception of image see William A. Scott, "Psychological and Social Correlates of International Images," *International Behavior,* ed. Kelman, pp. 70-103; esp. pp. 72ff. Cf. the somewhat different analysis of perception in discriminating situations by Michael Haas, "Communication factors in decision-making," Peace Research Society (International), Papers, XIII, 1969, pp. 65-86, especially the remarks about cognitive, affection, and evaluation aspects, their differentiation and their linkages.

8. Cf. here also Kenneth Boulding, "National Images and International Systems," *International Politics and Foreign Policy* ed. Rosenau, pp. 422-431; esp. pp. 423f. Of great interest in this article is also his perception matrix in which he demonstrates the significance of the affective friendliness-hostility dimension. John H. Sigler, "Cooperation and conflict in United States-Soviet-Chinese relations, 1966-1971: A quantitative analysis," Peace Research Society (International), Papers, XIX, 1972, pp. 107-128, made use of Boulding's hostility-friendliness scale.

9. For these preliminary conclusions see Ole R. Holsti, "The belief systems and national images: A case study," ibid., pp. 543-550. Cf. also his "Individual differences in 'definition of the situation'," Journal of Conflict Resolution, Vol. 14, No. 3, September 1970, pp. 303-310. Cf. also Boulding, "National Images and International Systems,"

pp. 424ff. See further John R. Raser, "Learning and Affect in International Politics," *International Politics and Foreign Policy* ed. Rosenau, pp. 432-441. Cf. here Volker Gold, Roland Koch, Christel Küpper, and Mathias R. Lohner, "Pädagogische und didaktische Uberlegungen zur Uberwindung von Bedrohungsvorstellungen in Erziehungsprozessen," Jahrbuch für Friedens- und Konfliktforschung, I, 1971, pp. 257-274; esp. p. 261 et passim. See the important paper by Leon Rappoport, "Cognitive conflict as a function of socially-induced cognitive differences," Journal of Conflict Resolution, Vol. 13, No. 1, March 1969, pp. 143-148. For a basic discussion of psychological aspects of cognition, communication, anxiety, pathological learning, and perception cf. Klaus Horn, "Zur Sozialpsychologie von Kommunikation und Interaktion unter Bedingungen von Konflikt und Aggression," Jahrbuch für Friedens- und Konfliktforschung, II, 1972, pp. 35-56; esp. pp. 42ff. Cf. also Newcombe, *Peace Research Around the World,* pp. 122ff. especially the summary of Festinger's hypotheses and findings about cognitive dissonance. Further, cf. Robert Axelrod, "Psycho-algebra: A mathematical theory of cognition and choice with an application to the British Eastern committee in 1918," Peace Research Society (International), Papers, XVIII, 1972, pp. 113-131. On the problem of attitudes and attitude change cf. Norman Alcock, and William Eckhardt, "Comparisons between the attitudes and behaviours of individuals and nations," Peace Research, Vol. 5, No. 2, April 1974, pp. 33-44. Cf. also Herbert C. Kelman, "International Interchanges: Some Contributions from Theories of Attitude Change," paper prepared for the Annual Meeting of the International Studies Association in St. Louis, Mo., March 1974.

10. An interesting study of the educational and professional background of foreign ministers is George Modelski, "The world's foreign ministers: A political elite," Journal of Conflict Resolution, Vol. 14, No. 2, June 1970, pp. 135-175.

11. A model of this kind of thorough analysis is Holsti's portrait of Dulles' thought and belief system. See Ole Holsti, "The belief system and national images: A case study," op. cit.

12. For a skeptical affirmation of this axiom cf. here C. F. von Weizsäcker's introduction to *Kriegsfolgen und Kriegsverhütung,* p. 19. The standard texts in diplomacy and strategic theory are overwhelmingly based on the rationality exiom.

13. For a strong argument against the thesis of rationality on strategic thinking see Anatol Rapoport, "Critique of Strategic Thinking," *International Conflict and Behavioral Science* ed. R. Fisher, esp. pp. 224ff. Karl W. Deutsch and Dieter Senghaas, "Die brüchige Vernunft von Staaten," *Kritische Friedensforschung* ed. Senghaas, pp. 105-163; esp. pp. 105-109 et passim offer a convincing critique of the conventional assumptions about "raison d'Etat" and rational foreign policies.

14. For the two basic matrices showing the various interrelationships and conflict possibilities on the individual psychological and on the collective political levels see ibid., pp. 121 and 148.

15. See ibid., pp. 121ff. and 132ff. For specific foreign policy-related applications see esp. pp. 145ff.

16. See here ibid., pp. 145ff. and 150ff.

17. It is worth pointing out that the autism hypothesis is formulated much more flexibly and tentatively in the Deutsch/Senghaas essay than in the latter's independent writings, e.g., in his *Abschreckung and Frieden,* esp. pp. 146ff., in his "Zur Analyse von Drohpolitik in den internationalen Beziehungen," Jahrbuch für Friedens- und Konfliktforschung I, 1971, esp. pp. 105ff., and in his *Rüstung und Militarismus,* esp. part I. For additional psychological background information cf. Horn, "Zur Sozial psychologie von Kommunikation und Interaktion unter Bedingungen von Konflikt und Aggression,"

Jahrbuch für Friedens- und Konfliktforschung II, 1972, pp. 42ff and 50ff. For general remarks critical of the autism hypothesis, as it relates to international politics and deterrence, cf. Hassner, "Paix et Guerre Entre les Théories," paper for the Ninth World Congress of the International Political Science Association, Montreal, August 1973, pp. 17 and 29 et passim, and Joffe, "Abschreckung und Abschreckungspolitik. Kritische Bemerkungen zu Dieter Senghaas' Beitrag," Jahrbuch für Friedens- und Konfliktforschung I, 1971, esp. pp. 141ff. See also Gerhard Wettig, "Die Wirkzusammenhang und die Konfliktfunktion von Bedrohungsvorstellungen in der zwischenstaatlichen Politik als wissenschaftliche Probleme," ibid., pp. 159-194, for a careful critique and moderation of Senghaas' theorem of perception and interaction. None of the critics, however, offers any stronger proof of his own viewpoint or against the Senghaas hypothesis than the latter had done for it.

18. This is taken from Ole R. Holsti, "The Belief System and National Images: A Case Study," *International Politics and Foreign Policy,* ed. Rosenau, p. 549.

19. Ibid., p. 545. This essay on belief systems and national images as well as Holsti, Richard A. Brody, and Robert C. North, "Measuring Affect and Action in International Reaction Models: Empirical Materials from the 1962 Cuban Crisis," ibid., pp. 679-696, and Holsti, "Time Alternatives, and Communications: The 1914 and Cuban Missile Crises," *International Crises,* ed. Hermann, pp. 58-80, are fine examples of the application of his conception of perception.

20. See Robert Jervis, "Hypotheses on Misperception," *International Politics and Foreign Policy,* ed. Rosenau, pp. 237-254 (first published in World Politics, Vol. 20, 1968, pp. 454-479).

21. On account of their significance these hypotheses by Jervis are here reproduced in summarized form:

Hypothesis 1: Decision-makers tend to fit incoming information into their existing theories and images.

Hypothesis 1a: A theory will have greater impact on an actor's interpretation of data (a) the greater the ambiguity of the data and (b) the higher the degree of confidence with which the actor holds the theory.

Hypothesis 2: Scholars and decision-makers are apt to err by being too wedded to the establishment view and too closed to new information, as opposed to being too willing to alter their theories.

Hypothesis 3: Actors can more easily assimilate into their established image of another actor information contradicting that image if the information is transmitted and considered bit by bit than if it comes all at once.

Hypothesis 4: Misperception is most difficult to correct in the case of a missing concept and least difficult to correct in the case of a recognized but presumably unfilled concept.

Hypothesis 5: When messages are sent from a different background of concerns and information than is possessed by the receiver, misunderstanding is likely.

Hypothesis 6: When people spend a great deal of time drawing up a plan or making a decision, they tend to think that the message about it they wish to convey will be clear to the receiver.

Hypothesis 7: Actors often do not realize that actions intended to project a given image may not have the desired effect because the actions themselves do not turn out as planned.

Hypothesis 8: There is an overall tendency for decision-makers to see other states as more hostile than they are.

Hypothesis 9: Actors tend to see the behavior of others as more centralized disciplined, and coordinated than it is.

Hypothesis 10: Because a state gets most of its information about the other state's policies from the other's foreign office, it tends to take the foreign office's position for the stand of the other government as a whole.

Hypothesis 11: Actors tend to overestimate the degree to which others are acting in response to what they themselves do when others behave in accordance with the actor's desires; but when the behavior of the other is undesired, it is usually seen as derived from internal forces.

Hypothesis 12: When actors have intentions that they do not try to conceal from others, they tend to assume that others accurately perceive these intentions.

Hypothesis 13: If it is hard for an actor to believe that the other can see him as a menace, it is often even harder for him to see that issues important to him are not important for others.

Hypothesis 14: Actors tend to overlook the fact that evidence consistent with their theories may also be consistent with other views.

22. For these and many other relevant propositions and recommendations see Robert C. North, "Axioms and Hypotheses Concerning Active and Passive Defense Systems and the Type of Response They Seem Likely to Evoke," *Weapons System Decisions* ed. Bobrow, esp. pp. 79ff.

23. See Dina A. Zinnes, "The Expression and Perception of Hostility in Prewar Crisis: 1914," *Quantitative International Politics,* ed. Singer, pp. 85-119.

24. See Dina A. Zinnes, Joseph L. Zinnes, and Robert D. McClure, "Hostility in Diplomatic Communication: A Study of the 1914 Crisis," *International Crises,* ed. Hermann, pp. 139-162. The authors warn that their findings are reasonable within the limits of the proviso that historical data are not easily manipulated for purposes of empirical verification; there would always be other factors that influence or determine the shaping of hostile responses, unaccounted for in the historical data and in the mathematical equation used in their inquiry.

25. See Holsti, Brody, and North, "Measuring Affect and Action in International Reaction Models: Empirical Materials from the 1962 Cuban Crisis," *International Politics and Foreign Policy,* ed. Rosenau, pp. 679-696. Also Holsti, North, and Brody, "Perception and Action in the 1914 Crisis," *Quantitative International Politics,* ed. Singer, pp. 123-158. The reader may have noted an interesting divergence between the finding by Zinnes that the decision-makers of the Dual Alliance continued to perceive no hostility, if they had no prior perception of hostility and received a hostile message, and the finding by Holsti, North, and Brody that the policy-makers of the Dual Alliance consistently overperceived the actions of the Triple Entente. We cannot reconcile this discrepancy, but we should emphasize that the findings are actually concerned with two slightly different aspects. The "if" condition in Zinnes' finding is not met by most of the material summarized in the Holsti result. To give a detailed answer to this question we would have to reconsider the data base and the data manipulation for both propositions.

26. See Holsti, "Individual differences in 'definition of the situation'," Journal of Conflict Resolution, Vol. 14, No. 3, September 1970, pp. 303-310.

27. See Holsti, "Time, Alternatives, and Communication: The 1914 and Cuban Missile Crises," *International Crises,* ed. Hermann, pp. 58-80.

28. See here Gordon Hilton, "Expressions of Hostility in Crisis," Journal of Peace Research, 1971, No. 3-4, pp. 249-262.

29. These findings are contained in Hilton, "A closed and open model analysis of perceptions in crisis," Proceedings of the IPRA Third General Conference, III, pp. 51-70.

30. See here Hilton, "The 1914 Studies–A Reassessment of the Evidence and Some Further Thoughts," Peace Research Society, (International), Papers XIII, 1970 pp. 117-141 for a very detailed examination of this issue of the use of data, methodologies, and statistics.

31. Randolph M. Siverson, "International conflict and perceptions of injury: The case of the Suez crisis," International Studies Quarterly, Vol. 14, No. 2, June 1970, pp. 157-165, has confirmed Holsti's and North's finding that decision-makers tend to perceive their own nation and their allies as the target of high levels of injury and that they see the enemy as operating in a favorable international environment. The findings for the Suez Crisis are reliable because the data base is large. Still a lot of methodological and analytical aspects remain open. We have to await more incoming studies before we can give a sounder and more conclusive judgment.

32. See Holsti, "The Belief System and National Images: A Case Study," *International Politics and Foreign Policy,* ed. Rosenau, pp. 543-550; in particular pp. 545f.

33. See Nazli Choucri, "The perceptual base of non-alignment," Journal of Conflict Resolution, Vol. 13, No. 1, March 1969, pp. 57-74.

34. For these findings and their discussion see Doris A. Graber, "Perceptions of Middle East conflict in the UN, 1953-1965," ibid., Vol. 13, No. 4, December 1969, pp. 454-484, and Randolph M. Siverson, "Role and perception in international crises: The case of Israeli and Egyptian decision-makers in national capitals and the United Nations," International Organization, Vol. 27, No. 3, Summer 1973, pp. 329-345.

35. For this interesting research report see Howard H. Lentner, "The Concept of Crisis as Viewed by the United States Department of State," *International Crises,* ed. Hermann, pp. 112-135.

36. For further details of this excellent experiment see Lars Dencik and Hakan Wiberg, "Strategic Thinking as a Function of Social Attitudes: An Experiment with Prisoner's Dilemma," *Conflict Control and Conflict Resolution,* ed. Höglund and Ulrich, pp. 39-71. Dencik and Wiberg compare their own findings with some recent American studies and state a general agreement with regard to the link of open-minded personality characteristics and cooperative behavior. For a review of attitudinal research in relation to situations of conflict and cooperation and some imaginative suggestions for better peace-promoting strategies see Alan Newcombe, "Initiatives and Responses in Foreign Policy," Peace Research Reviews, Vol. 3, No. 3, June 1969, esp. pp. 62 et passim.

37. This suggestion is, of course, far-fetched, because both political elites and career officials are not likely to accept such a standard of selection. Moreover, many communities want to be represented by aggressive spokesmen, since they are out for what they see to be their advantage. The argument that the role of external representation shapes the official while he carries out his duties, is not quite convincing, as the study by Henry H. Kerr, Jr., "Changing attitudes through international participation: European parliamentarians and integration," International Organization, Vol. 7, No. 1, Winter 1973, pp. 45-83, has revealed. The attitudinal predispositions clearly overshadow the shared educational, cultural, and professional experiences and inclinations that George Modelski has found among a large group of Foreign Ministers. See his "The world's foreign ministers: A political elite," Journal of Conflict Resolution, Vol. 14, No. 2, June 1970, pp.

135-175. The testing itself could easily become a part of the routine recruitment process or of the political access to public office.

38. For this passage see the very enlightening contribution by Urie Bronfenbrenner, "Allowing for Soviet Perceptions," *International Conflict and Behavioral Science,* ed. Fisher, pp. 161-178; esp. pp. 173ff. Cf. here also Ted Robert Gurr, "Psychological Factors in Civil Violence," *Anger, Violence, and Politics,* eds. Feierabend, Feierabend, and Gurr, pp. 31-57, where he relates deprivation and anger with the outbreak of civil violence. His propositions and findings are general enough to be applicable in international conflict situations.

39. See John R. Raser, "The Failure of Fail-Safe," *Peace and the War Industry* ed. Kenneth E. Boulding (Chicago: Aldine, 1970), pp. 105-124, where he reports and discusses recent American research and experimentation.

40. See Bronfenbrenner, "Allowing for Soviet Perceptions," op. cit., p. 163.

41. See Barbara F. Muney and Morton Deutsch, "The effects of role reversal during the discussion of opposing viewpoints," Journal of Conflict Resolution, Vol. 12, No. 3, September 1968, pp. 345-356. The essay includes a brief discussion of the literature on role reversal and bibliographical information. Cf. also the brief remark on role reversal by Peter Cooper, "Die Entwicklung von Vorstellungen über den Krieg," *Friedensforschung,* ed. Krippendorff, pp. 157-180; here p. 180, note 18.

Chapter 5

CONFLICT AS INTERACTION

The study of international interaction and bargaining is of central significance for the control and resolution of international conflict. Due to severe constraints with regard to the availability of in-depth empirical data and diplomatic personnel for intensive experiments (simulations, games, etc.), it is probably even more difficult to understand international interaction than perception. Considerable work has been done in this field, but each of the research directions tackles merely a narrow aspect of the problem, so that the cumulative output that might be relevant for the practitioner is at most a small step forward. The following discussion is inevitably going to reflect the tentative and diffuse condition of interaction research in international relations. However, taken individually, most recent findings and suggestions open up new and stimulating perspectives for further exploration. Moreover, a conscious attempt on both sides, research and policy-making, to incorporate mutually unusual propositions and experiences into their current work on a tentative basis might spur the development of better techniques of international conflict management.

Elements of an Interaction Model

The formulation of an interaction model is a difficult assignment because it it is probably impossible to select elements that would find general acceptance among all the experts. Major factors of uncertainty are whether the

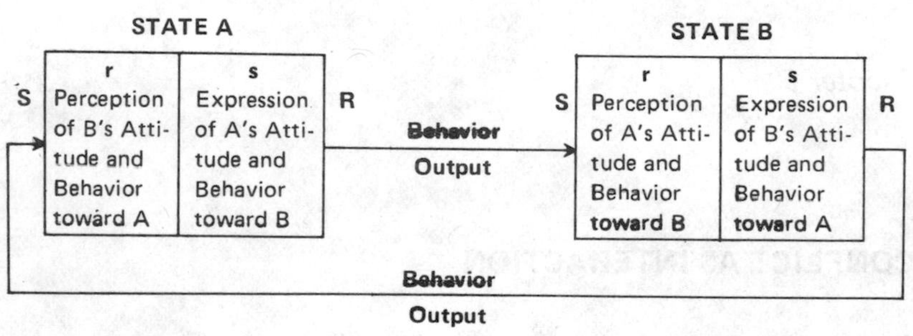

Figure 5.1: AN INTERACTION MODEL

representative role of the interacting official changes his behavior significantly from that of an average private citizen, to what extent the domestic collective decision-making process binds the foreign policy official in a way that is inimical to negotiation and conflict resolution, how the various levels of perception affect the interaction process, and what kind of objectives the interacting parties pursue and to what extent these goals change or can be changed in the interaction, especially bargaining, process. The impact of time and the intensity of the conflictual relationship further complicate the task of the model-builder.

Holsti, Brody, and North have proposed a general model at a high level of abstraction and without attention to the specific characteristics of interstate conflict.[1] A few words of explanation: "S" is an event in the environment which may or may not be perceived by a given actor, and which the actors may perceive and evaluate differently. The stimulus may be a physical event or a verbal act. The response (R) is an action of an actor, regardless of his intent or of how he or others may perceive it. The perception (r) of the stimulus (S) within the decision system of the state actor covers what we usually would call the definition of the situation requiring some decision. The (s) stage represents the actor's expression of his plans, intentions, actions, or attitudes toward another actor which, when carried out, becomes an action response (R).[2]

A special case is not covered by this conception; if A deludes itself into viewing something as an action by B against itself, although B has not engaged in any such behavior, A can initiate a decision sequence the result of which would be conflictual interaction between A and B. This kind of recurrent constellation adds already some complexity to an otherwise manageable interaction model. The distinction between S, the incoming information, and r, its interpretation by the receiver, strikes us as being rather hazy, since it is not clear how to differentiate between the two steps if the point of reference is the respective actor; it makes sense only if we introduce a difference between the perception of S in general and by the concerned actor. From these brief comments we may conclude that some of the systematic nomenclature and delineation is mainly due to the heuristic and methodological requirements of model-building. Nevertheless, this model can serve as an abstraction and systematization of the basic components of interaction. If we see it in conjunction with the major insights from the theory of perception, we have here an instrument that can help organize related research, but that serves little purpose in preparing and executing the practical measures in military or diplomatic interaction.

Most other attempts to depict the essential structural and procedural properties of international interaction are less comprehensive and more directly focused on specific aspects of the problem. Often they are of great interest not only because they reveal a different conception of interaction in general, but more so because they bring out crucial points that are neglected in the basic model.

In analyzing interaction patterns between the United States and the Soviet Union during the Cold War, two researchers suggest that the best explanation for the conflict behavior on both sides is that each side sees itself as pursuing a conciliatory policy; that each believes it is perceived in this way by the other side; and that each sees the adversary as expansionist.[3] What is relevant here is the emphasis on the perception by the other side of one's own image. It comprises a significant source of self-deception which is not included in the general model we have just described. In a recent review of interaction models, a student of cooperation and conflict pointed to the need to complement the customary models of interaction as reaction processes with cognitive and learning models, which should be integrated into one model that would treat both the cognitive view of the current situation and previous learning experience connected with it as determinants affecting current incentives, motives, and expectancies.[4] We have touched above upon the cognitive dimension of interaction. Learning entails the shifts in attitudes and behavioral options that result from the previous experiences in action and reaction. This aspect belongs in the problem area of the relationships among the cognitive, affective, and behavioral sides of perception and—we might add at this point—of interaction.

The changes in the behavior of interacting parties and in particular the reciprocity of these changes are the subject of a stimulating conceptual essay by Dean G. Pruitt. He has tried to develop a theory of interaction by sketching the actions and reactions of the two parties involved in the form of two curves. The point at which the two lines intersect, and which is at the same time most favorable in terms of the goals of the two actors, constitutes the equilibrium. The author holds that the interacting behavior can oscillate up to certain limits around the equilibrium point without endangering too much the equilibrium condition of peace and harmony. Beyond a certain limit that can easily be depicted in the reaction graph, stability would break down and a crisis would ensue. It follows that a distinction between fundamental and momentary behavioral reactions may be feasible and that stability here prevails, if the reacting party underreacts in order to restore the equilibrium. The author also suggests some explanations for the manner in which reactive processes may be pushed from conditions of stability through sudden change to points of overt conflagration, from which there is no easy return to peaceful stability.[5] The direct relevance of these propositions and considerations for the study of war and peace is obvious, even more so since the traditional balance of power theory has consistently failed to provide essential criteria for the definition of "power" and of the measures of the equilibrium. Further research along the lines of Pruitt's interaction equilibrium theory might eventually give us a better tool for the analysis and management of international reaction processes.

Focusing on the question of the incompatibility of values in conflictual interaction, Höglund and Ulrich hold that the degree of incompatibility can be determined as a combined measure of: (1) the number of value-dimensions on which incompatibilities exist; (2) the rank of these dimensions in the value hierarchies of the parties involved; and (3) the degree of offensivity of the goals on each dimension. In discussing the incompatibility of one value between two rivals, they introduce a helpful distinction between the actual position held by the actor on the value dimension, the desired position for which the actor strives, and the minimal position below which the actor will never go. If these three markings for one party on a value-dimension are complemented by the corresponding positions for the rival, a noticeably diversified structure for the interaction and bargaining range becomes visible. The difficult task of allocating numerical equivalents to the various positions on the value-dimension can be mastered. If we take the results together with the three measures of overall value incompatibility, we get a most helpful scheme which will enable researcher and policy-maker to describe more accurately the potential for conflict or cooperation, and to devise suitable strategies to maintain cooperation or to defuse and solve conflict.[6] It could be particularly beneficial in a program to detect conflict-prone international situations and incipient crises. Proposals for such conflict-monitoring programs have been voiced repeatedly in the recent past, but concerned public officials have usually frowned upon these ideas because, among other reasons, they think the task is unmanageable. An expanded program, including the analysis of events data and of goals and values, to be carried out under the auspices of the United Nations or interested states, could serve a major function in the universal peace-keeping effort.

Taking the cue from a recent development of the stimulus-response model, an American researcher has pointed to the impact of affective elements, e.g., hope-friendship and fear-hostility, in international interaction; he argues that these factors can be conditioned consciously, that they are crucial for the choice among available responses to incoming stimuli, and that even interstate behavior can be altered by the conscious manipulation of reward and punishment creating and reinforcing conditions that establish the milieu for future interaction behavior. Special emphasis is placed here on the milieu, which plays an important role in determining the interaction behavior.[7] This thrust of interaction analysis deserves considerable attention, because it helps fill a gap in the study of international conflict in that it focuses on the affective component of international relations. The same applies to Galtung's manifold contributions dealing with sociological conceptions translated into the conditions of international politics. We remind the reader once again of his hypotheses about asymmetry, rank-disequilibrium, imperialism and dependency, and their relationship to interstate conflict.[8]

Most of the principal models and theorems about international interaction focus exclusively on dyadic relations between two actors. The reason for this restriction is obvious, as the expansion to more than two parties results in a tremendous complication of the web of interaction alternatives. This has repercussions for the quantitative researcher who is hard put to attribute reliable numerical values to the various conceivable interrelationships among three or more parties. Such a difficulty is especially exacerbated in a situation of fluid alignments, where enmity and friendship are uncertain or absent. A simple reflection about the impact of cross-cutting conflicts on the overall level of tension shows that it will normally exert a moderating influence against the formation of rigid blocs and the dangerous rise in hostility.[9]

There lies ahead a large and rather unexplored field that invites intensive academic thinking and experimenting. As of now, we have to work with a widening set of hypotheses that still are predominantly derived from the dyadic interaction model, especially its stimulus-response version. We notice, however, as we turn to individual specific propositions, that the introduction of historical and contemporary international data has tended to enrich the somewhat barren basic interaction model and to increase the researcher's awareness of additional dimensions and measures of international conflict behavior.

Specific Propositions About Interaction

Let us begin once again with some of the findings that have resulted from the examination of the great crises of 1914 and 1962, as reported by North and his associates. A basic hypothesis that has been confirmed for several situations, initially for the outbreak of World War I, says that perceptions of its own inferior capability will fail to deter a nation from going to war if its perceptions of fear, threat, or injury are great enough.[10] Although this finding seemingly conforms with the intuitive expectation of the foreign policy expert, it does indeed run counter to the wisdom of traditional textbooks in international politics and diplomacy that policy-makers act rationally and calculate primarily their military capabilities before they engage in open warfare. History teaches us that wars and violent conflicts break out although the odds speak clearly against such engagements.

In an interesting manner, Zinnes' failure to confirm the following interaction hypotheses: [(a) If x expresses hostility toward y, then y will perceive that it is the object of x's hostility; and (b) if x expresses hostility toward y, then y will express hostility toward x.)] shows the significance of the North finding.[11] If we assume that the non-confirmation of Zinnes' common sense propositions is not just the consequence of inadequate data or insufficient methodology, then we have some indirect evidence for the overriding strength of what is perceived by decision-makers over what is real in the interaction. If the individual or the community is predisposed to see hostile behavior, the other side will be hard put to prove its friendly intentions. Hence the perception of injury, fear, or threat will not easily be outweighed by messages implying non-hostility and cooperation. It follows that parties to a conflict should always strive to make the meaning of their messages explicit if they want to avoid tragic misunderstanding.

These basic propositions, which deserve further discussion and empirical testing, have been expanded and refined by North, some of whose axioms on perception we have reported above. From among many more, we include here only a few:

(1) The higher the tension felt by the decision-makers in one state A and the more intense the interaction with another state B, the higher is the probability that the leaders of B will experience increasing tension and that interchanges between A and B will reach increasingly higher levels of violence and tension;

(2) The higher the tension generated by a reaction process, the greater the probability of violence, no matter what the consequences;

(3) The correlation between input action (S) and output action (R) will be better in a low reward, low penalty situation than in a high reward, high penalty situation;

(4) If a conflict spiral develops, the decision-makers must make every effort to control time, i.e., primarily to avoid succumbing to time pressure, to impressions that time is running out;

(5) If the policy-maker does not want to drive the opponent into the corner and to induce him to strike back whatever the cost, he must make certain that the opponent perceives at least one alternative that promises the avoidance of defeat and punishment.[12]

From these hypotheses, more than from many others, it becomes clear how relevant the work of the conflict researcher can be for the practitioner. Although the hypotheses may not deviate from what the experienced policy-maker and the diplomat know, they contribute to the advancement in knowledge in that they serve as guides for additional empirical research and as material for the foreign policy proccss, in which the urgency of the conflict situation or the personal conviction or competence of the participants may otherwise severely limit the recognition of policy options and alternatives. In addition, these academic insights might also help the official to be constantly aware of the crucial significance of the internal mechanism of the own decision-making process for the way the other party perceives the objectives and dimensions of the conflictual interaction. Beyond these general, characteristics, the North hypotheses are self-explanatory.

The emphasis on the behavioral and procedural dimension of interstate conflict, as it emerges from Zinnes, North, and Holsti's findings, is strengthened and justified by Rummel's research in which he has tried to ascertain the way national attributes affect foreign conflict behavior; he has found little or no evidence that the level of economic or technical development is significantly related to the external behavior of states. The same is true for the level of international communications or transactions, for the instability of a state, its military capabilities, its power, its values, or the psychological motivations of the people, even the nature of the political system and the number of borders a state shares with other states.[13] None of these state characteristics, which we customarily consider in explaining or predicting the involvement in international conflicts, withstand the empirical scrutiny of the computer-assisted researcher. This does not mean we have to discard all our beliefs and assumptions about the sources of state behavior, but we must reconsider our thinking as we approach each individual case. It is no longer warranted to assert premises such as that authoritarian and totalitarian regimes are more eager to start violent hostilities or that democratic systems, once involved in warfare, find it difficult to extricate themselves from the conflict, or to argue that a country with high technological, military, and economic capability is more aggressive than a community with low capabilities. We recognize that in the search for the explanation of international conflicts we have to turn to other more varied and more differentiating devices for exploration and understanding. In refocusing on the interaction process itself, we must keep in mind that the degree of uncertainty in accounting for specific patterns of interaction is considerably higher than it is in the study of national attributes, because the range of causal factors and their conceivable linkages is far wider and more complex.

For the examination of interaction and bargaining in conflict and crisis situations, Oran Young has formulated a list of hypotheses that provide a pertinent analytical framework for the decisive facets of the process of international politics. To illustrate the argument which we have submitted about the relative insignificance of elements extraneous to the process itself, we summarize a few major propositions from Young's study. In intense crisis situations, effective communication among the adversaries concerning their attitudes, expectations, intentions, and resolve will be based increasingly on physical actions in contrast to verbalized statements through diplomatic channels. Peripheral actors will play a minimal role during the beginning of a crisis, but their influence will increase as the conflict reaches its climax. The impact of bargaining impediments will increase with the onset of a crisis. Conditions of crisis will generate highly influential restraints on the usability of violence for the achievement of political objectives. In critical situations, the tactical "initiative that forces the opponent to initiate" tends to become a significant coercive device. Simple or partial bargains that leave many issues to be worked out at a later time are apt to be employed in terminating crises.[14]

Clearly the consequences that we may derive from these propositions, to some extent confirmed empirically, do not point in any single direction. They must reflect the perplexing and often seemingly contradictory symptoms and outcomes that we register in the chronicles of international conflict and crisis. The first finding about the nature of communications in crises is particularly important as it reveals the fragility and tenacity of verbal messages in comparison with the decisiveness of action, primarily the use of force. On the other hand, overt force has only a marginal utility for the furtherance of the goals in intense crisis situations. As a result, the range of possible action narrows appreciably, as the policy-maker steers a course that avoids too much violence without excluding the prudent employment of communication through action. Since bargaining is impeded in high-level crises, it is to be expected that simple or partial agreements will bring about the termination of the conflict; once that is achieved, the conditions for the negotiations will be favorable for a detailed long-term settlement. The recent history of international conflict contains many instances that fit this description.[15] One significant query that we merely note at this point has to do with the difficulty of the weaker party in achieving a fair and equitable long-term agreement once the initial partial agreement has been put into practice. It depends on the "good will" of the stronger party whether it acknowledges the principal objectives of the weaker side, and accedes to the essential requests of the opponent in order to support a mutually satisfactory arrangement. Here lies a large, rather unexplored issue area that is of urgent concern for modern peace research.

In Search of Conflict Resolution

Before we turn to specific findings, we take a brief look at suggestions that originate from a normative or policy perspective. We are aware of the fact that this short excursus seems to lack any connection with previous and subsequent discussions. But there is indeed an intimate link in that the normative reflections and policy proposals concerning modes of conflict resolution have become a major subject of empirical analysis by numerous researchers. This is especially true for Charles Osgood's scheme of GRIT (Graduated Reciprocation in Tension-Reduction), which has been widely debated and examined. Its focus coincides perfectly with the basic divisions in abstract and empirical works, i.e., with the issues of threats and promises, compliance and non-compliance, escalation and de-escalation and their utility in conflictual situations. In order to understand the full implications of the specific research, we must be cognizant of a few major models of conflict resolution. They are also of importance because they add background factors that are crucial for a balanced view of international conflict interaction and for modes of conflict control outside the immediate concern of the decision-maker.

Let us consider a few elements that impede conflict resolution. A conflict may be significantly exacerbated by cognitive differences between the parties, although the disagreement about the conflict matter is only minimal. If an international conflict has a component of considerable cognitive distance between the actors—and we must assume that this is the case in many conflicts—the openings for managing and repairing the rupture in international peace are few and narrow.[16] The same is true in situations where the state and its decision-makers are symbolically involved, especially in the initial phases of the confrontation.[17] This assumption is indirectly supported by another hypothesis that the maximization of power, defined as military and economic capability, is not the chief motivating factor in the behavior of states.[18]

If these assumptions are indeed pertinent, there is little doubt that significant aspects of conflictual interaction have received far too scant attention. The material and symbolic dimensions of state goals need more examination; special information is needed about the conditions under which states and governments are willing to forfeit military conflict and triumph, and to accept compromise or even defeat. These issues must be interpreted as problems that defy any solution unless they are put into the context of interaction. How else can we determine the relative overall strength of parties to a potential conflict and the significance of norms and symbols that might become the foundation for the termination of a conflict or crisis?[19]

These factors relate closely to the elaborate GRIT scheme formulated by Osgood.[20] The basic question which Osgood has confronted since the hey-day of the Cold War is how to initiate a process of interlocking concessions and commitments in a situation where each side expects the other to make the first move. The only feasible and justifiable escape from that deadlock arises, in his judgment, from the willingness of one party to engage in a unilateral initiative—or in several steps—that does not involve abandoning the possibility of retraction and the capability of severe retaliation. This qualification of whatever measure may be taken has frequently been overlooked, disregarded, or ridiculed by those who have opposed Osgood's peace strategy.

Due to the frequency and persistence of these misunderstandings it seems appropriate to describe the specific premises underlying GRIT;

(1) Unilateral initiatives must not reduce our capacity to inflict unacceptable nuclear retaliation on an opponent should we be attacked;

(2) Unilateral initiatives must not cripple our capacity to meet aggression by conventional weapons with appropriately graded conventional military responses;

(3) Unilateral initiatives must be graduated in risk according to the degree of reciprocation obtained from opponents;

(4) Unilateral initiatives must be diversified in nature, both as to sphere of action and as to geographical locus of application;

(5) Prior to announcement, unilateral initiatives must be unpredictable by an opponent as to their sphere, locus, and time of execution;

(6) Unilateral initiatives must represent a sincere intent to reduce and control international tensions;

(7) Unilateral initiatives must be announced publicly at some reasonable interval prior to their execution and identified as part of a deliberate policy of reducing and controlling tensions;

(8) In their announcement, unilateral initiatives should include explicit invitation to reciprocation in some form;

(9) Unilateral initiatives that have been announced must be executed on schedule regardless of prior commitment by the opponent to reciprocate;

(10) Unilateral initiatives must be continued over a considerable period, regardless of immediate reciprocation or events of a tension-increasing nature elsewhere;

(11) Unilateral initiatives must, wherever possible, take advantage of mutual self-interests, mutual self-restraints and opportunities for cooperative enterprise;

(12) Unilateral initiatives must be as unambiguous and as susceptible to verification as possible;

(13) Our initiatives and requested reciprocations should, wherever possible, involve transfer of sovereignty from national to international auspices;

(14) Our initiatives and requested reciprocations should, wherever feasible, be designed to reduce the imbalance between "have" and "have-not" countries; and

(15) Our initiatives and requested reciprocations should, wherever feasible, be designed to strengthen democratic as against totalitarian ways of life.[21]

The Osgood principles demonstrate that serious attention should be paid to the strategy of unilateral measures to open a systematic and concerted move away from high tension hostility and toward a stable system of peaceful interchange. While the first proposals would not endanger the ability of the initiating state to maintain its solid defense and to arrest the process, if necessary, their implementation could be expected to generate a momentum of their own that would pull a recalcitrant opponent into the experiment. As Osgood and his supporters have pointed out repeatedly, steps toward partial disarmament would commence only at the end of a successful series of reciprocated tension-reduction measures that would provide the basis of trust on which to tackle the decisive problems, implying far-reaching changes under balanced conditions. The suspicion that the other side is engaged in deception would be laid to rest at that stage; otherwise the parties would not have reached that point. A crucial expectation is, of course, that in the accelerating scheme of tension-reduction a learning process would set in, during which the adversaries would train their skills in trust and confidence-building. Moreover, it is reasonable to posit that the cognitive and perceptual premises of their behavior would undergo a slow, but marked transformation, in the course of which the antagonists would become capable of acknowledging the legitimacy of the other side's viewpoint and actual behavior.[22]

The major barriers against a large-scale successful application of GRIT to contemporary tensions and conflicts are the immense accumulation of ill will and mistrust that has hampered international relations since 1948, and the considerable practical problems connected with the implementation of the program. The latter factor requires some explanation. Osgood emphasizes throughout his writings that the program of tension-reduction can only succeed if it is carried out systematically and coherently. The structure of internal politics, as we observe it in most modern states, severely impairs the ability of the decision-makers in foreign policy to plan and execute a program that would enjoy public support and, more importantly, find reliable acceptance among the governmental and social elites. Open societies in which much of the governmental process takes place in full view of the general public or is leaked in some fashion, cannot gag the various pressure and interest groups, both within and without the realm of government, and cannot suppress dissent, especially not on issues that arouse high emotions and are the subject of bitter controversy. Similar pressures, although considerably subdued, are most likely to operate in closed political systems, where the dispute is essentially restricted to the circles of government and its supporting political organization. The consequence of the internal controversy is either a loud disavowal of the government's actions by its domestic enemies and critics or the adoption of a consensus measure that allows for a weak and doomed initiative, or results in side effects which negate the thrust of the policy of tension-reduction.

What, if anything, can be done to forestall these adverse factors and to foster the promotion of peace? Osgood and his supporters have tried to educate the public and its leaders so that they perceive GRIT as the only conceivable peace program that would not involve the disruption of the internal order of the main international actors or of the present structure of the international system. He has also emphasized that all sides need to grant the opponent what they claim for themselves; namely, that they labor under the constraints of domestic dissent and protest which cannot—and should not—be eliminated or brutally suppressed. The active involvement of opponents at home should not be taken as a sign that the responsible government is faltering in its resolve and prudence and that it is unable to implement what it has announced to the partner in the experiment. This insistence on the necessity of accommodation to the so-called "realities" of internal politics is the only possible approach to the problem if we want to see GRIT operate successfully. Previous scattered experiences should encourage the governments of the superpowers and of all other states to take the necessary first step and start a scheme of tension-reducing initiatives that will encourage their rivals to respond in kind. Peace researchers all over the world should join in such a great effort by studying the causes and patterns of specific tensions and conflicts between states and within states, because GRIT could be applied to internal disputes. The world needs a lot of practice-oriented research to equip the responsible officials with facts and to increase their awareness of the range and interrelationship of the problems involved, as well as to enlighten and encourage the general public so that the governments face increasing support and even demand for a fully developed tension-reducing peace strategy.

Interaction in Crises

One of the richest sources of interaction findings, and hypotheses is the volume of essays on international crises to which we have referred repeatedly.[23] The major difficulty with the book lies in its being addressed to the academic specialist, so that no attempt has been made to interpret the research language or the results of the various studies for the policy-maker, who is most intimately involved in the daily administration of his country's external relations and in the management of the all too frequent crises that shake the international order. It is impossible for us to carefully examine each research study and to discuss the many relevant assumptions and results. To the great benefit of the reader, Charles Hermann, the editor, has culled from the individual essays 311 empirically testable propositions which the authors have tested in their work or formulated on the basis of their research. From that list we have chosen a few examples that are of direct relevance to the nature of international interaction in conflict and war.[24] Each of the reported propositions would merit intensive consideration, but for our purposes it must suffice to briefly summarize them and to limit our comments to a few words.

Focusing on the beginning, duration, and abatement of international crises in Berlin and Taiwan since World War II, Charles McClelland, a leading analyst of events data and interaction, has confirmed that attempts to settle the crisis and interactions toward that goal increase as the crisis lessens. However, if the conflict situation stays below the crisis threshold, defined in terms of danger and urgency, a decline in the conflict tensions will result in a decrease of attempts to find a settlement.[25] This two-pronged finding has been echoed frequently in other studies. It strengthens the impression that the foremost task in volatile crisis conditions is to bring about a cessation of open hostilities in order to stop death and injury and to move the situation to the stage in which efforts toward a thorough settlement have a chance of success. On the other hand, it should reinforce the resolve of the policy-maker to be alert to developments that tend to result in a full-blown crisis. The warning by McClelland that in less than critical conflict the decline of the tension will be accompanied by a slackening of the search for a satisfactory settlement, should be of considerable interest to the foreign policy-makers in light of the likelihood that negligence in these low-level conflicts may well be a contributing element to their subsequent escalation up to the high crisis level. These insights should affect the behavior of the conflict parties as well as the third parties, including the universal and regional organizations.

Glenn Paige has compared the Korean war and the Cuban Missile Crisis. Among his results is this important point: by avoiding the issuance of an ultimatum and by acting slowly in relation to the main values held by the opponent, the party to the crisis can gain extended time for its decision.[26] In this connection, Hermann has confirmed a concurrent proposition that low threats tend to produce more communication than high threats and that, as the decision time increases, the rate of external communication increases.[27] We know that time and communication are among the scarcest commodities in severe crisis. Therefore, the decision-maker faces the imperative task of extending his available time, and maintaining and increasing the communication with the opponent. The Cuban Missile Crisis of 1962 is the most celebrated instance in which these rules were successfully observed. Supplementary research about other critical events in the recent past would certainly produce evidence to confirm these "laws" of crisis interaction. Thus it is wise for a party to a conflict to refrain from ultimatums and from threatening or injuring the cherished values of the other side. If this is done, communications will continue to flow at significant levels and will thereby mitigate the stress and tension under which the decision-makers operate.

In a brilliant and imaginative discussion of bargaining in crises, Glenn Snyder has submitted many fascinating arguments and hypotheses. We may begin with his observation that as wars become too costly and risky, they tend to be replaced by crises in the resolution of conflict, at least between great powers.[28] There is ample evidence in the history of superpower relations to verify that statement. Consequently, we recommend that both researchers and policy-makers take a look at the feasibility of increasing the costs of war so much that even small states will be reluctant to start full-fledged military action. It would lead us too far from our current concern to pursue this useful topic any further; even preliminary reflection proves the intricate and rewarding nature of the proposition.

Snyder also stipulates that the greater the uncertainty in each party's image of the other's alternatives and incentives, the greater is the possible effect on the outcome of the bargaining process.[29] Unfortunately, the author does not make clear whether the degree of uncertainty will affect the bargaining process negatively or positively. We would guess that the impact would be mainly negative, since uncertainty about the other's options and inclinations will force the actor to prepare for the worst case. Moreover, it will force him to hide his own possibilities. We might argue that a little uncertainty could be beneficial, as it would discourage rash judgment and reaction, while too much uncertainty would tend to reduce the opportunity for well-reasoned bargaining.

Snyder proposes that the public communication of threats and demands tends to increase their credibility.[30] The obvious conclusion must be that even in our time it would be desirable for the parties in an ongoing conflict to keep their communication of threats and demands secret and confidential, unless they are irrevocably committed to them. Once hostilities are ended or the crisis has passed the climax, the demands could be issued publicly, as they would not exacerbate the confrontation too much. This is particularly important, since emotional or irrational factors tend to produce "psychological" compulsions toward action and uncontrollable patterns of conflict behavior could develop, if tension is already high and violence is imminent.[31]

Discussing the value of threats as an instrument of bargaining, Snyder points out that a party is less likely to react emotionally or irrationally if it is warned that a change in its behavior is necessary to prevent things from getting out of control, rather than if it is simply threatened.[32] Here we learn that threats, upon which much international policy is based, are usually the wrong approach to bring about compliance by the adversary. When one side opts for more subtle ways of warning, the argument goes, it becomes easier for the other side to change its behavior for the benefit of both parties. This appeal to the "common good" is effective, because both sides understand that some response is implied if the other side does not heed the admonition. Snyder supports our reasoning with another proposition, that the parties in a crisis situation are often at least as much concerned about their common interest in avoiding war as they are about getting their way.[33] These last two insights tend to confirm the importance of a certain ambiguity, since it preserves policy options and generally cools the heat of conflictual interaction.[34]

Finally, a few psychological aspects of interaction in crises merit our attention. Thomas Milburn has explained that mild stress often facilitates performance in crisis situations. But as stress increases, it usually leads to a deterioration and ultimately to a complete disintegration of performance by the decision-makers.[35] Under greater stress, the number of cues of which the individual policy-maker is aware also decreases.[36] Moreover, crises increase a tendency toward rigidity of perception and thinking.[37] Milburn also argues that, under conditions of high stress, tacit bargaining and communication is less likely to be understood by the receiver in the way the initiator has intended.[38] Concurring with Hermann and others, he points out that if the actors increase their capacity to delay their response the crisis will tend to de-escalate.[39]

The impairment of the ability of the policy-maker to cope with high tension crises serves as a clear warning that the personality of the individuals involved weighs heavily for the outcome of the conflict. Milburn emphasizes that high levels of stress generally affect the decision-making process adversely, regardless of the particular social and decisional system in which the official operates. The main insight we get from his observations supports the suggestions made by the other students of crisis and conflict: the need to keep the tension and stress level low is imperative; this ties in with another major finding that the decidion time, i.e., the capacity to delay the response, must be extended so that the stress remains low.

In general, we recognize that none of the authors whose findings we have briefly summarized offer easy solutions, but they pinpoint the crucial pitfalls that impede the crisis management and cause escalatory measures, and as a consequence the margin of tension-reducing and conflict-solving operations is severely reduced. The foreign policy-maker, however, need not despair over the prospect that his opponent, through reckless actions, could make it impossible for him to pursue a moderate course favoring accommodative steps and a speedy abatement of the crisis. The willingness of one party to force war on the other side does not preclude the latter's pursuit of a policy averting violence and warfare, at least until all peaceful alternatives have been proposed or until the aggressor begins military actions.

To know the critical points in the crisis process is already a great advance, since this knowledge will improve and guide the search of researchers and practitioners for those cues that seem to strengthen the trends to avoid violent confrontation and to ease severe crises.

Interaction in Non-Crisis Situations

As Milburn indicates in one of his hypotheses, we have to make a clear distinction between crisis and non-crisis situations, since they are characterized by different symptoms in individual behavior and in the dynamics and meaning of the interaction process. The propositions from the volume edited by Hermann refer primarily, although not exclusively, to crisis conditions. But the relationships between states often are of a conflictual but non-critical nature, for which methods of conflict control and resolution are also needed. Many international negotiations belong in the category of conflict interaction, as do communications such as declarations of intent, threats, promises, etc. All these phenomena indicate that the parties pursue goals and values that do not quite match, so that some tension strains their relationship and they seek a solution. Researchers have been able to model typical examples of these conflicts in the forms of games and simulations, or they have attempted to detect and extract structural procedural characteristics in concrete cases, e.g., disarmament and arms control negotiations. A lot of work has been reported in academic periodicals, from which we have selected a few pieces that supplement and correct the approaches and findings we have presented.

The most significant finding of the Prisoner's Dilemma experiment that Dencik and Wiberg conducted is the strong evidence that interaction determines to a considerable degree the performance of the individual participant: socially rigid players behaved more cooperatively when they interacted with socially open-minded players; on the other hand, the latter acted less cooperatively in playing against the former. What is truly remarkable is the finding of an overall gain in cooperative behavior, since the rigid players increased more in cooperative performance than the open-minded ones lost.[40] This tends to confirm our suggestion that flexible cooperative attitudes will lead to a modification of the provocative or aggressive inclination on the side of even the most rigid adversary. There are, of course, some exceptions, but why should our whole thinking about interstate conflict and international relations in general be dominated by those few cases on the fringe of international conduct?

The same notion, that conciliatory behavior on one side serves to encourage reciprocation among the other parties, resulted from a careful investigation of the negotiations among the United States, the Soviet Union, and the United Kingdom in the Eighteen Nations Disarmament Conference in 1962-1963, which led to the Partial Test Ban Treaty. The author of that study also found that the negotiating behavior itself affected the outcome of the negotiations more than did the environmental situation, i.e., the general policies of the states involved and the global political development. With regard to the effect of the latter external factors, more cooperative behavior affected the disarmament negotiations positively, and more conflict outside was followed by a marked decline in concessions in the protracted talks. Overall the three parties showed a substantial symmetry and reciprocity in those negotiations.[41] From these results we can infer firmly that the direction and quality of the interaction process itself are crucial for the achievement of the objectives of the actors.

Certain decisive suggestions that reflect these experiences reappear throughout the theoretical and experimental literature. One researcher simulated disarmament negotiations and established that if the contentions issues were emphasized, the players acted far less cooperatively and made fewer concessions.[42] Hence international talks should always be conducted in full awareness of what the parties have in common and what they try to agree upon rather than what divides them. As we have noted previously, the whole theory of threats must be evaluated in the light of that insight. Ultimatum bargaining, a standard tactic in classical diplomacy, usually increases rather than diminishes the reluctance of the opponent to make concessions; therefore, a better strategy is to combine conflictive and conciliatory elements in the bargaining process.[43]

The rise of nuclear weapons since 1945 and in particular the development of the missile-based second strike capacity for both superpowers have revealed an intricate problem of interaction: To what extent does the "capacity to delay response" in a nuclear exchange affect the relationship between those who have that capacity and their opponents, allies, and non-aligned members of the international system? From among the numerous findings of a complex simulation exercise we mention only that the "capacity to delay response" increases the belligerency of the actors who wield it, and it deters the opponents to a considerable degree. It also emerged that it does not affect the negotiating ability of its wielder or of the other parties significantly, although it makes accidental and preemptive wars less likely.[44] The study, revealing as it is, is somewhat outdated in design, because for more than a decade two states have had a second strike capacity. It would be most welcome if a similar simulation could be carried out to incorporate this development and to check how this duopoly changes the perception and interaction between adversaries and allies. The historical record indicates a deadlock reducing sharply the degree of belligerency and less so the deterrence effect. Much more experimentation is necessary to arrive at some firm findings.

The whole issue of the relative utility of threats and promises is still little explored and awaits additional research. It has been suggested that among the factors affecting the compliance to threats and promises are the role position of the initiator, available resources and intentions, the degree of approval the initiator gains from his fellow actors, and the credibility and magnitude of the threat or promise, as well as status, attraction, prestige, esteem, and message utility on the side of the receiver. Research has shown that the magnitude of the threat must exceed the costs of compliance in order to bring about compliance. Moreover, when the target of the threat likes the threatener, he will not comply with low credibility threats but will usually comply with highly credible threats. When he dislikes the threatener, he will comply frequently with threats regardless of the level of threat credibility. Greater compliance will result if the threatener enjoys high status, as long as the target of the threat has a lower status. If promises are issued, the utility of the message loses in importance; it seems that the compliance with promises is due to normative elements that are aroused and lead to a general willingness to reciprocate the positive proposal for cooperation.[45] Taking Osgood's basic GRIT premise, another student of threats, promises, and compliance has tested the relative efficacy of escalation and de-escalation: he found out that an escalation of threats and punishments, whether systematic or sudden, is more effective than de-escalation. The only way a policy of de-escalation approximates somewhat the success of escalatory measures is if it is sudden and drastic, that means if the threatener "lays down his arms." In that condition, the threatener becomes credible to the other party because he increases his own vulnerability by not using the punishments actually available to him. Further experimental work along these lines has indicated that the whole question of escalation and de-escalation requires further inquiry. The differentiation of the causes for compliance with threats and promises could be of crucial significance for negotiations in conflictual situations. While only the powerful can enforce what he seeks, the weaker actors dispose of a richer set of instruments to influence the course of events than is commonly assumed. These suggestions offer support to the assumption that appeals to the "common good" might evoke considerable impartial sympathy and blunt the open and veiled threats that are issued by the powerful international actors. So far, we know too little to offer more than these general indications.

From these remarks it is obvious that toughness or softness as standards of bargaining behavior must be adjusted to the specific circumstances if a satisfactory agreement is to be reached. While individuals, even if they are tough, reciprocate concessions to some extent, teams show no such sign. Pure softness is a bad strategy as it fails completely in the attempts to achieve concessions. Pure toughness sharply decreases the chance for an agreement, although it may bring a rich payoff to the tough actor if the other side gives in completely. In general, toughness is an appropriate strategy for negotiations that begin in uncertainty about the opponent's interests and objectives. If the participants, however, have an accurate idea of each other's expectations, toughness may be a definitively bad strategy.[46] It depends on the nature of the accurate information: if the intentions of the other player make for sharp position incompatibility between the parties, the chances for an agreement will be slim, unless both are willing to change their perception of the situation and their goals.[47]

Our discussion of the problem of perception made clear that it is more or less impossible to determine with anything approaching absolute certainty which aspects are really decisive for the goals of the actors in negotiations. Experiments show that considerations of prestige, face, and credibility weigh heavily in how far an actor is willing to take risks or to press for his demands. It is hard to identify clearly the reactions of the co-players and observers. This is especially true for international crises. The attempt to save face may engender risky threatening actions for which the other parties might find no rational explanation. It may also prevent an actor from making a conciliatory gesture. Appropriate changes in experimental games whereby the players remain anonymous have introduced some relaxation into tense situations and have raised the level of cooperation on both sides.[48]

This would concur with several recent diplomatic constellations in which the negotiations were conducted by a mutually trusted intermediary, since a face-to-face meeting of responsible representatives was initially unthinkable. One reason for the success of indirect bargaining was the availability of an honorable fallback position for the opponents to which they could withdraw without directly taking the blame for their rigid stance. As the events demonstrate, the emphasis that researchers have put on the need for oral and face-to-face communications between opponent players[49] needs considerable reexamination and refinement before it can be accepted as a general rule of interaction behavior.

If outsiders involve themselves in a conflict situation, the question has been asked in many cases what their role can be to help promote a settlement. In a discussion of the Quaker effort in the Middle East, the following elements of such third party involvement were listed: The first stage is the collection of information and the identification of issues; second, insight is needed into the history and the emotional tone or affective load of the conflict; third, alternative positions are explored; fourth, possible partial or general solutions are proposed; and finally, public opinion must be mobilized. The advantage of having a private organization such as the Quakers involved in this elaborate effort is that the parties to the conflict can disavow that communication channel at any time, as they deem it necessary.[50] As a correlate, it is also self-evident that such disavowable involvement destroys the chance to coerce recalcitrant opponents into a mutual compromise. Recent events in the Middle East may be interpreted as a sign that at least in nearly intractable crisis situations the intermediary must be a symbol for the presence of a force that can coerce by deprivation and other sanctions.[51] Even then, the agreement that is reached covers only a minimal segment of the total dispute. This confirms Young's hypothesis that simple bargains will be used to terminate the crisis stage of a conflict, as reported above, and Fisher's well-known suggestion that "fractionating conflicts," i.e., separating issues into their smallest components and dealing with them separately, may reduce the crisis level significantly.[52] Another possible condition for the success of third party involvement is its timing: it has been suggested that the later a proposal is introduced in a bargaining session, the greater is its influence on the final decision.[53] Instances supporting that assumption come easily to our mind, but such random confirmation proves not more than its attractive potential for the researcher and for the policy-maker.

Even the most dramatic successes of third party intervention in the search for conciliation and agreement prove, at least implicitly, that the parties in conflictual interaction and the precise situation are the decisive aspects of the problem of conflict resolution. A recent essay has pointed to the crucial need for the maintenance of the freedom of decision; if that gets lost and if the "lock-in" effect results, the deterioration of the interaction is very likely to set in. It may lead the parties to war, or in a negotiating situation to a breakdown of the bargaining process.[54]

Mention should also be made of a recent examination of mutual disengagement as a step of confidence-building between parties in conflict. Its author proposes that if territories are conspicuous, i.e., clearly separate and open to the control of the parties, and economically, strategically, and symbolically worthless, their choice for disengagement is a most feasible, lasting and rewarding measure; in the recent past, disengagement of this type has been neglected, but it should be revived as an inexpensive way of upgrading the confidence between antagonistic states and alliances.[55] These measures and other equally simple steps, some of which have been discussed in the Conference on Security and Cooperation in Europe, could easily be initiated without exposing any of the major actors in international politics to sudden attack and defeat. If greater confidence grows from such efforts, international tensions may be eased in the future through more far-reaching initiatives.

A brief remark about the impact of a multinational set-up on the quality of the interaction. Most interaction of this kind occurs in international organizations or in multinational conferences. Little systematic study has been done in that field, although an increasing amount of diplomacy takes place in that setting. Several essays on the interaction process at UN headquarters have supported the assumption that it differs considerably from the traditional bilateral diplomatic situation in that the diplomats have contact with their colleagues from all other states, including those from hostile countries and those of lower or higher ranks, and that these contacts are mostly oral, more informal, and also less restricted in subject matter than in national capitals.[56] Although these findings are of a relatively formal nature and tell us little about the substantive outcome of this multinational interaction, we have reason to believe that there are small, but perceptible improvements in terms of collecting information and of bargaining flexibility in the committees and in informal discussions outside the conference rooms.

However, research on the decision-making process in the European community points to some negative consequences of multinational bargaining. A crucial characteristic of the decisions in the European community is their immutability once they are adopted after lengthy and difficult bargaining, because they have to be arrived at unanimously and because they are binding for all member states. In such a constellation, the structural complexity and the pluralism of authority hamper the decision-making capacity of the community which has turned to "package deals" to override the objections of the members to individual decisions that seem unfavorable to them and against which they exercise or threaten to exercise a veto.[57] At this point the state of our knowledge about the quality of multinational decision-making is still preliminary. The small but important benefits, as demonstrated in the case of the UN interaction structure, and the fact that a complex system like the European community has been able to move ahead in many highly important areas affecting the structure of each member state, tend to demonstrate that the multinational environment may be a positive element for the control and resolution of international conflict. It cannot replace bilateral diplomacy, but it surely complements the traditional approach and should be utilized more frequently and comprehensively. Moreover, as the European case proves, the danger that the goals and objectives of individual states suffer from compliance with binding decisions or from adoption of joint resolutions is certainly minimal, if the record of multinational and supranational policy-making is a reliable indicator.

As our survey so far has indicated, the thrust of interaction research with regard to conflict resolution is by no means unidirectional. Most of the diverse and stimulating hypotheses lack in adequate empirical verification, but they are at least closely related to the sphere of interstate conflict and interaction. A principal difficulty that has impeded academic research in the field is the scarcity of those data that would inform the analyst of conflictual interaction about the motivation, thinking, and bargaining techniques and objectives of those actively involved in diplomatic action. Even if the documents are made public after fifty years, the researcher still knows little about the processes that brought about a successful solution to a violent confrontation, a major crisis, or a tough negotiation. Considering how little we really learn about major international events, it is impressive what their detailed study has revealed. Many of our original beliefs about the pre-war crisis of 1914 had to be revised and similar changes will occur as we enter into systematic investigations of other crucial conflicts in the twentieth century. Nevertheless, the research community will never overcome completely the barriers that surround the actual making of foreign policy.[58]

NOTES

1. See Holsti, Brody, and North, "Measuring Affect and Action in International Reaction Models: Empirical Materials from the 1962 Cuban Crisis," *International Politics and Foreign Policy* ed. Rosenau, p. 684.

2. See ibid., pp. 683f.

3. This proposition stems from William A. Gramson and Andre Modigliani, *Untangling the Cold War. A Strategy for Testing Rival Theories* (Boston: Little, Brown, 1971). The analytical scheme lacks a time dimension for the action-reaction sequences and is only concerned with events, overt occurrences. The result is a dry numerical analysis.

4. Here see Martin Patchen, "Models of cooperation and conflict: A critical review," Journal of Conflict Resolution, Vol. 14, No. 3, September 1970, pp. 389-407.

5. See the excellent explanatory essay by Dean G. Pruitt, "Stability and sudden change in interpersonal and international affairs," ibid., Vol. 13, No. 1, March 1969, pp. 18-38. For an earlier background paper see his "Definition of the Situation as a Determinant of International Action," *International Behavior* ed. Kelman, pp. 393-432; here esp. pp. 420ff. Pruitt himself clearly points out that his thinking is still tentative and that several important issues require clarification. One crucial question is how to make his abstract argumentation suitable for application by the decision-maker.

6. For these important contributions to the analysis of the value dimension of conflict see Höglund and Ulrich, "Peace Research and the Concepts of Conflict–Summary and Criticism," *Conflict Control and Conflict Resolution* ed. Höglund and Ulrich, esp. pp. 18ff. and 30f.

7. See John R. Raser, "Learning and Affect in International Politics," *International Politics and Foreign Policy* ed. Rosenau, pp. 432-441; in particular p. 440.

8. In addition to what we have listed above, cf. the basic essay by Galtung, "Small Group Theory and the Theory of International Relations: A Study in Isomorphism" *New Approaches in International Relations* ed. Kaplan, pp. 270-302, where he discusses the transferability of propositions and findings from small-group research to the level of international politics. Cf. also his "A Structural Theory of Aggression," *Anger, Violence, and Politics* ed. Feierabend, Feierabend, and Gurr, pp. 85-97; esp. p. 87. Several of the hypotheses in Eric A. Nordlinger, Conflict Resolution in Divided Societies. Occasional Papers in International Affairs, No. 29 (Center for International Affairs, Harvard University, January 1972), esp. pp. 117ff., lend themselves well to interstate conflict. Of particular relevance are the hypotheses about elite behavior that are pertinent for international relations.

9. Cf. the remarks by Gould and Barkun, *International Law and the Social Sciences,* pp. 192f. For a stimulating effort to study friendship and hostility in a triadic rather than dyadic interaction pattern along conceptual lines cf. Hanna Newcombe and Gernot Koehler, "The Balance of Peace: Predicting International Friendship and Hostility from Cognitive Balance Triangles," paper prepared for the Annual Meeting of the International Studies Association in St. Louis, Mo., March 1974. A purely descriptive report on a triadic relationship is John H. Sigler, "Cooperative and conflict in United States-Soviet-Chinese relations, 1966-1971: A quantitative analysis," Peace Research Society (International), Papers, XIX, 1972, pp. 107-128. It is important that Newcombe and Koehler construe their triadic interaction pattern with the help of bilateral data beyond which they do not really advance in their analysis.

10. This finding was first reported in Zinnes, North, and Howard E. Koch, Jr., "Capability, Threat, and the Outbreak of War," *International Politics and Foreign Policy,* 1st ed., ed. Rosenau, p. 470. Cf. also North, "The Behavior of Nation States: Problems of Conflict and Integration," *New Approaches to International Relations* ed. Kaplan, pp. 346ff. The finding has been confirmed by Charles F. and Margaret G. Hermann, "An Attempt to Simulate the Outbreak of World War I," *International Politics and Foreign Policy* ed. Rosenau, pp. 622-639; p. 634.

11. See Zinnes, "The Expression and Perception of Hostility in Prewar Crisis: 1914," *Quantitative International Politics* ed. Singer, pp. 87 et passim, p. 119.

12. See North, "Axioms and Hypotheses Concerning Active and Passive Defense Systems and the Types of Response They Seem Likely to Evoke," *Weapons System Decisions* ed. Bobrow, pp. 57, 60, and 80. He concludes his list of propositions with a quote by Homans who defines the measure of successful human interchange as follows: "The open secret of human exchange is to give the other man behavior that is more valuable to him than it is costly to you and to get from him behavior that is more valuable to you than it is costly to him" (p. 81). Cf. here similar axioms in the light of their empirical validity, as discussed by Holsti, North, and Brody, "Perception and Action in the 1914 Crisis," *Quantitative International Politics* ed. Singer, pp. 152ff.

13. See for these astonishing results Rudolph J. Rummel, "The Relationship Between National Attributes and Foreign Conflict Behavior," ibid., pp. 187-214. For additional information, including a few minor U.S.-related deviations from the general results, see Rummel, "U.S. Foreign Relations: Conflict, Cooperation and Attribute Distances," *Peace, War, and Numbers,* ed. Russett, pp. 71-113. The discrepancies in the findings are due to an altered data base, different research designs, and the divergence in focus. Stephen A. Salmore and Charles F. Hermann, "The effects of size, development and accountability on foreign policy," Peace Research Society (International),

Papers, XIV, 1970, pp. 15-20, arrive at the opposite conclusion, that size, constitutional structure, and level of development do affect the foreign policy of a state, although the empirical evidence is not very strong. For the complexity of the interrelationship between domestic and international factors of conflicts and interaction, cf. Jonathan Wilkenfeld, "Domestic Conflict in the Middle East: An Analysis of International Inputs," paper prepared for the Ninth World Congress of the International Political Science Association in Montreal, August 1973.

14. See Oran R. Young, *The Politics of Force. Bargaining During International Crises,* pp. 116, 146, 244, 284, 311, 337. The author has tested these and other hypotheses in four case studies: Berlin 1948, Taiwan 1958, Berlin 1961, and Cuba 1962. All these conflicts involved the superpowers, but the hypotheses are at least for conceptual purposes of general relevance. Therefore they are reproduced here in full:

Conceptual factors:

Political fluidity: Periods of crisis tend to be politically fluid in two distinct senses: 1. Crises take place when the existing setting of international politics is significantly disturbed, and 2. Crises themselves generate pressures and prospects for important shifts and re-alignment of political forces in the international system.

The force of events: Under conditions of crisis, "force-of-events" considerations increase in prominence, a development stemming from: 1. Increases in the physical interdependence of the principal participants, and 2. Perceptions on the part of decision-makers that their ability to control the course of events is declining.

Problems of communication: As a crisis becomes more intense, "effective" communications among the protagonists concerning such matters as attitudes, expectations, intentions, and resolve will be based increasingly on physical actions in contrast to verbalized statements through diplomatic channels.

Peripheral actors: The role of peripheral actors such as international organizations, non-aligned states, and non-engaged allies or partners will generally be minimal during the upswing phase of a crisis; the influence of such actors, however, will increase once a crisis confrontation becomes full-blown in physical terms.

Tactical equations:

Resolve and prudence: Conditions of crisis raise incentives both to demonstrate resolve clearly and to react in a prudent fashion to the dangers of destructive outcomes. The resultant cross-pressures tend to produce bargaining patterns among the principals which are unpredictable and subject to erratic oscillations.

Freedom of choice: Conditions of crisis raise incentives, at any given moment, to utilize actions and diplomatic formulas designed to divide the issues at stake in ways facilitating the retention of freedom of choice in subsequent phases.

Bargaining impediments: The impact of bargaining impediments will increase with the onset of a crisis.

Political bargains: Simple or partial bargains that leave many issues to be worked out at a later time are apt to be employed in terminating crises.

Force, coercion, and violence: Conditions of crisis will generate highly influential restraints on the usability of violence for the achievement of political objectives.

The role of initiative: Under conditions of crisis, the tactical "initiative that forces the opponent to initiate" tends to become a critical coercive device.

Coercive uses of asymmetries: As alternatives to actions to structure the fundamental dimensions and specific issues of the clash in order to utilize or create advantages asymmetries are apt to become highly influential coercive procedures.

The determinants of emphasis: Conditions of crisis generate strong incentives for decision-makers to manipulate the perceptions of various parties concerning critical aspects of the clash. (Evidence does not lend clear-cut support to this hypothesis.)

For a somewhat different approach to the general structure of the interaction in conflict cf. Lincoln P. Bloomfield and Ameliá C. Leiss, *Controlling Small Wars: A Strategy for the 1970's* (New York: Knopf, 1969) esp. pp. 25ff. They list the following thirteen factors as bearing on international conflict: (1) degree of commitment; (2) autonomy of action; (3) environment; (4) information; (5) time; (6) military relationship; (7) internal cohesion; (8) internal control; (9) ethnic relationships; (10) ideology; (11) past relationships; (12) actions of international organizations; and (13) great power interests, commitments, and actions. Their main finding is that in the fourteen postwar conflicts which they examined, the number of conflict control measures of all types actually taken was roughly in inverse proportion to those that with the benefit of hindsight might have been taken in pursuit of a purposeful conflict-control strategy and the increase in such measures occurred only once the conflict had erupted openly (p. 38). It should be pointed out that Bloomfield includes factors that are tentatively ruled out by Rummel. But there are some interesting instances of concurrence between Young's and Bloomfield's analysis.

15. In the framework of this survey we cannot engage in a detailed examination of some historical cases in order to check the validity of Young's findings for other situations than those he has focused upon. It would be most worthwhile and promising in terms of additional knowledge and of possible corrections of current assumptions, if such a set of case studies could be initiated.

16. See Leon Rappoport, "Cognitive conflict as a function of socially-induced cognitive differences," Journal of Conflict Resolution, Vol. 13, No. 1, March 1969, pp. 143-148.

17. See the related proposition focusing on escalation, as reported by Michael P. Sullivan with the assistance of William Thomas, "Symbolic Involvement as a Correlate of Escalation," *Peace, War, and Numbers,* ed. Russett, pp. 185-212.

18. See Michael Brecher, Blema Steinberg, and Janice Stein, "A framework for research on foreign policy behavior," Journal of Conflict Resolution, Vol. 13, No. 1, March 1969, pp. 75-101. We should point out that the authors limit the hypothesis to middle powers; but it is probably warranted to expand it to all states, as long as we exclude rare instances of totally abnormal state behavior. Even in those few cases, it is by no means clear that the responsible decision-makers strive exclusively for the maximization of economic or military capability.

19. Cf. the crucial remarks by Lewis Coser, "The Termination of Conflict," *Social Processes in International Relations* ed. Kriesberg, pp. 43f.

20. The main essay about GRIT is Charles E. Osgood, *An Alternative to War or Surrender* (Urbana: University of Illinois Press, 1962). Cf. also his recent conference paper "GRIT for MBFR: A Proposal for Unfreezing Force-Level Postures in Europe," (1974), in which he restates his GRIT ideas and indicates ways to apply it to the process of détente in Europe.

21. For these points and their elaboration see ibid., pp. 89-132. Etzioni, who shares Osgood's view on tension-reduction, studied the case of the test ban treaty of 1963 for

evidence that some GRIT procedures has been used; he was able to show the presence of this approach in the actions of the American and Soviet governments. See Amitai Etzioni, "The Kennedy Experiment," *Social Processes in International Relations* ed. Kriesberg, pp. 415-437. Cf. also Alan Newcombe, "Initiatives and responses in foreign policy," Peace Research Reviews, Vol. 3, No. 3, June 1969, pp. 62ff.

22. Cf. here the remarks, made in a somewhat different, but related context, by Bertram H. Raven and Arie W. Kruglanski, "Conflict and Power," *The Structure of Conflict* ed. Swingle, pp. 69-109; esp. pp. 93ff.

23. The volume is *International Crises: Insights from Behavioral Research,* ed. Charles Hermann.

24. It is our great hope that as a consequence of our brief introduction to the manifold insights in this collection, the reader who lacks in the theoretical knowledge of this new academic discipline, will overcome his reluctance and acquaint himself with the book in its full extension.

25. See Charles A. McClelland, "The Beginning, Duration, and Abatement of International Crises: Comparisons in two Conflict Arenas," ibid., pp. 83-105; here pp. 97 and 101.

26. See Glenn D. Paige, "Comparative Case Analysis of Crisis Decision: Korea and Cuba," ibid., pp. 41-55, here p. 52.

27. See Charles Hermann, "Threat, Time, and Surprise: A Simulation of International Crisis," ibid., pp. 203f. Cf. here also Hermann and Brady, "Alternative Models of International Crisis Behavior," ibid., pp. 291ff.

28. See Glen H. Snyder, "Crisis Bargaining," ibid., pp. 217-256; here p. 220.

29. See ibid., pp. 222 and 247.

30. See ibid., p. 237.

31. See ibid., p. 241.

32. See ibid., p. 244.

33. See ibid., p. 241.

34. Cf. here ibid., p. 247.

35. See Thomas W. Milburn, "The Management of Crisis," ibid., pp. 259-277; here p. 264.

36. See ibid., p. 265.

37. See ibid., p. 274.

38. See ibid., p. 275.

39. See ibid., p. 274. Cf. here also William C. Mitchell, "The role of stress in the war in Vietnam: An analysis of United States actions and public statements, 1964-1967," Peace Research Society (International), Papers, XVII, 1971, pp. 47-60.

40. See Lars Dencik and Hakan Wiberg, "Strategic Thinking as a Function of Social Attitudes: An Experiment with Prisoner's Dilemma," *Conflict Control and Conflict Resolution* ed. Höglund and Ulrich, pp. 56 et passim.

41. See P. Terrence Hopmann, "Internal and External Influences on Bargaining in Arms Control Negotiations: The Partial Test Ban," *Peace, War, and Numbers* ed. Russett, pp. 213-237. Cf. here also Hopmann and Charles Walcott, "Bargaining in International Negotiations," paper prepared for the Midwest meetings of the International Studies Association and the Peace Science Society (International), in St. Louis, Mo., April 1973.

42. See G. Matthew Bonham, "Simulating international disarmament negotiations," Journal of Conflict Resolution, Vol. 15, No. 3, September 1971, pp. 299-315.

43. Cf. the recent argument by Edward Saraydar, "A certainty-equivalent model of bargaining," ibid., pp. 281-297; esp. p. 296.

44. See for these interesting results John R. Raser and Wayman J. Crow, "A Simu-

lation Study of Deterrence Theories," *Social Processes in International Relations* ed. Kriesberg, pp. 327-389.

45. For this innovative perspective see James T. Tedeschi, "Threats and Promises," *The Structure of Conflict* ed. Swingle, pp. 155-191; esp. pp. 185ff. On the question of escalation and deescalation see Thomas V. Bonoma, "Deescalating Two-Party Conflict: Accommodation and Timing as Indices of Source Intent and Mediators of Target Compliance," Institute for Juvenile Research, 1974; and his "A Social Psychological Perspective on the Escalation and Deescalation of Conflict: A Review and Reconceptualization," Institute for Juvenile Research, 1973; also Bonoma and Tedeschi, "The Relative Efficacies of Escalation and Deescalation for Compliance-Gaining in Two-Party Conflicts," 1974.

46. These experimental results are from Otomar J. Bartos, "Determinants and Consequences of Toughness," *The Structure of Conflict* ed. Swingle, pp. 45-68, esp. pp. 57ff.

47. Cf. here Daniel Druckman's review article "The influence of the situation in inter-party conflict," Journal of Conflict Resolution, Vol. 15, No. 4, December 1971, pp. 523-554; here p. 548.

48. See for these points Paul G. Swingle, "Dangerous Games," *The Structure of Conflict*, pp. 235-276; esp. pp. 244, 267ff. Swingle discusses a lot of experimental evidence, some of which is rather contradictory.

49. Cf. Druckman, "The Influence of the Situation in Inter-Party Conflict," p. 547, where he reports the results of Ellis and Wichman.

50. See the richly detailed description of the Mideast mission and the discussion of its impact in *Observations in International Negotiations.*

51. This observation does not deny the validity of Milstein's finding that the influence of America and the Soviet Union on the Arab-Israeli conflict is tenuous and restricted (see Milstein, "American and Soviet Influence, Balance of Power, and Arab-Israeli Violence," *Peace, War, and Numbers* ed. Russett, pp. 139-166). Cf. also his "Soviet and American influences on the Arab-Israeli arms race: A quantitative analysis," Peace Research Society (International), Papers, XV, 1970, pp. 6-27. We merely have to realize at what expense the disengagement agreements have been achieved and that even the direct commitment of a superpower can be disavowed. The utmost complexity of the political situation in the Middle East conflict is amply demonstrated in numerous research papers dealing with the determinants of the interaction process. Cf. here e.g., Azar, "The dimensionality of violent conflict: A quantitative analysis," ibid., pp. 122-167, also Thomas Sloan, "Dynamics of Conflict Reduction in the Middle East: An Exploratory Study," paper prepared for the Annual Meeting of the International Studies Association in St. Louis, Mo., March 1974; further, Michael Brecher, "Environmental Inputs and Decisions for War and Peace: The Israeli Experience," paper prepared for the Ninth World Congress of the International Political Science Association in Montreal, August 1973, and Frederic Pearson, "Interaction in an international political subsystem,: 'The Middle East,' 1963-64," Peace Research Society (International), Papers, XV, 1970, pp. 73-99.

52. See Roger Fisher, "Fractionating Conflict," *International Conflict and Behavioral Science* ed. Fisher, pp. 91-109; here esp. p. 103.

53. Cf. the brief discussion, including an evaluation of older studies by Schelling and Walton and McKersie (*A Behavioral Theory of Labor Negotiations,* 1965), by Gould and Barkun, *International Law and the Social Sciences,* pp. 240f.

54. See Paul Smoker, "A time series analysis of Sino-Indian relations," Journal of Conflict Resolution, Vol. 13, No. 2, June 1969, pp. 172-191. His attempt to analyse the problem in a time series, although very interesting, is of no direct concern in this study.

55. See this very interesting suggestion and the relevant data in Daniel Frei, "De-escalation–the Geographical Approach. Tension-Reduction and Confidence Building by Mutual Disengagement," paper prepared for the international conference of the International Institute for Peace in Vienna, December 15-17, 1972.

56. See here Chadwick F. Alger, "Personal Contact in International Organizations," International Behavior ed, Kelman, pp. 523-547; cf. also his "Interaction and negotiation in a committee of the United Nations General Assembly," Peace Research Society (International), Papers, 6, 1966, pp. 141-159, and his "Interaction in a Committee of the United Nations General Assembly," *Quantitative International Politics* ed. Singer, pp. 51-84.

57. See here the recent essay by Arild Underdal, "Multinational negotiation parties: The case of the European community," Cooperation and Conflict, Vol. 8, No. 3/4, 1973, pp. 173-182. This article is one example of a fast-growing body of literature about decision-making in the European Community, but it is focused on the specific question of the impact of a multinational policy-making structure on the quality of the decision outcomes.

58. Two comprehensive empirical essays demonstrate what research on interaction in international conflict has achieved so far and where the important challenges lie in trying to advance our knowledge about these vital processes. Cf. Warren R. Phillips, "The dynamics of behavioral action and reaction in international conflict," Peace Research Society (International), Papers, XVII, 1971, pp. 31-46, and Tanter and William C. Potter, "Modelling alliance behavior: East-West conflict over Berlin," ibid., XX, 1973, pp. 25-41. In selecting the material included in this chapter we have deliberately excluded decision-making studies. Two reasons for that exclusion are the enormous scope of this area of academic specialization and the relative dearth of conceptual and empirical studies that reach beyond the level of intrastate decision-making and shed light on the dynamics of conflict interaction and conflict resolution. With regard to the first reason it is assumed that the reader is familiar with the major premises and findings of decision-making research and that there is no need to refer to this kind of common knowledge in the present context.

Chapter 6

GAMES AND SIMULATIONS

Games Researchers Play: Some Recent Findings

We have referred repeatedly to games and simulations, from which many students of conflict behavior have drawn their findings and hypotheses. It is self-evident that these experiments are merely a crutch, an auxiliary device that permits the replication of typical interaction conditions, as seen and selected by the researcher, in controlled laboratory settings, and usually employs easily available participants from the student body or from other social groups. In rare cases diplomats and foreign policy officers serve as participants, but even in such semi-ideal conditions the experimental behavior and interaction is still remote from reality. In the following, we briefly report some recent results from such games. Once that is done, we will try to discuss the merits of this research approach.

The principal question underlying all experimental games is how to secure cooperation among the players who are engaged in a situation where the pursuit of the own maximal advantage is juxtaposed to the uncertain benefit from mutual cooperation without a prior indication of the general attitude of either player. The ability of the researcher to manipulate the given situation to strengthen or weaken the foundation of cooperative behavior, and to repeat the same experiment many times with different players, provides for fascinating research designs and often intriguing results.

Due to the variability of the purposes and outcomes of the games it is hard to systematize the research results. Most of the games use realistic conflict situations in which the stakes are not expressed in abstract numbers and the players pursue more than one objective. It is of interest in this context to learn that in realistic situations the participants achieve a much higher level of cooperation than in a pure numbers' game.[1] But if the game implies too many possible strategies, the comparative utility and feasibility of which the players have to weigh, the degree of stable cooperation declines, since the participants are concerned that the payoffs in the complex situation will be divided unequally.[2] Since most international conflicts correspond to the complex multiple-strategy game, it is certainly not astonishing that cooperative behavior is not all too frequent in international politics, even though foreign policy officials are tuned to these conditions.

Questions of personality and pairing have aroused considerable attention in experimental gaming. What kind of individual attitude tends toward cooperation or competition? In one experiment the players were randomly put into one of three conditions: one third played a regular game with their partners; one third played against highly cooperative but random strategies, and the last third were subjected to a delayed matching strategy in which they received the choices that they had made on the previous move. Out of these three groups those in the last one developed the most favorable image of their "partners" and saw in them the same personality traits they attributed to themselves.[3] This is a nice illustration for the impact of cognitive and behavioral similarity on perception and action in conflict interaction. Another experiment tested the willingness to take risks among cooperative and competitive friends. The friends who played cooperatively were far more willing to make risky decisions.[4] What this stipulates, at least indirectly, is the expansion of the range of choices in conditions of mutual friendship. The emphasis on mutual sympathy is also underscored in a recent finding that coalitions in games are formed primarily according to the degree of compatibility between the potential coalition partners, and far less so for reasons of an expected dominant position or of equality.[5] If the coalition partner is not engaged in the game, he still commands the loyalty of the player; in a game situation in which the outside partner had indicated his idea of a "fair" agreement benefitting mostly the own side, the player offered a smaller concession to the opponent who made a cooperative move than when he felt not accountable to the suggestions of the partner.[6] Can one translate this tentative insight into the relevance of friendship and coalition directly into the realm of state interaction? At the least, we should take them as signs that the conventional diplomatic "realism" needs to be reexamined and revised, if that is feasible and desirable.

The same suggestion flows from the numerous studies about the effect of threats and concessions, including pacifist policies, on the strengthening of cooperative behavior by the other player. Morton Deutsch and his associates have developed a trucking game in which both sides dispose of a threat capacity through which they can try to coax the other side into concessions or to deter him from direct confrontation. Their results indicate that the ability to issue threats and its employment usually increases hostility and conflict.[7] But other students have found that if both sides possess the ability to punish, e.g., in one experiment the availability of an electrical shock rather than the denial of the opponent's possible gain, this warning signal produced a clearly increased cooperative attitude on both sides.[8] In conjunction with this experimental result we should refer to another game in which the threat was used more often when both sides wielded it than when only one side possessed it.[9] There appears to prevail a modicum of fairness and empathy in threatening conflicts, in that the party that enjoys a clear-cut advantage is reluctant to exploit it ruthlessly. This does not mean that if one player pursues a pure pacifist strategy, i.e., issues cooperative moves regardless of whether the other player acts in the same spirit or in hostile competition, mutual cooperation will follow; most experiments show to the contrary that pacifism encourages ruthless exploitation by the opponent.[10] Only if the pacifist enjoys large-scale outside support and if the other side cannot expect a considerably higher payoff through a course of exploitative non-cooperation, there may be a chance that total cooperation unilaterally might succeed.[11] In general, the belief that threats contribute to the final realization of a cooperative solution must be abandoned, although their availability might help maintain a condition free of overt conflict and prevent its deterioration into overt and mutually damaging confrontation. The failure of pacifism, even when its moral dimension is fully known to the opponent, serves as a shocking reminder that the states have to be prepared in some fashion, whether it is armaments or programs of civilian defense, against the ill intentions of the other actors in the interaction system.[12]

As our remark indicates, the need for constant caution—or suspicion—is obvious. It is fascinating that two researchers have argued that caution acts like an amplifier: if the trend is toward tolerant, non-retaliative behavior, it enhances the growth of mutual trust and cooperation; if retaliation and intolerance prevail, it pushes both sides further into unremitting struggle.[13]

What then is the best strategy to entice the co-players into cooperative behavior? The crucial factor is the social-psychological relationship of the participants, i.e., their initial attitudes toward each other and their experience as the game progresses.[14] Results indicate that players usually trust partners from their own group noticeably more than members of other groups. They rate a cooperative partner much more favorably on his motives and on his personality traits than a competitive opponent and react much more strongly to his signals. If they themselves pursue a non-cooperative strategy, they view the partner negatively and tend to blame him for the conflict course. The best strategy to achieve mutual cooperation is a tit-for-tat strategy which results in an increase of cooperative moves on both sides. Previous competitive plays strengthen the cooperative interaction in subsequent games.[15] In addition, previous contact, even if it is only visual, influences the attitude of the players positively, at least in the first round of the game.[16] The discrepancy in game behavior between players who play for the first time and those who have had previous game experience is indeed startling: the latter group overwhelmingly pursued a strategy of mutual cooperation, whereas in the former group half the games ended in the elimination of the rival.[17] This is as strong a proof for the learning process in interaction behavior as any we are likely to get in an experiment. It should strengthen our hope that internationally a similar development, though slow and hardly perceptible, is currently going on. Such a permanent change through learning would constitute a strong move towards wider and more effective cooperation.

A last note on the place of mediation, as it emerges from some experimental games: the clearest proof of the importance of mediation results from a game in which the identical offer for a compromise settlement was submitted by the spokesman for the one party (here the management) and by the "impartial" mediator; the first version was rejected as unacceptable, while the mediated version was accepted.[18] Unfortunately, little additional information of such direct relevance has been reported elsewhere. But this particular result could give new impetus to the study of the circumstances and requirements under which mediation can open the path to a mutually satisfactory agreement that would portend more cooperative behavior in the future.

Our selection is representative of the state of the art in gaming. Most of the experiments do not allow for communication during the actual game except for the moves that signal to the partner the cooperative or competitive intent. This practice is consistent with the theoretical premises of the most frequently played games, Prisoner's Dilemma and, to a lesser extent, Chicken games. A recent critic has warned that these game conditions actually remove the research efforts from the sphere of relevance, because social and political conflict, as a rule, occurs under conditions of full-fledged communication. Beyond the purely pragmatic adjustment to the empirical givens of human conflictual interaction, the author argues that we should focus on the social mechanisms that groups of interacting individuals develop to resolve their disputes over conflicting interests. His assumption, for which he cites evidence, is that social sanctions for non-cooperation will become more intense as the conflict continues. The actor who resists the social pressure for its peaceful termination and settlement will increasingly encounter moral sanctions sustained by the solidarity of the group.[19] The proposition that such social forces are involved in conflicts between individuals and groups and that their persuasion can and does only function through directly related communication is hard to deny. The really intricate problem is how far these pressures affect large social groups and, even more critically, states and societies in their external relations. To hold that no such factors are present is too simple and disregards remarkable indicators of some cohesion in the political and social ethic of the "world community." What counts is the relative strength of the moral factor compared with the thrust and bitterness of interstate hostility and conflict. To learn more about this elusive phenomenon, we need expanded research in the direction suggested in that article and intensive examination of the "world community" as a peace-enhancing force in historical and contemporary conflict situations.

A Note on Gaming

How meaningful and relevant are the results of the experimental research that we have reported? This question is a central issue that has been debated vigorously and inconclusively since gaming and similar research techniques were introduced. As we have explained in the introduction to this study, it is not our intention to try to contribute to the debate because many of the specific questions are of purely methodological and heuristic significance, which to explain would be difficult in the context of our effort. What we propose to do in the following is to describe the most important categories of gaming and simulation and to reflect as concisely as possible on the uses of these experiments in the search for better methods of international conflict control and resolution. We therefore consider only a few contributions by main spokesmen in the academic debate without judging the quality of underlying conceptual and methodological principles. For our purpose, the main criterion of evaluation is the question of whether the tests are operational, i.e., whether they are designed in such a way that the results are not only consistent in terms of the research design, but that they also provide an answer to the concrete issue that is the reason for the experiment.[20]

In view of this criterion, what are the principal uses of experimental gaming for the practice of conflict resolution? In general terms, such questions as the communications process, the effect of personality on the decision process, negotiating behavior, the choice of objectives and strategies, etc., may be elucidated.[21] Anatol Rapoport, who has written extensively on the merits of game theory and gaming, warns against exaggerated expectations, and pleads for the simple case study approach to experimentation, since it allows a rich and diverse input without being too concerned with the general applicability of the questions asked and answers received. He even goes so far as to stipulate that laboratory experiments can demonstrate the "enormous complexity of the dynamics of conflict" by showing that any hypothesis can be verified or falsified by an appropriate experiment.[22] This is due to the wide gap between laboratory and real life conditions, which even the best research design cannot overcome. One significant instance of this incomparability is the structure of payoffs; even such an experienced spokesman for experimental games as Morton Deutsch has acknowledged that this is an open problem which has not yet been adequately dealt with.[23] Some academic specialists take a dim view of the value of gaming and explain their critical attitude by referring to the ease with which gaming has been applied for war planning and war games.[24] We do not have to subscribe to this argument, but there is no denying the fact that the military profession has adopted the technique, not to seek better ways of avoiding conflict and of making peace, but to improve its skills in warfare.

GAME THEORY: "CHICKEN" AND "PRISONER'S DILEMMA"

Before we enter into a detailed evaluation of some of these judgments, we should finally separate small games that derive from game theory, and large games including simulations that are meant to test interaction systems rather than narrowly circumscribed hypotheses about choice in bilateral competition. Game theory proper is a theory of rational behavior, in which all sides are assumed to behave rationally, i.e., to choose actual policies according to a set of well-defined and mutually consistent basic objectives.[25] From this basic premise it is clear that game theory is a formal or prescriptive, but not a descriptive, theory of conflict, as the assumption of fully rational behavior is not at all in conformity with the social and political reality.[26]

Game theory classifies games into three groups: games with identical interests, with opposite interests, and with mixed interests. The basic experiment uses two persons who play in one of the three configurations against each other. Leaving out the first group as it is unrelated to international conflict, we have two basic game situations: if the interests of the two players are opposed, we speak of a two-person zero-sum game; if the interests are mixed, some identical and some opposite, we call the game a non-zero-sum or mixed-motive (or mixed-interest) game. The first type is unusual in international life, but the second type appropriately reflects fundamental international conflict patterns. Within non-zero-sum games we can distinguish two basic forms, the so-called Chicken game and the Prisoner's Dilemma game (see Figure 6.1). There are two players in each case, with two strategies: 1 stands for cooperation, 2 for non-cooperation or competition. The payoffs in the four matrix cells (left of the comma for player A, right of the comma for B) are arbitrary; they exhaust the possible strategy combinations. The

Prisoner's Dilemma

		B 1	B 2
A	1	5, 5	−10, 10
A	2	10, 10	−5, −5

Chicken

		B 1	B 2
B	1	0, 0	−10, 10
B	2	10, −10	−20, −20

Figure 6.1.

premise is that both players act completely rationally and that both seek the maximum payoff. Usually it is also assumed that they cannot communicate with each other and that they act simultaneously.

As the two matrices show, the decisive difference between the two games lies in the rewards for mutual cooperation (both play 1) and in the penalties for mutual non-cooperation (both play 2). In the Prisoner's Dilemma game mutual cooperation is rewarded, although unilateral non-cooperation promises a higher payoff, if the other side cooperates. The penalty for mutual non-cooperation is less severe than the penalty for unilateral cooperation, if the other plays the non-cooperative offensive strategy. Thus both sides have two incentives not to play cooperatively: the offensive one to gamble for the highest payoff, and the defensive one of keeping the losses as low as possible. The uncertainty about the choice by the other partner makes it more of less mandatory to opt for non-cooperation. The consequence is that if the goal is indeed the maximization of profit or value, the rationality inherent in the game situation favors the mutual choice of non-cooperation resulting in a mutual loss of –5.

In the Chicken game, the payoff for cooperation is simply the avoidance of losses, while the penalties for mutual non-cooperation constitute the biggest loss. Therefore, surrender before the non-cooperating partner is still less costly than the counter-strategy of non-cooperation. Here rationality favors the adoption of the cooperative strategy to avoid disaster for both, whereas the cooperative solution in the Prisoner's Dilemma game is least likely to materialize.[27] The Cuban Missile Crisis of 1962 is a close approximation of the Chicken game. History abounds with situations à la Prisoner's Dilemma, since most conflicts do not present an acute threat of mutual annihilation or other irreparable damage that would deter from non-cooperative policies.

It is possible to expand the game structure to encompass three or more players and more than two strategies, but as an easy mathematical calculation will tell, the increase in complexity is such that it requires automatic data-processing or a large auxiliary staff to conduct the experiment and to evaluate its outcome. The addition of one more player to the simple 2 x 2 game is already helpful, because it enables the researcher to take an experimental approach to the concrete question of how coalitions and alignments are formed and reversed in the course of the interaction sequence.[28]

Most of the games reported in academic literature are variations of the basic models we have described. As a rule, students participate in the series of experiments, in which some nominal rewards and penalties are fixed to increase the incentive for the players to enact the scenario as faithfully as possible. Still the simplicity of the modelled situation and–in most cases–its remoteness from the reality of international conflict make it impossible to produce findings that are directly relevant to the day-to-day duties of the foreign policy-maker. What the games can achieve, aside from the empirical validation of theoretical analysis, an indispensible element in the scientific process, is to force the researcher, his players, and his audience to think about interstate tensions and crises in a novel manner by conceptualizing the issues in a fashion suitable for the approach that is expressed in the matrix, i.e., by defining them in terms of basic strategies and outcomes and of their rank according to overall policy and specific payoff. In trying to determine these figures, the analyst will recognize symmetries and asymmetries in the bilateral or trilateral relationship and change his test matrix accordingly.

Another even more important insight from games is the recognition that the standard of rationality is ambiguous and does not serve as a guide to the best solution. Is it rational to seek the one-sided maximum payoff if it causes severe losses to the other player? What are the payoffs? Are they not often incompatible even for the one side? The relevance of these questions is easy to see in a concrete international situation in which the actors pursue multiple values and strategies; we could conceive of these as variously overlapping payoff matrices. The task of the researcher is considerably easier because he can simply hold constant all the values and options except for the one which is tested in the experiment. The decision-maker cannot do so, but in planning and evaluating the policies of his government he can embrace some of the basic conceptions of the researcher to get a simplified view of the various components of the specific case within the framework of the total foreign policy.

Rationality is only a secondary standard, as its thrust derives from primary values and goals. Game theory and experimental games help the foreign policy-maker to accept that insight. Beyond that, they allow a systematic reiterated check on certain hypotheses and axioms about the impact of the conflict situation on the interacting and negotiating behavior. In the

Prisoner's Dilemma game, for instance, the researcher can arbitrarily change the payoff structure, in particular the differential between reward and penalty and the balance or imbalance between the participants, to determine how far the actors are willing to go in risking a mutually detrimental outcome in order to achieve the largest payoff for their own side. Here game designs can manipulate the interaction conditions widely and to great effect. If the academic specialist is willing to sacrifice some measure of conceptual validity, he can indeed offer substantial findings and suggestions to the policy-maker.[29] This is particularly true for the search for improved cooperative solutions, as the summary of recent experimental games has shown.

We could elaborate at great length about the theoretical aspects of game theory and small games and about the various special ways in which these experiments could be diversified to bring maximum return to the policy-makers. But such a detailed review and analysis is beyond the scope of this survey. May it suffice to conclude that small experimental games, primarily of the Prisoner's Dilemma type, have offered considerable results that are of great use in the understanding and promotion of better methods of conflict resolution and that hold even greater promise for the future, if governments are willing to support continued conflict-focused research and experiments of this kind without expecting overly quick or immediately policy-relevant prescription-like findings.

SIMULATIONS AND LARGE GAMES

Large games, including simulations, are of a different order. The experts face larger and more difficult problems, and the uses of games and simulations are distinct from those of experimental small games. Therefore, it is necessary to consider the meaning of the term "simulation," a frequently misunderstood technique, to describe its application and to evalaute its usefulness.

If we take "simulation" in its broad interpretation, we can distinguish three basic types: all-man simulation, man-computer simulation, and all-computer simulation. The first is often called a large game. Especially in this case, the goal of the exercise may be diffuse: some games merely serve the purpose of educating the participants in their recognition of the quantity and quality of policy alternatives; others assign representative roles to the players with the intent of replicating actual policy behavior; a more demanding type is to test hypotheses about characteristics of the international system and of interstate interaction which the researcher has formulated from theoretical or case studies. The strictly scientific purpose is more predominant in man-computer and all-computer simulations, although this does not mean that they are useless for the foreign policy-maker. As Harold Guetzkow, the leading American simulation expert, has explained, the crucial difference between simulations is how far the operations are explicitly programmed; in the all-man simulation, very little is pre-programmed and much leeway is given to the initiative and intuition of the players, whereas in the all-computer simulation everything is programmed. The intention of the researcher either to validate his underlying theory or to make the results of the exercise applicable for the practitioner is decisive for the specific shape and direction of the simulation. If he has the former in mind, he has to provide for explicit formal controls and reliable data collection; if he tries to achieve the latter, he can rely on informal supervision and random reporting.

While war games, decision-making exercises, and all-man conflict simulations have become quasi-routine with many government agencies and economic organizations, the recent research interest has increasingly focused on the conceptual, methodological and empirical aspects of man-computer and all-computer simulations that constitute a theoretical construction of the system of international relations in its global or regional dimension.[30] The concentration upon these large-scale models has been made possible by the widespread availability of computer facilities whereby more data and far larger simulation environments can be handled easily without a big staff. Guetzkow's original construction, the Inter-Nation Simulation (INS), started out as an all-man simulation, was used in numerous college and university courses as an educational tool, but as the dimensions were enlarged and as relatively inexpensive computers came into the reach of university researchers, computerized information and control processes were introduced and pure computer models were developed. It should not come as a surprise that the heuristic and methodological issues are still most urgent for those who have abstracted and programmed their exercises in that direction, due to the immensity and complexity of the simulated universe and to the resulting uncertainty about the validity of the conceptual and quantitative assumptions.[31]

For the policy-maker, those simulations merit most attention that maintain a close and precise focus on actual decision-making problems or on factors impinging directly on his decisional capacity. One prominent category here is the series of simulations that have been conducted about the events of 1914, from which quite a few findings about perception and interaction originate.[32] Many other similar cases and problem areas can be the subject of a simulation, but they all have to offer a rich data base to justify the preparation and execution of multiple program runs, especially because they may be too idiosyncratic for deriving basic system-wide findings from them.[33] A recent report about an all-man simulation of disarmament negotiations proves, however, that policy-relevant and theory-relevant assumptions can be examined within a simple and inexpensive experimental framework.[34]

Such endeavors that are intimately related to policy issues and meet average standards of scientific validity would go far to meet the manifold criticism from practitioners, fellow teachers, and researchers that the larger simulations fail to give enough attention to the hard problems, e.g., lengthy and arduous bargaining between tough negotiators, or the tensions and conflicts in domestic bureaucratic politics that often impede rather than facilitate the setting of policies.[35]

From all available indications we must conclude that the uses of simulation are still limited and tentative. Nevertheless, great progress has been made, especially in more complex models,[36] and it seems likely that further advances of significance will occur if the research community finds adequate funds to carry on the background research and to broaden the range of theoretically sound and politically relevant exercises. Only if the governments and other financial backing lend their support to this growing field of academic expertise without forcing the scholars to hew too closely to the official line of policy and to return easy and speedy answers to a multitude of questions, ranging from a future world peace order to the effect of personal beliefs and attitudes on the policy choices, can it be anticipated that simulation research will bear rich fruit that would be available to both practitioner and scholar.

Many additional comments and suggestions could be made, but since we have reported and evaluated simulation findings throughout this study, we hold that such continued discussion would not serve the main objective of our survey effort appreciably. If as a result of this essay policy-makers feel more inclined to investigate the question further along the lines of their own needs and priorities, our goal will have been fully met.

The review of some theories and findings of perception and interaction has shown that although many research efforts and approaches are exploratory and tentative and that some of the outcomes are "merely" a confirmation of traditional historical and intuitive knowledge, a second, closer look reveals the amount of innovative thinking and novel methodology that has gone into these endeavors and the significance of the minor and major changes that have resulted from the research for the foundations and directions of the science of international relations. The focus on these difficult aspects of the behavior of individual and collective actors is of particular importance for the students of peace and conflict, since it enables them to develop systematic comparative models and to conduct their specific research projects accordingly. Aside from this internal element of scientific conceptual and methodological advances, the literature contains a strong component of policy-relevant suggestions, hypotheses, and findings. Our selection is just a small fraction of what has been written and discussed in recent years. But it gives a comprehensive view of the universe of interstate conflict and of instruments of its control and resolution. It must be said that researchers have sometimes neglected practical issues and have focused too much on large systems and models. But that may be due to the fact that specific suggestions for better or different policies and procedures in their judgment can only be drawn from sound theories. As the history of the theory of international relations proves, the quest for comprehensive conceptions is far from ended. This is illustrated for instance by the lack of a broad theory of the measurement of interrelationships between interaction systems comprising more than two actors. Peace researchers and international relations specialists are just beginning to grapple with this intricate problem.

If the policy-maker expresses genuine interest and concern, but does not demand easy answers or conformist propositions, and if he makes accessible the "secrets" of the inner working of the men and agencies shaping foreign policies, he can be confident that the study of perception and interaction as it relates to conflict management and conflict resolution will continue to grow remarkably, and will turn much more directly to the hard issues that confront the foreign policy officials throughout the world and threaten to upset the fragile peace that we better call "non-war."

NOTES

1. For this interesting result see Carol J. and Jack E. Orwant, "A comparison of interpreted and abstract mixed-motive games," Journal of Conflict Resolution, Vol. 14, No. 1, March 1970, pp. 91-97.

2. See here F. T. Dolbear, L. B. Lave, G. Bowman, A. Lieberman, E. Prescott, F. Rueter, and R. Sherman, "Collusion in the Prisoner's Dilemma: Number of strategies," ibid., Vol. 13, No. 2, June 1969, pp. 252-261.

3. See Philip S. Gallo, "Personality impression formation in a Maximizing Difference game," ibid., Vol. 13, No. 1, March 1969, pp. 118-122.

4. See Michael Lupfer, Mark Jones, Lionel Spaulding, and Richard Archer, "Risk-taking in cooperative and competitive dyads," ibid., Vol. 15, No. 3, September 1971, pp. 385-392.

5. See Lawrence H. Nitz and James L. Philips, "The effects of divisibility of payoff on confederative behavior," ibid., Vol. 13, No. 3, September 1969, pp. 381-387.

6. See Charles L. Gruder, "Relationships with opponent and partner in mixed-motive bargaining," ibid., Vol. 15, No. 3, September 1971, pp. 403-416.

7. From Morton Deutsch's numerous writings see his recent *Resolution of Conflict. Constructive and Destructive Processes* (New Haven: Yale University Press, 1973), which contains lectures on the theoretical aspects of conflict resolution and several revised papers from earlier years. For the results of the trucking games see in particular pp. 215ff. See also William P. Smith and Timothy D. Emmons, "Outcome information and competitiveness in interpersonal bargaining," Journal of Conflict Resolution, Vol. 13, No. 2, June 1969, pp. 262-270, where the authors used a slightly changed trucking game and also noticed higher conflict and non-cooperation as a result of the use of threats. They recommend, however, to reexamine the use of the gates as signals for cooperation.

8. See Bruce John Morrison, Michael Enzle, Kenneth Kneisel, and John Gimperling, "The effect of electrical shock and warning on cooperation in a non-zero-sum game," ibid., Vol. 15, No. 1, March 1971, pp. 105-108.

9. See James T. Tedeschi, Thomas Bonoma, and Noel Novinson, "Behavior of a threatener: Retaliation vs. fixed opportunity costs," ibid., Vol. 14, No. 1, March 1970, pp. 69-76.

10. See here Richard Ofshe, "The effectiveness of pacifist strategy: A theoretical approach," ibid., Vol. 15, No. 2, June 1971, pp. 261-269. Also Jack E. Vincent and Edward W. Schwerin, "Ratios of force and escalation in a game situation," ibid., Vol. 15, No. 4, December 1971, pp. 489-511. Cf. also P. G. Swingle, "Dangerous Games," *The Structure of Conflict* ed. Swingle, p. 251.

11. Cf. the cautious remarks about the possible use of a strategy of pacifism by Robert J. Meeker and Gerald H. Shure, "Pacifist bargaining tactics: Some 'outsider' influence," Journal of Conflict Resolution, Vol. 13, No. 4, December 1969, pp. 487-493.

12. Cf. on the issue of threat effects also Roderick Ogley and David Thomas, "New hypotheses in game experiments," Peace Science Society (International), Papers, XXII, 1974, pp. 75-110; also Ogley, "Investigating the effects of threats," ibid., XVI, 1971, pp. 61-93, and Gerald H. Shure and Robert J. Meeker, "Bargaining processes in experimental territorial conflict situations," ibid., XI, 1969, pp. 109-122.

13. See Edwin Bixenstine and Jacquelyn W. Gaebelein, "Strategies of 'real' opponents in eliciting cooperative choice in a Prisoner's game," Journal of Conflict Resolution, Vol. 15, No. 3, June 1971, pp. 157-166. In conclusion, they offer four rules of thumb to achieve more cooperation from the partner: (1) if you can tolerate another's defections, do so, but tax with caution his overtures of cooperation; (2) if you cannot tolerate another's defections and must retaliate, at least avoid caution in responding to his cooperative overtures; (3) if you cannot avoid suspicion of another's cooperative overtures, above all do not immediately retaliate when he defects; (4) if you can neither tolerate defection nor avoid exercising suspicion of cooperative overtures, at least eschew defecting from mutual cooperation (i.e., avoid trapping) (p. 165).

14. For these points cf. Donnel Wallace and Paul Rothaus, "Communication, group, loyalty, and trust in the PD game," ibid., Vol. 13, No. 3, September 1969, pp. 370-380.

15. These interesting findings are reported in Warner Wilson, "Cooperation and the cooperativeness of the other player," Journal of Conflict Resolution, Vol. 13, No. 1, March 1969, pp. 110-117; and his "Reciprocation and other techniques for inducing cooperation in the Prisoner's Dilemma game," ibid., Vol. 15, No. 2, June 1971, pp. 167-195.

16. See Ronald L. Michelini, "Effects of prior interaction, contact, strategy, and expectation of meeting on game behavior and sentiment," ibid., Vol. 15, No. 1, March 1971, pp. 97-103.

17. See David W. Conrath, "Experience as a factor in experimental gaming behavior," ibid., Vol. 14, No. 2, June 1970, pp. 195-202.

18. See the excellent article by Jerome E. Podell and William M. Knapp, "The effect of mediation on the perceived firmness of the opponent," ibid., Vol. 13, No. 4, December 1969, pp. 511-520.

19. See Phillip Bonavich, "Putting the dilemma back into the Prisoner's Dilemma," ibid., Vol. 14, No. 3, September 1970, pp. 379-387.

20. Martin Shubik and Garry D. Brewer, Reviews of Selected Books and Articles on Gaming and Simulation, a report prepared for the Advanced Research Projects Agency (R-732-ARPA) (Santa Monica, Calif.: RAND Corp., 1972), strongly emphasize the criterion of operationality as the measurement for the evaluation of the experimental results.

21. Cf. Gould and Barkun, *International Law and the Social Sciences,* p. 35, for some of these items and relevant critical remarks.

22. See Rapoport, "Games which simulate deterrence and disarmament," Peace Research Reviews, Vol. 1, No. 4, August 1967, pp. 67- and 76.

23. See Morton Deutsch, *The Resolution of Conflict,* pp. 208ff., where he discusses some research results by other gaming experts that fail to support the customary setting of incentives in games. His own experiments have not weakened the assumptions underlying the payoff structure of his trucking game.

24. One such judgment is voiced by Irving Louis Horowitz, "Deterrence Games: From Academic Codebook to Military Codebook," *The Structure of Conflict* ed. Swingle, pp. 277-296; esp. p. 294.

25. For basic information about game theory cf. John C. Harsanyi, "Game Theory and the Analysis of International Conflict," *International Politics and Foreign Policy* ed. Rosenau, pp. 370-379. A classic in the field is Rapoport, *Fights, Games, and Debates* (Ann Arbor: University of Michigan Press, 1960). For a brief account of game theory in international relations cf. his "International Relations and Game Theory," *Disarmament and Arms Control,* ed. Barnaby and Schaerf, pp. 241-252. Cf. also Morton Kaplan, "A Note on Game Theory and Bargaining," *New Approaches to International Relations* ed. Kaplan, pp. 483-518 for a very informative description of major tenets of game theory.

26. See here, e.g., Rapoport, "Directions in Peace Research," *Conflict Control and Conflict Resolution* ed. Höglund and Ulrich, pp. 233f.

27. Cf. here the discussion in Harsayni, "Game Theory and the Analysis of International Conflict," op. cit., and Shubik, "Game theory, behavior, and the paradox of the Prisoner's Dilemma: Three solutions," Journal of Conflict Resolution, Vol. 14, No. 2, June 1970, pp. 181-193. See in particular the fine article by Glenn H. Snyder, "Prisoner's Dilemma and 'Chicken' models in international politics," International Studies Quarterly, Vol. 15, No. 1, March 1971, pp. 66-103; esp. pp. 84ff. This last essay is most useful for the direct linkage of game theory and the history of major international conflicts.

28. One example for the use of game theory in the study of coalition behavior is S. Groenningen, E. M. Kelley, and Michael Leiserson (eds.), *The Study of Coalition Behavior: Theoretical Perspectives and Cases from Four Continents* (New York: Holt, Rinehart, and Winston, 1970). Cf. a review about this collection by Shubik and Brewer, *Reviews of Selected Books and Articles on Gaming and Simulation,* pp. 15f.

29. For these evaluating remarks cf. Rapoport, "Conflict Resolution in the Light of Gaming Theory," *The Structure of Conflict* ed. Swingle, pp. 1-43; esp. p. 41 et passim. Cf. also Tanter, "The policy relevance of models in world politics," Journal of Conflict Resolution, Vol. 16, No. 4, December 1972, pp. 568f. Shubik, Brewer, and E. Savage, *The Literature of Gaming, Simulation, and Model-building: Index and Critical Abstracts.* A report prepared for Advanced Research Projects Agency (Santa Monica, Calif.: RAND Corp., 1972) (R-620-ARPA) has compiled a useful set of reviews that indicate in a representative fashion the merits and weaknesses of major American contributions to gaming. As our notes show, the best source for current games that have some relationship to international politics is the Journal of Conflict Resolution, although it does not address itself to the non-specialist audience outside universities and research institutions.

30. For basic information about the theory of simulation and about its practical and empirical problems see Harold Guetzkow, "Some Correspondences Between Simulations and 'Realities' in International Relations," *New Approaches to International Relations* ed. Kaplan, pp. 202-269. See also his remarks in *Observations on International Negoti-*

ations, op. cit., pp. 92ff., esp. pp. 94f. Cf. also Shubik's and Brewer's reviews of some of Guetzkow's work in *Reviews of Selected Books and Articles on Gaming and Simulation,* pp. 16ff. Cf. also their useful comments on other large games and simulations in *The Literature of Gaming, Simulation, and Model-Building,* op. cit.

31. A leading representative of the large computer-modelling approach is Paul Smoker who himself has contributed two abstract constructions, the World Politics Simulation (WPS) and the International Processes Simulation (IPS). See for these and for general aspects of simulation his excellent "International relations simulation," Peace Research Reviews, Vol. 3, No. 6, 1970. See here also the critical review by Alker and Ronald D. Brunner, "Simulating international conflict: A comparison of three approaches," International Studies Quarterly, Vol. 13, No. 1, March 1969, pp. 70-110. For a typical scholarly essay on the theory of simulation cf. Richard W. Chadwick, "An inductive, empirical analysis of intra- and international behavior, aimed at a partial extension of inter-nation simulation theory," Journal of Peace Research, 1969, No. 3, pp. 193-214. These academic studies show clearly what has been achieved and where knowledge is still lagging; quite a few of the basic tenets of simulation turn out to be unsupported in trial runs; others are deficient in conceptual rigor or in propositional coherence.

32. Charles and Margaret Hermann are the principal authors of 1914 simulations. See their informative "An Attempt to Simulate the Outbreak of World War I," *International Politics and Foreign Policy* ed. Rosenau, pp. 622-639. They also emphasize the tenuous quality of the simulation results.

33. For some feasible policy areas see Smoker, "International Relations Simulations," op. cit., pp. 4f.

34. See Bonham, "Simulating international disarmament negotiations," Journal of Conflict Resolution, Vol. 15, No. 3, September 1971, pp. 299-315. This is one of the finest instances of an interesting and manageable simulation which could easily be replicated by research and educational institutions.

35. One of many such complaints is voiced by Gould and Barkun, *International Law and the Social Sciences,* pp. 37f.

36. Reference should be made here to the recurrent publication of articles about simulations that focus on major foreign policy issues in the Papers of the Peace Science Society (International) (former Peace Research Society), e.g., on Vietnam and the Middle East: Cf. here Milstein and William C. Mitchell, "Dynamics of the Vietnam conflict: A quantitative analysis and predictive computer simulation," ibid., X, 1968, pp. 163-213; also Milstein and Mitchell, "Computer simulation of international processes: The Vietnam war and the pre-World War I naval race," ibid., XII, 1969, pp. 117-136; and Jong Ryool Lee and Milstein, "A political economy of the Vietnam war, 1965-1972," ibid., XXI, 1973, pp. 41-63. On the problem of forecasting which is greatly significant in computer simulations, cf. the excellent paper by Nazli Choucri, "Applications of economic analysis to forecasting in international relations," ibid., XXI, 1973, pp. 15-39.

CONCLUSION

The issues and aspects of peace research that we have discussed, although they are only a small piece of the ongoing academic work, reflect roughly the dominant trends of peace and conflict analysis. Major problems that have divided the camp of the peace researchers and that are equally felt in the peace movement throughout the world and the North American and West European regions in particular, have to do with the ideas and future objectives underlying research and practical work. We have briefly alluded to these dimensions, and after having traversed some parts of the universe of peace and conflict research, we can pick up these threads of argument once again and take a broader look at the present and future foci of academic research as well as the implications of the theoretical results for the policies of governments and the involvement of the social groups who try to contribute to the creation of a more peaceful and just world order.

Peace Through Change

We address ourselves in principal terms to the quest for peace through change, an issue that reaches beyond the more customary recommendations that researchers derive from their inquiries for the policy-maker, and beyond the obligatory suggestions for specific future research. It is obvious that the following concluding remarks cannot do more than touch upon a few crucial points that could and should guide the researcher, the policy-maker, and the peace activist in the years to come.[1]

The general normative foundation of peace research is, as we have already mentioned, not beyond dispute. While the traditionalist and the "realist" emphasize the short-range objective of maintaining or restoring a condition of non-war, the critical and radical students of peace and conflict hold that this focus is far too limited because it does not expose the deeper causes of social and political violence and therefore contributes, at least indirectly, to the continuation of war and hostility. They argue that the mission of peace researchers reaches beyond advice to the policy-makers and must be free of the shackles of overt public constraint. Depending on their general political attitude, a few of them advocate that the committed student of peace defined as social justice join the struggle against those forces that they hold responsible for the severe shortcomings of the international order.[2] Others remain in a more academic vein and propose that the scientific task includes as a major responsibility the detailed study of ways and means of social and political change that would lead to a new system of peace.[3] The idea of peace through change also permeates the work of many researchers who are strongly opposed to the use of violence in pursuit of that goal.[4]

Even the staunchest defender of the notion of peace as non-war will not dissent from those who pronounce the conception of "peaceful change," since he insists on a stringent definition of the word "peaceful." If we were to accept that narrow definition, domestic social and political reforms and basic changes in the international political and economic structure would never come about. This static approach to the realization of the highest ambition of man, to make wars impossible, is nothing less than self-defeating, as the history of warfare amply demonstrates. This has been apparent since the end of World War II. The call for fundamental changes in the organization of society and of the international system was issued in 1948 by a group of social scientists that had been convened by UNESCO; these scholars pointed out that continued colonial rule and the suppression of minorities would rule out the establishment of stable world peace.[5] This conviction has been repeated and amplified by religious, philosophical, and scholarly advocates of peace in the nearly three decades since 1945.[6] The critical peace researchers have done a lot to explain and specify the major factors of political imbalance, economic inequality, and social inequity that are the greatest threat to the "negative peace" of our time as well as the largest barrier to the "positive peace" that visionaries, missionaries, and intellectuals have depicted since the early days of human civilization.[7]

In view of the historical developments and the urgent message that recent analyses by students of peace and conflict have generated, we have to ask ourselves whether we can afford to base the theory and practice of foreign policy and international relations on the long-embedded traditional viewpoint that the avoidance of violent confrontation, whatever its origin and outcome, constitutes an exhaustive definition of peace, or whether we should embrace a dynamic understanding of peace, which implies that we have to incorporate the element of constant transformation into our image of the world peace order. Constant transformation does not mean that we should passively accept change as an inescapable fate for the global community, but it signals our active reorientation toward that goal as the only feasible strategy of peace. The establishment of such a long-range policy vision is complemented by the pursuit of short-range day-by-day measures to prevent the outbreak of costly military engagements and to promote fair and equitable solutions to unsettled conflicts as long as the immediate policy does not contravene the eventual approximation of the ultimate objective.

The Utilization of Peace Research

If we posit a goal of "peace through change" and conceive of peace in the dynamic sense, as we have circumscribed it briefly, we have to take a new look at the crucial question of the utilization of peace research. The whole complex of science and policy is still far from an adequate overall structured interrelationship. The same applies even more to the social sciences and the policy sciences, which offer not only policy-relevant insights but which focus analytically on the structure, process, and outcome of policy-making. In this dual function of applied social science lies a dichotomy that has continually strained the link between the researcher and the practitioner.

From what has been said about the various groups in peace research, it is rather easy to divide them into three main lines of thinking on the issue of research utilization. One group, among them many traditionalists, deems it a major task of researchers to advise governments and to make their policy-related findings available to the fullest extent. The second group, which combines academic purists and those who take a critical attitude toward some or all of the activities of their governments, wants to steer clear of policy involvement and rejects it as unscientific. The third group condemns the advisory role as support for the established elites and urges the scholar to act according to his conscience and actively oppose the ruling regime, if his insights from his academic work so command. The principal debate among peace researchers in America, Europe, and elsewhere fully reflects this split.[8]

The dangers in the first position are obvious. As one recent essay shows, the researcher has to adopt more or less the definition of the problem by the sponsor, i.e., the governmental agency that engages his cooperation, if he wants to be heard and understood.[9] Many students of war and peace have accepted some of these restrictions on the direction of their inquiry because they are fully aware of the danger of nuclear destruction and want to do their share to avert this catastrophe.[10] This need overrides their "innate" suspicion of governmental bias and helps them to try to meet the expectations of the practitioner.

Others view the whole problem in a more detached manner and insist on complete independence in their determination and execution of worthwhile research themes. They do so either because they believe that to accept governmental terms of reference would violate their code of scientific behavior or because they do not share the views of those in power, but nevertheless recognize the urgency of a thorough examination of the policy issues and of the formulation of some remedial and corrective action guidelines.[11] This position is probably sound and safe in that the researcher cannot fall into disfavor as governments change and he can keep his intellectual orientation consonant with the research needs, even though his convictions may tend to push him into dissent from and opposition to governmental actions and objectives.

The third position involves implicitly or explicitly adverse relations with the governing elites. As we have pointed out, this attitude pervades the work of numerous peace researchers in the industrialized societies of the West. The large majority of these students of the social and political bases of conflict and peace refrains from endorsing the openly radical posture that calls for bringing about revolutionary change through revolutionary means.[12] Most "critical" peace researchers openly avow their conviction that government to a large extent needs drastic overhaul, but they see their mission fulfilled in carrying out practice-oriented studies and in publishing their findings under the umbrella of scientific truth and objectivity. If, as they hope, their activity affects the evolution of the political and social system domestically and internationally, the direct steps executing the practical changes will be taken by those sociopolitical forces sharing the perspective of the peace researchers. Thus those in the critical group in peace research play an ambivalent role enabling them to function as scholars and citizens in their societies without either becoming the intellectual servants of the ruling elites or breaking the boundaries of loyalty, minimally defined, within which their academic freedom is protected constitutionally. It needs no additional explanation that their attitude toward the utilization of their research is clearly apart from that of the two other groups.[13]

The various positions on how to use research results for policy-making are in themselves coherent and well-founded. In the context of our study we would propose that if certain conditions are fulfilled on both sides, the utilization of insights from peace and conflict studies is desirable and feasible. The main problem dividing the researchers and the policy-makers relates to the nature and degree of influence that the latter might try to exert over the design, subject matter, and outcome of governmentally funded and supported research projects. How can the decision-maker procure pertinent information without impeding the initiative and the free flow of thought and analysis of the scholar? There cannot be a fully satisfactory solution to this intricate issue. However, we are justified in believing that the difficult condition of the international situation, as reflected in the nuclear threat, the current economic turmoil, the recurrent outbreak of dangerous local and regional conflagrations, the huge disparity in socioeconomic development throughout the world, has sharpened the awareness of governments that the potential of academic expertise and insight even in controversial central political issues must be realized to the fullest extent. The policy-makers can expect the collaboration from the scholar, if they indicate precisely what the problem areas are for which they need additional study and suggestions. They should not try to impose their own conception of how to approach the questions, how to conduct the research nor how to analyze and present the findings to the government. Non-conformist policy-related argumentation should not be discouraged, but strongly solicited and welcomed. For the scholar, some limitations would also apply; he could not deviate from the jointly agreed topical framework nor could he demand automatic compliance from the official agency with his own policy findings and suggestions. Another premise of scholarly participation is the expectation that the researcher maintains his own detached critical attitude so that his views and ideas do not get colored by the inescapable biases affecting official governmental programs and decisions. The major benefit of scholarly policy research is its independence from those institutionalized patterns.

If these criteria of the interaction between decision-makers and scholars are fulfilled, their relationship will be smooth enough under circumstances that would define their separate functions as clearly as possible. Considering the range of research and policy issues that we have listed, we can safely say that most of them would not give cause for controversy. Here we are thinking of most issues involving perception and interaction, including bargaining and dealing with the various aspects of the impact of the international system as a whole on interstate conflict behavior. Some aspects that directly impinge on the argument about the preservation of the status quo or the shaping of a strikingly different political and economic world order are more likely to arouse disagreement about their researchability as well as utilization if they are examined. We cannot suggest any general standards of judgment in these disputed cases, but in light of the utmost urgency of the problem of peace for every responsible government on this earth we hold that both sides must undertake every effort to reconcile their different views and to promote vital research projects for the benefit of their communities. We plead for the committed but at the same time detached scholar who accepts his share of the public responsibility for the protection of an imperfect peace and the achievement of a just and equitable world order.[14]

The Need for Peace Education

Even if academic specialists take divergent stands on many heuristic and practice-related questions, they share the conviction that their work serves first of all educational purposes. This reflects not only their professional commitment, but it is enhanced by the widely held premise that the best, if not the only, approach to peace and social justice is via specific peace education programs ranging from kindergarden programs through post-graduate study. The need for peace education was already strongly emphasized by Quincy Wright, the leading student of war and peace.[15] In recent years UNESCO and the International Peace Research Association, as well as several national organizations and institutes, have begun to develop a general conceptual framework for peace education as a whole and for its various levels.[16] The range of issues is enormous, and despite encouraging advances the development of specific educational programs is still in the early stages.[17]

Most of the work done so far has not transcended the perspective of the individual country in which and for which the researcher does his thinking. The international organizations, some of which we have mentioned, have concentrated on coordinating the country-specific study endeavors, but as of now no major cross- or transnational program structure for peace education has been submitted, although the IPRA Education Committee is involved in transnational discussions and projects. Here is indeed a major lacuna in the field of peace studies, and if the belief in the force of education is generally shared, we feel that a much larger concerted effort toward the elaboration of transnational peace programs and curricula is urgently needed.

The idea of peace education is closely related to the problem of research utilization. The world organization together with governments and researchers all over the globe should actively promote educational schemes that rise beyond the parochial perspective of national societies, and communicate the goals of peace and social justice on the level of the world community without abstracting too much from the legacy of national involvement and achievement. The adoption of such a large research and study project under the auspices of the United Nations could become an important milestone in the evolution of this planet from a mass of independent actors in disarray and conflict to the community of mankind in stable peace, as envisaged in the charters of the United Nations and its affiliated agencies and in the constitutional documents of most states.

Researchers cannot offer panaceas to reach this lofty goal. They can develop the ideas on the basis of better and deeper understanding. The decision-makers must enact programs and apply research findings in their policies. If the general public learns to view the world in its global dimensions of opportunity and risk, the policy-makers, supported by the academic community, will be enabled and probably compelled to depart from the route of an uncertain "national interest" and to join with their colleagues in other governments in negotiating and implementing a new world peace order that assures the survival and dignity of all men.

NOTES

1. This aspect of the uses of peace research underlies the writings of the "critical" peace researchers, among them Galtung, Senghaas, Gene Sharp, and many others, but it is implicit in the thinking and working of quite a few of the other students of peace and conflict, e.g., Singer, Russett, Weizsäcker, and Karl Deutsch. For an emphasis on the practice-related focus of peace research as instrument for social change cf. the introductory remarks in Paul Wehr, Conflict Regulation, AAAS Study Guides, op. cit. The fact that the theme of "peace through change" has emerged over the last few years is indirectly confirmed by the absence of this theme in the peace-action and peace-education oriented review by Hanna and Alan Newcombe, *Peace Research Around the World,* esp. p. 191.

2. Among these voices are Lars Dencik and Herman Schmid. Cf. here Schmid, "Peace research as a technology for pacification," Proceedings of the IPRA Third General Conference, I, esp. pp. 68f.

3. For many such statements see here Krippendorff's editorial introduction to *Friedensforschung,* esp. pp. 21ff., and Senghaas, "Conflict formations in contemporary international society," Journal of Peace Research, 1973, No. 3, pp. 163-184, and his "Friedensforschung–Theoretische Fragestellungen und praktische Probleme," Jahrbuch für Friedens- und Konfliktforschung, II, 1972, pp. 10-22.

4. Cf. here e.g., Karl Deutsch, "Abschreckungspolitik und gesellschaftliche Ordnung. Zum Problem der sich wandelnden Gesellschaft," ibid., I, 1971, pp. 41-53, and his *Peace Research, the Need, the Problems, and the Prospects* (Middlebury, Vermont: Middlebury College, 1972).

5. See the "Common Statement," reprinted in Hedley Cantril (ed.) *Tensions that Cause Wars,* pp. 17-21.

6. To give a few good examples, cf. Francois Visine, *De la Paix,* esp. p. 214, Walter Dirks (ed.) *Friede im Atomzeitalter,* Daniel Frei, *Kriegsverhütung und Friedenssicherung,* esp. pp. 249f., and Ernst-Otto Czempiel, *Schwerpunkte und Ziele der Friedensforschung.* All of these publications contain a clear warning that only substantial change in the international and internal order will advance mankind toward a meaningful peace.

7. Here we refer again to the major writings by Galtung and other West European researchers. Cf. e.g., Galtung, "Peace Thinking," *The Search for World Order* ed. Lepawsky et al., pp. 120-153, his "La science de la paix. Historique et perspectives," Science et Paix, 1973, No. 1, pp. 38-63, and his "Violence, peace, and peace research," Journal of Peace Research, 1969, No. 3, pp. 167-192. Cf. also Senghaas, "Kompositionsprobleme in der Friedensforschung," *Kritische Friedensforschung* ed. Senghaas, pp. 313-361, and the two essays mentioned in note 3 above. Cf. further Fritz Vilmar, "Systematischer Entwurf zur Kritischen Friedensforschung," ibid., pp. 362-395, and Schmid, "Politics and Peace Research," Journal of Peace Research, 1968, pp. 217-232, and Krippendorff, "Peace research and the Industrial Revolution," ibid., 1973, No. 3, pp. 185-202. For some theoretical considerations cf. Rapoport, "Is peace research applicable?" Journal of Conflict Resolution, Vol. 14, No. 2, 1970, pp. 277-286. Last, cf. pertinent remarks by Dominique Simons, "Fondements de la science de la paix," Science et Paix, 1973, No. 1, pp. 27-37.

8. For a description and analysis of these tensions in peace research see Asbjorn Eide, "Dialogue and confrontation in Europe," Journal of Conflict Resolution, Vol. 16, No. 4, December 1972, pp. 511-522, esp. pp. 512f.

9. See Tanter, "The policy relevance of models in world politics," ibid., pp. 557ff.

The author sees the danger of manipulation by the government, but he does not argue against the involvement of the researcher in policy advice.

10. This motivation underlies the work of many distinguished scientists who serve in some contractual form for a governmental agency. Cf. here Singer, "Modern International War. From Conjecture to Explanation," *The Search for World Order* ed. Lepawsky et al., pp. 47-71. Cf. also the introduction by Hanson and Russett to *Peace, War, and Numbers* ed. Russett, esp. pp. 9 and 17.

11. Rapoport takes the view that serious peace research is not applicable in policy decisions. Cf. his "Is peace research applicable?" Journal of Conflict Resolution, 1970, pp. 277-286, and his "Les différentes conceptions d'une science de la paix," Science et Paix, 1973, No. 1, pp. 5-26. A great reluctance to engage in policy research emerges in many other cases. Cf. here the cautious attitude expressed by Deutsch indirectly in his "Abschreckungspolitik und gesellschaftliche Ordnung. Zum Problem der sich wandelnden Gesellschaft," Jahrbuch für Friedens- und Konfliktforschung, I, 1971, pp. 41-53. Cf. also the policy-detached view of relevant conflict research in Höglund and Ulrich, "Peace Research and the Concepts of Conflict–Summary and Criticism," *Conflict Control and Conflict Resolution* ed. Höglund and Ulrich, esp. pp. 32ff.

12. Even such a sharp critic as Schmid shrouds his call for anti-governmental activism into so many dialectical qualifications that the thrust of his arguments is considerably mitigated. Cf. Schmid, "Peace research as a technology for pacification," Proceedings of the IPRA Third General Conference, I, pp. 20-69, and his "Politics and peace research," Journal of Peace Research, 1968, pp. 217-232. The same is true for Lars Dencik, "Peace research: Pacification or revilution," Proceedings, I, pp. 74-89.

13. In our judgment, the whole Scandinavian-West German "critical school" belongs into that group. Cf. again Senghaas, "Conflict formations in contemporary international society," Journal of Peace Research, 1973, No. 3, pp. 163-184, his "Kompositionsprobleme in der Friedensforschung," *Kritische Friedensforschung,* pp. 313-361, and his *"Friedensforschung–Theoretische Fragestellungen und praktische Probleme,"* Jahrbuch für Friedens- und Konfliktforschung, II, 1972, pp. 10-22. This yearbook is a special issue devoted entirely to the question of peace research and political practice and offers many pertinent essays, especially those by Ebert and Benedict. Galtung's scholarly work is also characteristic for the ambivalent position. Cf. here his "Violence, peace, and peace research," Journal of Peace Research, 1969, No. 3, pp. 167-192, and his "La science de la paix. Historique et persepctives," Science et Paix, 1973, No. 1, pp. 38-63. For a fairly comprehensive review of this fundamental problem in the European context cf. Simons, "Fondements de la science de la paix," Science et Paix, 1973, No. 1, pp. 27-37.

14. This is the spirit that characterizes the attitude of many American members of the peace research community. The components of what they see as their research and action commitment are expressed, e.g., in Paul Wehr's *Conflict Regulation.* We could add many other references showing similar traits.

15. Cf. here, e.g., Quincy Wright, "Building a Social System for Mankind," *World-society* ed. Landheer et al., pp. 178-196, here esp. pp. 195f.

16. UNESCO had held several conferences and sponsored additional activities. IPRA's Education Committee published a *Handbook on Peace Education* ed. Christoph Wulf (Frankfurt: IPRA Education Committee, 1974) which is currently the best introduction to the issue and to the major experiences, described in twenty-four essays from all regions and continents of the globe. The predominance of North American, Scandinavian, and West German peace education studies is illustrated by the fact that the volume was issued in cooperation with the Institute for World Order (New York), the German Society for Peace and Conflict Research, and the German Institute for Education Research.

Cf. on the IPRA developments Eide, "Dialogue and confrontation in Europe," Journal of Conflict Resolution, Vol. 16, No. 4, 1972, p. 519.

Foremost in North America is the Institute for World Order which has separate program sections for elementary, secondary, and university peace education. The Consortium on Peace Research, Education and Development (COPRED), which is very active in the United States and to a lesser extent in Canada, has also established several groups of specialists in the various fields of peace education.

17. Next to the interesting material in the *Handbook on Peace Education,* cf. here two West German contributions to get an impression of the wide topical range: Klaus Horn, "Approaches to social psychology relevant to peace research as developed in the FRG," Journal of Peace Research, 1973, No. 3, pp. 305-316, and Gold, Koch, Küpper and Lohner, "Pädagogische und didaktische Uberlegungen zur Uberwindung von Bedrohungsvorstellungen in Erziehungsprozessen," Jahrbuch für Friedens- und Konfliktforschung, I, 1971, pp. 257-274. On the other hand, cf. Paul Wehr and Michael Washburn, "Toward the Study of Peace. A Guide to Peace Studies Development (COPRED: no date) for an effort to formulate a framework for university-level peace education.

A NOTE ON THE BIBLIOGRAPHY

The selected bibliography is, as its title indicates, by no means complete. It lists the literature to which I refer in this study, and includes in addition a few items that have been of direct significance for my argumentation, although I do not quote them explicitly. General background literature has been excluded. To give a rough guideline, I have emphasized developments from 1968 to 1973 with primary attention to published books and articles.

My search for material was supported by librarians at UNITAR, at Hammarskjold Library, and at the Carnegie Endowment. Due to constraints in terms of time and access to highly specialized university collections, and due to my own choices regarding scope and subject matter of the critical survey, I do not claim to offer a comprehensive or representative bibliography, nor should it be understood in such a manner.

In the Supplementary Bibliography I have updated and expanded the original bibliography without in any way trying to compile a comprehensive listing. Material of the period until Spring 1975 is included.

SELECTED BIBLIOGRAPHY

Abrahamsson, Bengt. "A Model for the Analysis of Inter-Group Conflict," in: *Conflict Control and Conflict Resolution,* ed. Höglund and Ulrich, pp. 72-85.

Afheldt, Horst. "Analyse der Sicherheitspolitik durch Untersuchung der kritischen Parameter," in: *Kriegsfolgen und Kriegsverhütung,* ed. C. F. von Weizsäcker, pp. 25-74.

---. "Political conclusions of the study 'The consequences of war and the prevention of war'," Journal of Peace Research, No. 3, pp. 259-264. (Hereinafter abbreviated JPR)

--- and Philipp Sonntag. "Stabilität und Abschreckung durch strategische Kernwaffen –eine Systemanalyse," in: *Kriegsfolgen und Kriegsverhütung,* ed. C. F. von Weizsäcker, pp. 303-415.

--- and ---. "Stability and deterrence through strategic nuclear arms," JPR, 1973, No. 3, pp. 245-250.

Albrecht, Ulrich. *Der Handel mit Waffen* (Munich: Hanser, 1971).

---. "The costs of armamentism," JPR, 1973, No. 3, pp. 265-284.

--- and Birgit A. Somner. *Deutsche Waffen für die Dritte Welt. Militärhilfe und Entwicklungspolitik* (Reinbek: Rowohlt, 1972).

---, Johan Galtung, Pertti Joenniemi, Dieter Senghaas, Sergiu Verona. "Is Europe to demilitarize?" Instant Research on Peace and Violence, 1972, No. 4, pp. 181-246.

Alcock, Norman Z. *The Emperor's New Clothes* (Oakville, Ont.: CPRI Press, 1971).

——— and Keith Lowe. "The Vietnam war as a Richardson process," JPR, 1969, No. 2, pp. 105-112.

Alger, Chadwick F. "Interaction and negotiation in a committee of the United Nations General Assembly," Peace Research Society (International) Papers 5, 1966, pp. 141-159.

———. "Interaction in a Committee of the United Nations General Assembly," in: *Quantitative International Politics,* ed. Singer, pp. 51-84.

———. "The multinational corporation and the future international system," Annals of the American Academy of Political and Social Science, Vol. 403, September 1972, pp. 104-115.

———. "Personal Contact in Intergovernmental Organizations," in: *International Behavior,* ed. Kelman, pp. 523-547.

———. "The United States in the United Nations," International Organization, Vol. 27, No. 1, Winter 1973, pp. 1-23.

——— and David Hoovler. "Regional Participation in International Organizations (Governmental, Nongovernmental, Corporations, and Banks)," paper prepared for the Ninth World Congress, International Political Science Association, Montreal, August 19-25, 1973.

Alker, Hayward R., Jr. "The Long Road to International Relations Theory: Problems of Statistical Nonadditivity," in: *New Approaches to International Relations,* ed. Kaplan, pp. 137-169.

——— and Ronald D. Brunner, "Simulating international conflict: A comparison of three approaches," International Studies Quarterly, Vol. 13, No. 1, March 1969, pp. 70-110.

——— and Donald Puchala. "Trends in Economic Partnership: The North Atlantic Area, 1928-1963," in: *Quantitative International Politics,* ed. Singer, pp. 287-316.

——— and Bruce M. Russett. *World Politics in the General Assembly* (New Haven: Yale University Press, 1965).

Almond, Gabriel. "National Politics and International Politics," in: *The Search for World Order,* ed. Lepawsky et al., pp. 283-297.

Angell, Robert C. *Peace on the March. Transnational Participation* (New York: Van Nostrand Reinhold Co., 1969).

Ardrey, Robert. *African Genesis* (New York: Athenaeum, 1961).

———. *Territorial Imperative* (New York: Athenaeum, 1966).

Azar, Edward E. Towards the development of an early warning model of international violence. Studies of Conflict and Peace, Report No. 13, Department of Political Science, University of North Carolina, Chapel Hill, 1973.

Bahr, Hans-Eckehard. "Frieden ohne Revolution?" in: *Weltfrieden und Revolution,* ed. Bahr, pp. 7-22.

———, ed. *Weltfrieden und Revolution in politischer und theologischer Perspektive* (Frankfurt: Fischer Bücherei, 1970).

Barnaby, Frank and Carlo Schaerf, eds. *Disarmament and Arms Control. Proceedings of the Third Course given by the International Summer School on Disarmament and Arms Control of the Italian Pugwash Movement* (New York: Gordon and Breach Science Publishers, 1972).

Barrea, Jean. "The counter-core role of middle powers in processes of external political integration," World Politics, Vol. 25, No. 2, January 1973, pp. 274-287.

Barsegov, Yuri and Rustem Khairov. "A study of the problems of peace," JPR, 1973, No. 1-2, pp. 71-80. With a "Rejoinder" by Kjell Skjelsbaek, pp. 121f.

Bartos, Otomar J. "Determinants and Consequences of Toughness," in: *The Structure of Conflict,* ed. Swingle, pp. 45-68.

van Benthem van den Berg, Gottfried. "Theory or taxonomy? Some critical notes on Johan Galtung's 'A structural theory of imperialism'," JPR, 1972, No. 1, pp. 77-86. With a "Rejoinder" by Johan Galtung, pp. 87-90.

Bertalanffy, Ludwig von. "General Systems Theory," *Yearbook of the Society for General Systems Research* I, 1956, pp. 1-10.

Bixenstine, Edwin V. and Jacquelyn W. Gaebelein. "Strategies of 'real' opponents in eliciting cooperative choice in a Prisoner's Dilemma game," Journal of Conflict Resolution, Vol. 15, No. 2, June 1971, pp. 157-166. (Hereinafter abbreviated JCR)

Black, Cyril E. and Richard A. Falk. *Conflict Management. The Future of the International Legal Order,* Vol. III. (Princeton, N.J.: Princeton University Press, 1971).

Bloomfield, Lincoln P. and Amelia C. Leiss. *Controlling Small Wars: A Strategy for the 1970's* (New York: Knopf, 1969).

Boasson, Charles, Johan Galtung, and Adnan Amad. "Discussion on Galtung's 'The Middle East and the theory of conflict'," JPR, 1973, No. 1-2, pp. 133-154.

Bobrow, Davis B. ed. *Weapons System Decisions* (New York: Praeger, 1969).

Bonacich, Phillip. "Putting the dilemma into Prisoner's Dilemma," JCR, Vol. 14, No. 3, September 1970, pp. 379-387.

Bonham, G. Matthew. "Simulating international disarmament negotiations," JCR, Vol. 15, No. 3, September 1971, pp. 299-315.

Boulding, Elise. "Peace research: Dialectics and development," JCR, Vol. 16, No. 4, December 1972, pp. 469-473.

Boulding, Kenneth E. "The Learning of Peace." Presidential Address delivered at the International Studies Association Annual Meeting, St. Louis, Missouri, March 20, 1974.

---. "A Pure Theory of Conflict Applied to Organizations," in: *Conflict Management in Organizations,* ed. Elise Boulding (Ann Arbor, Mich.: Foundation for Research on Human Behavior, 1961), pp. 43-51.

---. "National Images and International Systems," in: *International Politics and Foreign Policy,* Rosenau, pp. 422-431.

Bouthoul, Gaston. *La Guerre* (Paris: Presses Universitaires de France, 1953).

---. *L'Infanticide Différé* (Paris: Hachette, 1970).

---. *Traité de Polémologie. Sociologie des Guerres* (Paris: Payot, 1970; first published in 1951 under the title *Les Guerres*).

Brecher, Michael, Blema Steinberg, and Janice Stein. "A framework for research on foreign policy behavior," JCR, Vol. 13, No. 1, March 1969, pp. 75-101.

Bredow, Wilfried von. *Vom Antagonismus zur Konvergenz. Studien zum Ost-West-Problem* (Frankfurt/Main: Metzner, 1972).

---, ed. *Zum Charakter internationaler Konflikte. Studien aus West- und Osteuropa.* Schriften des Internationalen Institute für den Frieden Wien. (Cologne: Pahl-Rugenstein, 1973).

Bretton, Philippe and Jean-Pierre Chaudet. *La Coexistence Pacifique.* Collection U (Paris: Librairie Armand Colin, 1971).

Brofenbrenner, Urie. "Allowing for Soviet Perceptions," in: *International Conflict and Behavioral Science,* ed. Fisher, pp. 161-178.

Burton, John W. *Conflict and Communication. The Use of Controlled Communication in International Relations* (New York: Free Press, 1969).

---. *Peace Theory. Preconditions of Disarmament* (New York: Knopf, 1962).

---. *World Society* (London: Cambridge University Press, 1972).

Burton, John W., A.J.R. Groom, C. R. Mitchell, and A.V.S. De Reuck. The Study of World Society: A London Perspective. A discussion. International Studies, Occasional Paper No. 1 (International Studies Association, 1974).

Campbell, Thomas W. "Nationalism in America's UN Policy, 1944-1945," International Organization, Vol. 7, No. 1, Winter 1973, pp. 25-44.

Cantori, Louis J. and Steven L. Spiegel. "The analysis of regional international politics: The integration versus the empirical systems approach," International Organization, Vol. 27, No. 4, Autumn 1973, pp. 465-494.

Cantril, Hadley, ed. *Tensions that Cause Wars* (Urbana: University of Illinois Press, 1950).

Chadwick, Richard W. "An inductive, empirical analysis of intra- and international behavior, aimed at a partial extension of inter-nation simulation theory," JPR, 1969, No. 3, pp. 193-214.

Chi Hsi-sheng, "The Chinese Warlord System as an International System," in: *New Approaches to International Relations,* ed. Kaplan, pp. 405-425.

Choucri, Nazli. "The perceptual base of nonalignment," JCR, Vol. 13, No. 1, March 1969, pp. 57-74.

--- with the collaboration of Robert C. North. "In Search of Peace Systems: Scandinavia and the Netherlands, 1870-1970," in: *Peace, War, and Numbers,* ed. Russett, pp. 239-274.

Conrath, David W. "Experience as a factor in experimental gaming behavior," JCR, Vol. 14, No. 2, June 1970, pp. 195-202.

Cooper, Peter. "Die Entwicklung von Vorstellungen über den Krieg," in: *Friedensforschung,* ed. Krippendorff, pp. 157-180.

Coser, Lewis A. *The Functions of Social Conflict* (New York: Free Press, 1964).

---. "The Termination of Conflict," in: *Social Processes in International Relations,* ed. Kriesberg, pp. 37-44.

Curle, Adam. *Making Peace* (London: Tavistock, 1971).

Czempiel, Ernst-Otto. *Macht und Kompromiss. Die Beziehungen der Bundesrepublik Deutschland zu den Vereinten Nationen. 1956-1970* (Düsseldorf: Bertelsmann, 1971).

---. *Schwerpunkte und Ziele der Friedensforschung* (Munich: Kaiser; Mainz: Matthias-Grünewald, 1972).

Delbrück, Jost. "Modelle eines gesamteuropäischen Sicherheitssystems," Jahrbuch für Friedens- und Konfliktforschung, Vol. II, 1972, pp. 87-102.

Dencik, Lars. "Peace research: Pacification or revolution?" Proceedings of the International Peace Research Association Third Conference, Vol. I, pp. 74-89.

--- and Hakan Wiberg. "Strategic Thinking as a Function of Social Attitudes: An Experiment with Prisoner's Dilemma," in: *Conflict Control and Conflict Resolution,* ed. Höglund and Ulrich, pp. 39-71.

Denker, Rolf. "Zum gegenwärtigen Stand der Aggressionsforschung: Versuch einer Synthese," in: *Aggressionstrieb und Krieg.* Symposium des Internationalen Instituts für Frieden, Wien, ed. Hollitscher, pp. 7-33.

Deutsch, Karl W. "Abschreckungspolitik und gesellschaftliche Ordnung. Zum Problem der sich wandelnden Gesellschaft," Jahrbuch für Friedens- und Konfliktforschung, Vol. I, 1971, pp. 41-53.

---. *Nationalism and Social Communication: An Inquiry into the Foundations of Nationality* (Cambridge, Mass.: MIT Press, 1966).

---. *Nerves of Government. Models of Political Communication and Control* (New York: Free Press, 1966).

---. "The Propensity in International Transactions," in: *Social Processes in International Relations,* ed. Kriesberg, pp. 246-254.

Deutsch, Karl W. and Dieter Senghaas. "Die brüchige Vernunft von Staaten," in: *Kritische Friedensforschung,* ed. Senghaas, pp. 105-163.

––– and –––. "A Framework for a Theory of War and Peace," in: *The Search for World Order,* ed. Lepawsky et al., pp. 23-46.

––– et al. *France, Germany and the Western Alliance: A Study of Elite Attitudes on European Integration and World Politics* (New York: Scribner's Sons, 1967).

––– et al. *Political Community and the North Atlantic Area* (Princeton, N.J.: Princeton University Press, 1957).

Deutsch, Morton. *The Resolution of Conflict. Constructive and Destructive Processes* (New Haven: Yale University Press, 1973).

Dirks, Walter, ed. *Friede im Atomzeitalter* (Mainz: Matthias-Grünewald, 1967).

Dolbear, F. T., L. B. Lave, G. Bowman, A. Lieberman, E. Prescott, F. Rueter, and R. Sherman. "Collusion in the Prisoner's Dilemma: Number of strategies, JCR, Vol. 13, No. 2, June 1969, pp. 252-261.

Druckman, Daniel. "The influence of the situation in interparty conflict," JCR, Vol. 15, No. 4, December 1971, pp. 523-554.

Duchrow, Ulrich. " 'Gerechte Gewalt,' Gewalttätigkeit und Gewaltlosigkeit im B-Waffen-Zeitalter," in: *BC-Waffen und Friedenspolitik,* ed. E. von Weizsäcker, pp. 112-136.

Ebert, Theodor. "Friedensbewegung und Friedensforschung–Historische und aktuelle Wechselwirkungen," Jahrbuch für Friedens- und Konfliktforschung, Vol. II, 1972, pp. 156-172.

–––. *Gewaltfreier Aufstand: Alternative zum Bürgerkrieg* (Frankfurt: Fisher, 1970).

–––. *Ziviler Widerstand. Fallstudien zur gewaltfreien direkten Aktion. Aus der innenpolitischen Friedens- und Konfliktforschung* (Düsseldorf: Bertelsmann, 1970).

–––. "Verteidigung ohne Drohung. Praxeologien der gradualistischen Abrüstung und gewaltfreien Verteidigung," Jahrbuch für Friedens- und Konfliktforschung, Vol. I, 1971, pp. 213-246.

Efroimson, Wladimir Pawlowitsch. "Die Genealogie des Altruismus," in: *Aggressionstrieb und Krieg,* ed. Hollitscher, pp. 129-164.

Eide, Asbjorn. "Dialogue and confrontation in Europe," JCR, Vol. 16, No. 4, December 1972, pp. 511-522.

–––. "La guerre technologique contre les faibles et la conscience de l'homme de science," Science et Paix, 1973, No. 2-3, pp. 82-91.

Etzioni, Amitai. "The Epigenesis of Political Communities at the International Level," in: *Social Processes in International Relations,* ed. Kriesberg, pp. 446-465.

–––. "The Kennedy Experiment," in: *Social Processes in International Relations,* ed. Kriesberg, pp. 415-437.

Everts, Philip P. "Developments and trends in peace and conflict research, 1965-1971: A survey of institutions," JCR, Vol. 16, No. 4, December 1972, pp. 477-510.

Falk, Richard A. "Bipolarity and the Future of World Society," in: *Worldsociety,* ed. Landheer et al., pp. 103-114.

–––. "New Approaches to the Study of International Law," in: *New Approaches to International Relations,* ed. Kaplan, pp. 357-380.

–––. "The Trend Toward World Community: An Inventory of Issues," in: *The Search for World Order,* ed. Lepawsky et al., pp. 353-370.

Feierabend, Ivo K., Rosalind L. Feierabend, and Ted Robert Gurr, eds. *Anger, Violence and Politics. Theories and Research* (Englewood Cliffs, N.J.: Prentice-Hall, 1972).

Fisher, Roger. "Fractionating Conflict," in: *International Conflict and Behavioral Science,"* ed. Fisher, pp. 91-109.

———. ed. *International Conflict and Behavioral Science* (New York: Basic Books, 1964).

Fock, Niels. "Regulation of Conflicts in American Societies," in: *Conflict Control and Conflict Resolution,* ed. Höglund and Ulrich, pp. 143-155.

Forndran, Erhard. *Abrüstung und Friedensforschung.* Kritik an Krippendorff, Senghaas und Ebert (Düsseldorf: Bertelsmann Universitätsverlag, 1971).

Franke, Winfried. "The Italian City-State System as an International System," in: *New Approaches to International Relations,* ed. Kaplan, pp. 426-458.

Frei, Daniel. "De-escalation–the Geographical Approach. Tension Reduction by Mutual Disengagement," paper for the international conference of the International Institute for Peace, Vienna, December 15-17, 1972.

———. *Kriegsverhütung und Friedenssicherung* (Frauenfeld and Stuttgart: Huber, 1970).

Fritsch, Bruno. "The Problem of a Global Social Order," in: *Worldsociety,* ed. Landheer et al., pp. 148-154.

Gallo, Philip S. "Personality impression formation in a Maximizing Difference game," JCR, Vol. 13, No. 1, March 1969, pp. 118-122.

Gallois, Pierre M. *Paradoxes de la Paix* (Paris: Presses du Temps Present, 1967).

Galtung, Johan. "East-West Interaction Patterns," in: *Social Processes in International Relations,* ed. Kriesberg, pp. 272-307.

———. "Europe–bipolar, bicentric, cooperative?" JPR, 1972, No. 1, pp. 1-26.

———. "Japan and future world politics," JPR, 1973, No. 4, pp. 355-385.

———. "The Middle East and the theory of conflict," JPR, 1971, No. 3-4, pp. 173-206.

———. "Nichtmilitärische Verteidigungsmassnahmen," in: *Soziale Verteidigung,* ed. Ebert, pp. 84-94.

———. "Peace Thinking," in: *The Search for World Order,* ed. Lepawsky et al., pp. 120-153.

———. "Pluralismus und die Zukunft der menschlichen Gesellschaft," in: *Kritische Friedensforschung,* ed. Senghaas, pp. 164-231.

———. "La science de la paix. Historique et perspectives," Science et Paix, 1973, No. 1, pp. 38-63.

———. "Small Group Theory and the Theory of International Relations: A Study in Isomorphism," in: *New Approaches to International Relations,* ed. Kaplan, pp. 270-302.

———. "A Structural Theory of Aggression," in: *Anger, Violence, and Politics,* ed. Feierabend et al., pp. 85-97.

———. "A structural theory of imperialism," JPR, 1971, No. 2, pp. 81-118.

———. "Theorien des Friedens," in: *Kritische Friedensforschung,* ed. Senghaas, pp. 235-246.

———. "Violence, peace and peace research," JPR, 1969, No. 3, pp. 167-192.

———. "World indicators program," Bulletin of Peace Proposals, 1973, No. 4, pp. 354-358.

———, Manuel Mora y Araujo, and Simon Schwartzman. "The Latin American System of Nations: A Structural Analysis," in: *Conflict Control and Conflict Resolution,* ed. Höglund and Ulrich, pp. 86-113.

Gamson, William A. and Andre Modigliani. *Untangling the Cold War* (Boston: Little, Brown, 1971).

Gantzel, Klaus Jürgen. "Dependency structures as the dominant pattern in world society," JPR, 1973, No. 3, pp. 203-216.

Gantzel, Klaus Jürgen. "Zu herrschaftssoziologischen Problembereichen von Abhängigkeitsbeziehungen in der gegenwärtigen Weltgesellschaft," in: *Imperialismus und strukturelle Gewalt. Analysen über abhängige Reprodution,* ed. Senghaas, pp. 105-120.

Gift, Richard E. "Trading in a threat system: the U.S.-Soviet case," JCR, Vol. 13, No. 4, December 1969, pp. 418-437.

Glagolev, Igor and Makar Goryainov. "Some problems of disarmament research," JPR, 1964, No. 2, pp. 150-154.

Gleditsch, Nils Petter. "Time Differences and International Interaction," *Cooperation and Conflict,* Vol. 9, No. 1, 1974, pp. 35-51.

Glenn, Edmund S., Robert H. Johnson, Paul R. Kimmel, and Bryant Wedge. "A cognitive interaction model to analyze culture conflict in international relations," JCR, Vol. 14, No. 1, March 1970, pp. 35-48.

Gold, Volker, Roland Koch, Christel Küpper, Mathias R. Lohner. "Pädagogische und didaktische Uberlegungen zur Uberwindung von Bedrohungsvorstellungen in Erziehungsprozessen," Jahrbuch für Friedens- und Konfliktforschung, Vol. I, 1971, pp. 257-274.

Goryainov, Makar and Igor Glagolev. "Concerning research on peace and disarmament conducted in the USSR," International Social Science Journal, Vol. 17, No. 3, 1965, pp. 417-419.

Gould, Wesley L. and Michael Barkun. *International Law and the Social Sciences* (Princeton, N.J.: Princeton University Press, 1970).

Graber, Doris A. "Perceptions of Middle East conflict in the UN, 1953-1965," JCR, Vol. 13, No. 4, December 1969, pp. 454-484.

Groenningen, S., E. M. Kelley, and Michael Leiserson, eds. *The Study of Coalition Behavior: Theoretical Perspectives and Cases from Four Continents* (New York: Holt, Rinehart, and Winston, 1970).

Gruder, Charles L. "Relationships with opponent and partner in mixed-motive bargaining," JCR, Vol. 15, No. 3, September 1971, pp. 403-416.

Guetzkow, Harold. "Some Correspondences Between Simulations and 'Realities' in International Relations," ed. Kaplan, pp. 202-269.

Gurr, Ted Robert. "Psychological Factors in Civil Violence," in: *Anger, Violence, and Politics,* ed. Feierabend et al., pp. 31-57.

Gutteridge, W. "Arms Control and Developing Countries," in: *Disarmament and Arms Control,* ed. Barnaby and Schaerf, pp. 121-141.

---. "Arms to Developing Countries," in: *Disarmament and Arms Control,* ed. Barnaby and Schaerf, pp. 141-158.

Haas, Ernst B. "The Study of Regional Integration: Reflections on the Joy and Anguish of Pretheorizing," in: *Regional Integration: Theory and Research,* ed. Lindberg and Scheingold, pp. 3-42.

---, Robert L. Butterworth, and Joseph S. Nye. *Conflict Management by International Organizations* (Harristown, N.J.: General Learning Press, 1972).

---, and Edward Thomas Rowe. "Regional organizations in the United Nations: Is there externalization?" International Studies Quarterly, Vol. 17, No. 1, March 1973, pp. 3-54.

Hanrieder, Wolfram F. "The international system, bipolar or multibloc?" JCR, Vol. 9, No. 3, September 1965, pp. 299-307.

Hansen, Erland Brun and Jörgen Wilian Ulrich. "A Weapons Transfer System for Inter-National Conflict Regulation: A Proposal," in: *Conflict Control and Conflict Resolution,* ed. Höglund and Ulrich, pp. 156-173.

Hanson, Betty Crump and Bruce M. Russett, "Introduction," in: *Peace, War, and Numbers,* ed. Russett, pp. 9-17.

Harsanyi, John C. "Game Theory and the Analysis of International Conflict," in: *International Politics and Foreign Policy,* rev. ed. Rosenau, pp. 370-379.

Hassner, Pierre. "Paix et Guerre Entre les Théories: Combats, Jeux et Débats sur la Maîtrise des Armements," paper for the Ninth World Congress of the International Political Science Association, Montreal, August 1973.

Hermann, Charles F., ed. *International Crises: Insights from Behavioral Research* (New York: Free Press, 1972).

———. "International Crisis as a Situational Variable," in: *International Politics and Foreign Policy,* Rosenau, pp. 409-421.

———. "Some Issues in the Study of International Crises," in: *International Crises,* ed. Hermann, pp. 3-17.

———. "Threat, Time, and Surprise: A Simulation of International Crisis," in: *International Crises,* ed. Hermann, pp. 187-211.

——— and Linda B. Brady. "Alternative Models of International Crisis Behavior," in: *International Crises,* ed. Hermann, pp. 281-303.

——— and Margaret G. Hermann. "An Attempt to Simulate the Outbreak on World War I," in: *International Politics and Foreign Policy,* rev. ed. Rosenau, pp. 622-639.

Hill, Gary. *General Patterns of Interaction Throughout the International System.* Annual Report: World Event/Interaction Survey–WEIS–, 1972.

Hilton, Gordon, "A closed and open model of perceptions in crisis," in: Proceedings of the IPRA Third Conference, Vol. III, pp. 51-70.

———. "Expressions of hostility in crisis," JPR, 1971, No. 3-4, pp. 249-262.

Hoffman, Stanley. "Choices," Foreign Policy, No. 12, Fall 1973, pp. 3-42.

Höglund, Bengt and Jörgen Wilian Ulrich, eds. *Conflict Control and Conflict Resolution. Interdisciplinary Studies from the Scandinavian Summer University,* Vol. 17 (Copenhagen: Munksgaard, 1972).

——— and ———. "Peace Research and the Concepts of Conflict–Summary and Criticism," in: *Conflict Control and Conflict Resolution,* ed. Höglund and Ulrich, pp. 13-36.

Hollitscher, Walter, ed. *Aggressionstrieb und Krieg. Symposium des Internationalen Instituts für den Frieden, Wien. Mit einer Einleitung von Rolf Denker* (Stuttgart: Deutsche Verlags-Anstalt, 1973).

Holsti, Ole R. "The Belief System and National Images: A Case Study," in: *International Politics and Foreign Policy,* rev. ed. Rosenau, pp. 543-550.

———. "Individual differences in 'definition of the situation'," JCR, Vol. 14, No. 3, September 1970, pp. 303-310.

———. "Time, Alternatives, and Communications: The 1914 and Cuban Missile Crises," in: *International Crises,* ed. Hermann, pp. 58-80.

———, Richard A. Brody, and Robert C. North. "Measuring Affect and Action in International Reaction Models: Empirical Materials from the 1962 Cuban Crisis," in: *International Politics and Foreign Policy,* Rosenau, pp. 679-696.

———, Robert C. North and Richard A. Brody. "Perception and Action in the 1914 Crisis," in: *Quantitative International Politics,* ed. Singer, pp. 123-158.

Hopmann, P. Terrence. "Internal and External Influences on Bargaining in Arms Control Negotiations: The Partial Test Ban," in: *Peace, War, and Numbers,* ed. Russett, pp. 213-237.

Horn, Klaus. "Approaches to social psychology relevant to peace research as developed in the Federal Republic of Germany," JPR, 1973, No. 3, pp. 305-316.

———. "Zur Sozialpsychologie von Kommunikation and Interaktion unter Bedingungen von Konflikt und Aggression," Jahrbuch für Friedens- und Konfliktforschung, Vol. II, 1972, pp. 35-56.

Horowitz, Irving Louis. "Deterrence Games: From Academic Notebook to Military Codebook," in: *The Structure of Conflict,* ed. P. Swingle, pp. 277-296.

Hugo, Grant. *Appearance and Reality in International Relations* (New York: Columbia University Press, 1970).

Hveem, Helge. "The global dominance system," JPR, 1973, No. 4, pp. 319-340.

Hymer, Stephen. "The Multinational Corporation and the Law of Uneven Development," in: *Economics and World Order,* ed. Jagdish N. Bhagwati (New York: Macmillan, 1972), pp. 113-140.

Iklé, Fred Charles. *Every War Must End.* (New York: Columbia University Press, 1971).

International Peace Research Association. Proceedings of the Third Conference, (Assen: Van Gorcum, 1970).

---. Proceedings of the Fourth Conference (Oslo: International Peace Research Association Secretariat, 1973).

International Political Communities. An Anthology (Garden City, N.Y.: Doubleday Anchor, 1966).

International Repertory of Institutions for Peace and Conflict Research. Reports and Papers in the Social Sciences, No. 28 (Paris: UNESCO, 1973).

Jahn, Egbert. "Civilian defense and civilian offensive," JPR, 1973, No. 3, pp. 285-294.

Jahrbuch für Friedens- und Konfliktforschung. Herausgegeben in Auftrag des Vorstandes der Arbeitsgemeinschaft für Friedens- und Konfliktforschung e.V., Vol. I: "Bedrohungsvorstellungen als Faktor der Internationalen Politik" (Düsseldorf: Bertelsmann Universitätsverlag, 1971).

---, Vol. II: "Friedensforschung und politische Praxis" (Düsseldorf: Bertelsmann Universitätsverlag, 1972).

Jervis, Robert. "Hypotheses on Misperception," in: *International Politics and Foreign Policy,* Rosenau, pp. 237-254.

Joffe, Josef. "Abschreckung und Abschreckungspolitik. Kritische Bemerkungen zu Dieter Senghaas' Beitrag," Jahrbuch für Friedens- und Konfliktforschung, I, 1971, pp. 133-158.

Kahn, Herman. "The Alternative World Futures Approach," in: *New Approaches to International Relations,* ed. Kaplan, pp. 83-116.

Kaiser, Karl. *Friedensforschung in der Bundesrepublik.* Im Auftrag der Stiftung Volkswagenwerk (Göttingen: Vandenhoeck and Ruprecht, 1970).

---. "Transnational politics: Toward a theory of multinational polities," International Organization, Vol. 25, No. 4, Autumn 1971, pp. 790-817.

Kaldor, M. "Factors governing the supply and demand of major weapons," in: *Disarmament and Arms Control,* ed. Barnaby and Schaerf, pp. 159ff.

Kaplan, Morton A., ed. *New Approaches to International Relations* (New York: St. Martin's Press, 1968).

---. "A Note on Game Theory and Bargaining," in: *New Approaches to International Relations,* ed. Kaplan, pp. 483-518.

---. *System and Process in International Politics* (New York: Wiley, 1957).

---. "The Systems Approach to International Politics," in: *New Approaches to International Relations,* ed. Kaplan, pp. 381-404.

---. "Traditionalism vs. Science in International Relations," in: *New Approaches International Relations,* ed. Kaplan, pp. 1-18.

Kelman, Herbert C., ed. *International Behavior. A Social-Psychological Analysis.* Published for the Society for the Psychological Studies of Social Issues (New York: Holt, Rinehart and Winston, 1965).

Kerr, Henry H., Jr., "Changing attitudes through international participation: European parliamentarians and integration," International Organization, Vol. 27, No. 1, Winter 1973, pp. 45-83.

Korbonski, Andrzej. "Theory and Practice of Regional Integration: The Case of Comecon," in: *Regional Integration,* ed. Lindberg and Scheingold, pp. 338-373.

Kramer, Heinz. "Transaktion zwischen Ost- und Westeuropa als Mittel kooperationsförnder Systemveränderung," Jahrbuch für Friedens- und Konfliktforschung, II, 1972, pp. 117-143.

Kriesberg, Louis, ed. *Social Processes in International Relations* (New York: Wiley, 1968).

Krippendorff, Eckehart, ed. *Friedensforschung.* Neue Wissenschaftliche Bibliothek 29. (Cologne-Berlin: Kiepenheuer and Witsch, 1970).

---. "Peace research and the industrial revolution," JPR, 1973, No. 3, pp. 185-202.

Kumar, Mahendra. *Current Peace Research and India* (Rajghat, Varanasi: Gandhian Institute of Studies, 1968).

Landheer, B. "Industrial Society as the Basis of Worldsociety," in: *Worldsociety,* ed. Landheer et al., pp. 168-177.

---. J.H.M.M. Loenen, Fred L. Polak, eds. *Worldsociety. How is an Effective and Desirable World Order Possible? A Symposium* (The Hague: Nijhoff, 1971).

Langholm, Sivert. "On the concepts of center and periphery," JPR, 1971, No. 3-4, pp. 273-278.

Laszlo, Ervin. *The Systems View of the World. The Natural Philosophy of the New Developments in the Sciences* (New York: Braziller, 1972).

Lentner, Howard H. "The Concept of Crisis as Viewed by the United States Department of State," in: *International Crises,* ed. Hermann, pp. 112-135.

Lentz, Theo F. *Towards A Science of Peace* (London: Halycon Press, 1955).

Lepawsky, Albert, Edward H. Buehrig, and Harold D. Lasswell, eds. *The Search for World Order. Studies by students and colleagues of Quincy Wright* (New York: Appleton-Century-Crofts, 1971).

Levy, Paul M.G., Marie-Dominique Simons, and Jorge d'Oliveira e Souza. Le Colloque de Louvain (mars 1971) ou Polémiques de Polémologues. Extrait de Res Publica 1972, No. 4, pp. 725-744. Centre de Recherches sur la Paix, Louvain, 1972.

Lieberman, Bernhardt. "i-Trust: A Notion of Trust in Three-Person Games and International Affairs," in: *Social Processes in International Relations,* ed. Kriesberg, pp. 359-371.

Lindberg, Leon N. "Political Integration as a Multidimensional Phenomenon Requiring Multivariate Measurement," in: *Regional Integration,* ed. Lindberg and Scheingold, pp. 45-127.

---, and Stuart A. Scheingold, eds. *Regional Integration: Theory and Research* (Cambridge: Harvard University Press, 1971).

Lorenz, Konrad. *Das Sogenannte Böse. Zur Naturgeschichte der Aggression* (Vienna, 1963); English: *On Aggression* (New York: Harcourt, Brace and World, 1966).

Lumsden, Malvern. "Some Factors Affecting Local Acceptance of a UN Force: A Pilot Report from Cyprus," in: *Conflict Control and Conflict Resolution,* ed. Höglund and Ulrich, pp. 117-142.

Lupfer, Michael, Mark Jones, Lionel Spaulding, and Richard Archer. "Risk-taking in cooperative and competitive dyads," JCR, Vol. 15, No. 3, September 1971, pp. 385-392.

Lüschen, Günther. "Cooperation, association, and contest," JCR, Vol. 14, No. 1, March 1970, pp. 21-34.

McClelland, Charles A. "The Beginning, Duration, and Abatement of International Crises: Comparisons in Two Conflict Arenas," in: *International Crises,* ed. Hermann, pp. 83-105.

---. "Field Theory and System Theory in International Relations," in: *The Search for World Order,* ed. Lepawsky et al., pp. 371-385.

---. and Gary D. Hoggard. "Conflict Patterns in the Interactions Among Nations," in: *International Politics and Foreign Policy,* rev. ed. Rosenau, pp. 711-724.

Meeker, Robert J. and Gerald H. Shure, "Pacifist bargaining tactics: some 'outsider' influence," JCR, Vol. 13, No. 4, December 1969, pp. 487-493.

Michelini, Ronald L. "Effects of prior interaction, contact, strategy, and expectation of meeting on game behavior and sentiment," JCR, Vol. 15, No. 1, March 1971, pp. 97-103.

Milburn, Thomas W. "The Management of Crisis," in: *International Crises,* ed. Hermann, pp. 259-277.

Miller, James G. "The nature of living systems," Behavioral Science, Vol. 16, July 1971, pp. 277-301.

Milstein, Jeffrey S. "American and Soviet Influence, Balance of Power, and Arab-Israeli Violence," in: *Peace, War, and Numbers,* ed. Russett, pp. 139-166.

Mitchell, C. R. "Conflict resolution and controlled communication," JPR, 1973, No. 1-2, pp. 123-132.

Mitchell, John D. "Cross-cutting memberships, integration, and the international system," JCR, Vol. 14, No. 1, March 1970, pp. 49-55.

Mitteilungen der Hessischen Stiftung Friedens- und Konfliktforschung, No. 4, 1972: "Die Rüstungsdynamik im Ost-West-Konflikt und die Möglichkeiten ihrer Beeinflussung," Projektskizzen. Frankfurt, April 1972.

Modelski, George. "The world's foreign ministers: A political elite," JCR, Vol. 14, No. 2, June 1970, pp. 135-175.

Molimart, Jean. *Sauver la Paix* (Paris: Promotion et Edition, 1966).

Montagu, Ashley, ed. *Man and Aggression.* (London: Oxford University Press, 1973).

Morris, Desmond. *The Naked Ape* (New York: McGraw-Hill, 1968).

Morrison, Bruce John, Michael Enzle, Diana Dunaway, Michael Griffin, Kenneth Kneisel, and John Gimperling. "The effect of electrical shock and warning on cooperation in a non-zero-sum game," JCR, Vol. 15, No. 1, March 1971, pp. 105-108.

Muney, Barbara F. and Morton Deutsch. "The effects of role-reversal during the discussion of opposing viewpoints," JCR, Vol. 12, No. 3, September 1968, pp. 345-356.

Mytelka, Lynn K. "The salience of gains in Third-World integrative systems," World Politics, Vol. 25, No. 2, January 1973, pp. 236-250.

Newcombe, Alan G. "Initiatives and responses in foreign policy," Peace Research Reviews, Vol. 3, No. 3, June 1969.

--- and Hanna Newcombe. "Approaches to peace research," Alternative Approaches to Peace Research, Peace Research Reviews, Vol. 4, No. 4, February 1972, pp. 1-23.

Newcombe, Hanna. *Patterns of Nations: Interactions in the UN 1946-1971* (Oakville, Ont.: CPRI Press, 1973).

--- and Alan G. Newcombe. *Peace Research Around the World* (Oakville, Ont.: Canadian Peace Research Institute, 1969).

Nitz, Lawrence H. and James L. Philips. "The effects of divisibility of payoff on confederative behavior," JCR, Vol. 13, No. 3, September 1969, pp. 381-387.

Nordlinger, Eric A. Conflict Resolution in Divided Societies. Occasional Papers in International Affairs, No. 29. (Center for International Affairs, Harvard University, January 1972).

North, Robert C. "Axioms and Hypotheses Concerning Active and Passive Defense Systems and the Types of Response They Seem Likely to Evoke," in: *Weapons System Decisions,* ed. Bobrow, pp. 35-91.

---. "The Behavior of Nation-States: Problems of Conflict and Integration," in: *New Approaches to International Relations,* ed. Kaplan, pp. 303-356.

Northedge, F. S. and M. D. Donelan. *International Disputes. The Political Aspects* (New York: St. Martin's Press, 1971).

Nye, Joseph S., Jr. "Comparing Common Markets: A Revised Neo-Functionalist Model," in: *Regional Integration,* ed. Lindberg and Scheingold, pp. 192-231.

---. "Multinational enterprises and prospects for regional and global integration," Annals of the American Academy of Political and Social Science, Vol. 403, September 1972, pp. 116-126.

---. *Peace in Parts. Integration and Conflict in Regional Organization* (Boston: Little, Brown, 1971).

Observations on International Negotiations. Transcript of an informal Conference, Greenwich, Conn., June 1971. AED: The Schweppe Research and Education Fund; Academy for Educational Development.

Offshe, Richard, "The effectiveness of pacifist strategies: A theoretical approach," JCR, Vol. 15, No. 2, June 1971, pp. 261-269.

D'Oliveira e Sousa, Jorge. "Les métamorphoses de la guerre," Science et Paix, 1973, No. 2-3, pp. 3-19.

Olson, Mancur. "Increasing the incentives for international cooperation," International Organization, Vol. 25, No. 4, Autumn 1971, pp. 845-865.

Orwant, Carol J. and Jack E. Orwant. "A comparison of interpreted and abstract versions of mixed-motive games," JCR, Vol. 14, No. 1, March 1970, pp. 91-97.

Osgood, Charles E. *An Alternative to War or Surrender* (Urbana: University of Illinois Press, 1962).

Paige, Glenn D. "Comparative Case Analysis of Crisis Decisions: Korea and Cuba," in: *International Crises,* ed. Hermann, pp. 41-55.

Patchen, Martin. "Models of cooperation and conflict: A critical review," JCR, Vol. 14, No. 3, September 1970, pp. 389-407.

Peace and the Sciences, March 1973, No. 1: Scientific Symposium: "Principles, possible structures and perspectives for a system of collective security and cooperation in Europe," International Institute for Peace, Vienna, October 14-15, 1972.

Podell, Jerome E. and William M. Knapp. "The effect of mediation on the perceived firmness of the opponent," JCR, Vol. 13, No. 4, December 1969, pp. 511-520.

Pruitt, Dean G. "Definition of the Situation as a Determinant of International Action," in: *International Behavior,* ed. Kelman, pp. 393-432.

---. "Stability and sudden change in interpersonal and international affairs," JCR, Vol. 13, No. 1, March 1969, pp. 18-38.

---, and Richard C. Snyder, eds. *Theory and Research on the Causes of War* (Englewood Cliffs, N.J.: Prentice-Hall, 1969).

Puchala, Donald J. "Europeans and Europeanism in 1970," International Organization, Vol. 27, No. 3, Summer 1973, pp. 387-392.

Puchala, Donald J. "International Transactions and Regional Integration," in: *Regional Integration,* ed. Lindberg and Scheingold, pp. 128-159.

---. "Patterns of West European Integration," revision of a paper originally prepared for delivery at the Annual Meeting of the American Political Science Association in 1970.

Rapoport, Anatol. "Conflict Resolution in the Light of Game Theory and Beyond," in: *The Structure of Conflict,* ed. Swingle, pp. 1-43.

---. "Critique of Strategic Thinking," in: *International Conflict and Behavioral Science,* ed. Fisher, pp. 211-237.

---. "Les différentes conceptions d'une science de la paix," Science et Paix, 1973, No. 1, pp. 5-26.

---. "Directions in Peace Research," in: *Conflict Control and Conflict Resolution,* ed. Höglund and Ulrich, pp. 217-238.

---. *Fights, Games, and Debates* (Ann Arbor: University of Michigan Press, 1960).

---. "Games which simulate deterrence and disarmament," Peace Research Reviews, Vol. 1, No. 4, August 1967.

---. "International Relations and Game Theory," in: *Disarmament and Arms Control,* ed. Barnaby and Schaerf, pp. 241-252.

---. "Is peace research applicable?" JCR, Vol. 14, No. 2, 1970, pp. 277-286.

Rappoport, Leon. "Cognitive conflict as a function of socially induced cognitive differences," JCR, Vol. 13, No. 1, March 1969, pp. 143-148.

Raser, John R. "The Failure of Fail-Safe," in: *Peace and the War Industry,* ed. Kenneth E. Boulding (Chicago: Aldine, 1970), pp. 105-124.

---. "Learning and Affect in International Politics," in: *International Politics and Foreign Policy,* Rosenau, pp. 432-441.

---, and Wayman J. Crow. "A Simulation Study of Deterrence Theories," in: *Social Processes in International Relations,* ed. Kriesberg, pp. 372-389.

Raven, Bertram H. and Arie W. Kruglanski. "Conflict and Power," in: *The Structure of Conflict,* ed. Swingle, pp. 69-109.

Rittberger, Volker. "International organization and violence," JPR, 1973, No. 3, pp. 217-226.

Robinson, James A. "Crisis: An Appraisal of Concepts and Theories," in: *International Crises,* ed. Hermann, pp. 20-35.

Rohrl-Wedge, Vivian J. and Bryant Wedge. "The role of perception in international politics," International Studies Newsletter, Preliminary Issue A, Fall 1973, pp. 32-50.

Röling, Bert v.a. *Inleiding tot de Wetenschap van Oorlog en Vrede. Teleac cursus Polemologie* (Assen: Van Gorcum, 1968). German edition: *Krieg ist kein Schicksal.* (Neukirchen-Vluyn: Neukirchener Verlag, 1971).

Rosen, Steven. "War Power and the Willingness to Suffer," in: *Peace, War, and Numbers,* ed. Russett, pp. 167-183.

Rosenau, James N., *International Politics and Foreign Policy. A Reader in Research and Theory* (New York: Free Press, 1969).

---, and George H. Ramsey, Jr. "External vs. Internal Sources of Foreign Policy Behavior: Testing the Stability of an Intriguing Set of Findings," paper prepared for delivery at the Ninth World Congress of the International Political Science Association, Montreal, August 1973.

Rummel, Rudolf J. "The Relationship Between National Attributes and Foreign Conflict Behavior," in: *Quantitative International Politics,* ed. Singer, pp. 187-214.

---. "United States Foreign Relations: Conflict, Cooperation and Attribute Distances," in: *Peace, War, and Numbers,* ed. Russett, pp. 71-113.

Russett, Bruce M., ed. *Peace, War, and Numbers* (Beverly Hills: Sage, 1972).

---. "The Revolt of the Masses: Public Opinion on Military Expenditures," in: *Peace, War, and Numbers,* ed. Russett, pp. 299-319.

---, and John D. Sullivan. "Collective goods and international organization," International Organization, Vol. 25, No. 4, Autumn 1971, pp. 845-865.

dos Santos, Theotonio. "The structure of dependency," American Economic Review, Vol. 60, No. 3, pp. 203-216.

Saraydar, Edward. "A certainty-equivalent model of bargaining," JCR, Vol. 15, No. 3, September 1971, pp. 281-297.

Savage, Richard and Karl W. Deutsch. "A statistical model of the gross analysis of transaction flows," Econometrica, Vol. 28, No. 3, July 1960, pp. 551-572.

Scheingold, Stuart A. "Domestic and International Consequences of Regional Integration," in: *Regional Integration,* ed. Lindberg and Scheingold, pp. 374-398.

Schmid, Herman. "Peace research as a technology for pacification," Proceedings of the International Peace Research Association Third Conference, Vol. I, pp. 20-69.

---. "Politics and peace research," JPR, 1968, pp. 217-232.

Schmitter, Philippe C. "A Revised Theory of Regional Integration," in: *Regional Integration,* ed. Lindberg and Scheingold, pp. 232-264.

Schnippenkoetter, Swidbert. "Gewaltdrohung und Gewaltverbot als Probleme der internationalen Politik," Jahrbuch für Friedens- und Konfliktforschung, I, 1971, pp. 67-81.

Schwartz, David C. "Decision-Making in Historical and Simulated Crises," in: *International Crises,* ed. Hermann, pp. 167-184.

Scott, William A. "Psychological and Social Correlates of International Images," in: *International Behavior,* ed. Kelman, pp. 70-103.

Senghaas, Dieter. *Abschreckung und Frieden. Studien zur Kritik organisierter Friedlosigkeit* (Frankfurt: Fischer, 1972).

---. "Armement par une politique de maîtrise des armements? Réflexions sur les négociacions MBFR," Science et Paix, 1973, No. 2-3, pp. 20-48.

---. "Conflict formations in contemporary international society," JPR, No. 3, pp. 163-184.

---. "Friedensforschung–Theoretische Fragestellungen und praktische Probleme," Jahrbuch für Friedens- und Konfliktforschung, II, 1972, pp. 10-22.

---, ed. *Imperialismus und strukturelle Gewalt. Analysen über abhängige Reproduktion* (Frankfurt: Suhrkamp, 1972).

---. "Kompositionsprobleme in der Friedensforschung," in: *Kritische Friedensforschung,* ed. Senghaas, pp. 313-361.

---, ed. *Kritische Friedensforschung* (Frankfurt: Suhrkamp, 1971).

---. *Rüstung und Militarismus* (Frankfurt: Suhrkamp, 1972).

---. "Zur Analyse von Drohpolitik in den internationalen Beziehungen," Jahrbuch für Friedens- und Konfliktforschung, I, 1971, pp. 89-132.

---, ed. *Zur Pathologie des Rüstungswettlaufs. Beiträge zur Friedens- und Konfliktforschung* (Freiburg: Rombach, 1970).

---. "Zur Pathologie organisierter Friedlosigkeit," in: *Friedensforschung,* ed. Krippendorff, pp. 217-259.

---, Volker Rittberger, and Burkhard Luber. "MBFR: Aufrüstung durch Rüstungskontrolle," Aus politik und zeitgeschichte, Beilage zu: Das Parlament, March 31, 1973, pp. 26-54.

Sharp, Gene. *Exploring Nonviolent Alternatives* (Boston: Porter Sargent, 1973).

---. *The Politics of Nonviolent Action* (Boston: Porter Sargent, 1973).

Shubik, Martin. "The Dollar Auction game: A paradox in non-cooperative behavior and escalation," JCR, Vol. 15, No. 1, March 1971, pp. 109-111.

---. "Game theory, behavior, and the paradox of the Prisoner's Dilemma: Three solutions," JCR, Vol. 14, No. 2, June 1970, pp. 181-193.

---, and Garry D. Brewer. Reviews of Selected Books and Articles on Gaming and Simulation. A Report prepared for Advanced Research Projects Agency–R-732-ARPA (Santa Monica, Calif.: RAND Corp., 1972).

---, G. Brewer, and E. Savage. The Literature of Gaming, Simulation, and Model-Building: Index and Critical Abstracts. A Report prepared for Advanced Research Projects Agency–R-620-ARPA (Santa Monica, Calif.: RAND Corp., 1972).

Simons, Dominique. "Fondements de la science de la paix," Science et Paix, 1973, No. 1, pp. 27-37.

Singer, J. David. "The correlates of war project: Interim report and rationale," World Politics, Vol. 24, No. 2, January 1972, pp. 243-270.

---. "Modern International War. From Conjecture to Explanation," in: *The Search for World Order,* ed. Lepawsky et al., pp. 47-71.

---, ed. *Quantitative International Politics: Insights and Evidence* (New York: Free Press, 1968).

---, Stuart Bremer, and John Stuckey. "Capability Distribution, Uncertainty, and Major Power War, 1820-1965," in: *Peace, War, and Numbers,* ed. Russett, pp. 19-48.

---, and Melvin Small. "Alliance Aggregation and the Onset of War, 1815-1945," in: *Quantitative International Politics,* ed. Singer, pp. 247-286.

--- and ---. *The Wages of War. A Statistical Handbook, 1816-1965* (New York: Wiley, 1972).

Siverson, Randolph M. "International conflict and perceptions of injury: The case of the Suez crisis," International Studies Quarterly, Vol. 14, No. 2, June 1970, pp. 157-165.

---. "Role and perception in international crises: The cases of Israeli and Egyptian decision makers in national capitals and the United Nations," International Organization, Vol. 27, No. 3, Summer 1973, pp. 329-345.

Skjelsbaek, Kjell. Peace and the System of International Organizations. Magister's Thesis. Institute of Political Science, University of Oslo; International Peace Research Institute, Oslo, 1970.

Small, Melvin and J. David Singer. "Formal alliances, 1816-1965: An extension of the basic data," JPR, 1969, No. 3, pp. 257-282.

--- and ---. "The diplomatic importance of states, 1816-1970: An extension and refinement of the indicator," World Politics, Vol. 25, No. 4, July 1973, pp. 577-599.

Smith, William P. and Timothy D. Emmons. "Outcome information and competitiveness in interperson bargaining," JCR, Vol. 13, No. 2, June 1969, pp. 262-270.

Smoker, Paul. "International relations simulations," Peace Research Reviews, Vol. 3, No. 6, 1970.

---. "Nation State Escalation and International Integration," in: *Social Processes in International Relations,* ed. Kriesberg, pp. 486-504.

---. "A time series analysis of Sino-Indian relations," JCR, Vol. 13, No. 2, June 1969, pp. 172-191.

Snyder, Glenn H. "Crisis Bargaining," in: *International Crises,* ed. Hermann, pp. 217-256.

---. "Prisoner's Dilemma and 'Chicken' models in international politics," International Studies Quarterly, Vol. 15, No. 1, March 1971, pp. 66-103.

Starke, J. G., Q. C. *An Introduction to the Science of Peace (Irenology)* (Leyden: Sijthoff, 1968).

Stegenga, James A. "Peacekeeping: Post-mortems or previews?" International Organization, Vol. 27, No. 3, Summer 1973, pp. 373-385.

---. "United Nations Peace-Keeping: Patterns and Prospects," in: *The Process of International Organization,* ed. Robert S. Wood, (New York: Random House, 1971), pp. 299-314.

Storr, Anthony. *Human Aggression* (New York: Athenaeum, 1968).

Sullivan, John D. "Cooperating to Conflict: Sources of Informal Alignments," in: *Peace, War, and Numbers,* ed. Russett, pp. 115-138.

Sullivan, Michael P. with the assistance of William Thomas. "Symbolic Involvement as a Correlate of Escalation: The Vietnam Case," in: *Peace, War, and Numbers,* ed. Russett, pp. 185-212.

Sunkel, Osvaldo. "Big business and 'dependencia'; A Latin American view," Foreign Affairs, Vol. 50, No. 3, April 1972, pp. 517-531.

---. "Intégration capitaliste transnationale et désintégration nationale en Amérique latine," Politique Etrangère, Vol. 35, No. 6, 1970, pp. 641-700.

Swingle, Paul G. "Dangerous Games," in: *The Structure of Conflict,* ed. Swingle, pp. 235-276.

---, ed. *The Structure of Conflict* (New York: Academic Press, 1970).

Tanter, Raymond. "The policy relevance of models in world politics," JCR, Vol. 16, No. 4, December 1972, pp. 555-583.

Tedeschi, James T. "Threats and Promises," in: *The Structure of Conflict,* ed. Swingle, pp. 155-191.

---, Thomas Bonoma, and Noel Novinson. "Behavior of a threatener: Retaliation vs. fixed opportunity costs," JCR, Vol. 14, No. 1, March 1970, pp. 69-76.

Terhune, Kenneth W. "The Effects of Personality in Cooperation and Conflict," in: *The Structure of Conflict,* ed. P. Swingle, pp. 193-234.

---, and Joseph M. Firestone. "Global war, limited war and peace: Hypotheses from three experimental worlds," International Studies Quarterly, Vol. 14, No. 2, June 1970, pp. 195-218.

Terrell, Louis M. "Societal stress, political instability, and levels of military efforts," JCR, Vol. 15, No. 3, September 1971, pp. 329-346.

Thompson, William R. "The regional subsystem. A conceptual explication and a propositional inventory," International Studies Quarterly, Vol. 17, No. 1, March 1973, pp. 89-117.

Tompkins, E. Berkeley, ed. *Peaceful Change in Modern Society* (Stanford, Calif.: Hoover Institution Press, Stanford University, 1971).

Toynbee, Arnold J. "War in Our Time," in: *The Search for World Order,* ed. Lepawsky et al., pp. 3-22.

Tromp, Hylke. "Notes sur la science de la paix et le movement pour la paix," Science et Paix, 1973, No. 1, pp. 64-70.

Tsipis, K. "U.S. Strategic Weapons–Offensive and Defensive," in: *Disarmament and Arms Control,* ed. Barnaby and Schaerf, pp. 23-40.

Underdal, Arild. "Multinational negotiation parties: The case of the European community," Cooperation and Conflict, Vol. 8, No. 3-4, 1973, pp. 173-182.

Verwey, Wil D. *Economic Development, Peace, and International Law* (Assen: Van Gorcum, 1972).

Vilmar, Fritz. "Kommutation–Friedenspolitische und friedenspädagogische Bedeutung produktiver Lernprozesse zwischen Ost und West," Jahrbuch für Friedens- und Konfliktforschung, II, 1972, pp. 103-116.

———. "The military-industrial complex in West Germany and the consequences for peace policy," JPR, 1973, No. 3, pp. 251-258.

———. "Systematischer Entwurf zur Kritischen Friedensforschung," in: *Kritische Friedensforschung,* ed. Senghaas, pp. 362-395.

Vincent, Jack E. and Edward W. Schwerin. "Ratios of force and escalation in a game situation," JCR, Vol. 15, No. 4, December 1971, pp. 489-511.

Visine, Francois. *De la Paix* (Paris: la pensée universelle, 1972).

Wall, G. R. Bipolarization and the International System: 1946-1970. Research Report UI-72-2. The Swedish Institute of International Affairs, Stockholm, 1972.

Wallace, Donnel and Paul Rothaus. "Communication, group loyalty, and trust in the PD game," JCR, Vol. 13, No. 3, September 1969, pp. 370-380.

Wallace, Michael D. "Status, Formal Organization and Arms Control as Factors Leading to the Onset of War, 1820-1964," in: *Peace, War, and Numbers,* ed. Russett, pp. 49-69.

———. *War and Rank Among Nations* (Lexington, Mass.: D. C. Heath, 1973).

Waskow, Arthur I. "Nonlethal Equivalents of War," in: *International Conflict and Behavioral Science,* ed. Fisher, pp. 123-141.

Waterkamp, Rainer. *Konfliktforschung und Friedensplanung* (Stuttgart: Kohlhammer, 1971).

Wehr, Paul. Conflict Management in Social Systems: A Guide for Teaching and Research. Prepared for the American Association for the Advancement of Science (AAAS) and for the Consortium on Peace Research, Education and Development. University of Colorado, 1973.

———. "Creative Conflict Management," AAAS Short Guide (no date, circa 1972/1973).

———, and Michael Washburn. *Toward the Study of Peace. A Guide to Peace Studies Development* (COPRED: mimeo, no date).

Weichelt, E. and J. Kirsten, eds. *Zu den völkerrechtlichen Prinzipien der friedlichen Koexistenz.* Aktuelle Beiträge zur Staats- und Rechtswissenschaft aus den sozialistischen Ländern, Heft 7. (Potsdam-Babelsberg, 1964).

Weizsäcker, Carl Friedrich Freiherr von. "Bedrohungsvorstellungen als Faktor der internationalen Politik. Eine Einführung," Jahrbuch für Friedens- und Konfliktforschung, I, 1971, pp. 15-29.

———, ed. *Kriegsfolgen und Kriegsverhütung.* (Munich: Hanser, 1971).

Weizsäcker, Ernst von, ed. *BC-Waffen und Friedenspolitik.* Studien zur Friedensforschung, Vol. 5 (Munich: Kösel; Stuttgart: Klett, 1970).

Wettig, Gerhard. "Der Wirkzusammenhang und die Konfliktfunktion von Bedrohungsvorstellungen in der zwischenstaatlichen Politik als wissenschaftliche Probleme," Jahrbuch für Friedens- und Konfliktforschung, I, 1971, pp. 159-194.

Wilkenfeld, Jonathan. "Models for the Analysis of Foreign Conflict Behavior of States," in: *Peace, War, and Numbers,* ed. Russett, pp. 275-298.

Wilson, Warner. "Cooperation and the cooperativeness of the other player," JCR, Vol. 13, No. 1, March 1969, pp. 110-117.

———. Reciprocation and other techniques for inducing cooperation in the Prisoner's Dilemma game," JCR, Vol. 15, No. 2, June 1971, pp. 167-195.

Wohlstetter, Albert. "Is there a strategic arms race?" Foreign Policy, No. 15, Summer 1974, pp. 3-20; No. 16, Fall 1974, pp. 48-81.

———. "Theory and Opposed-Systems Design," in: *New Approaches to International Relations,* ed. Kaplan, pp. 19-53.

Wolf, Peter. "International organization and attitude change: A re-examination of the functionalist approach," International Organization, Vol. 27, No. 3, Summer 1973, pp. 347-371.

Wright, Quincy. "Building a Social System for Mankind," in: *Worldsociety,* ed. Landheer et al., pp. 178-196.

Wulf, Christoph, ed. *Handbook on Peace Education* (Frankfurt-Oslo: IPRA Education Committee, 1974).

Yalem, Ronald J. "Controlled communication and conflict resolution," JPR, 1971, No. 3-4, pp. 263-272.

Young, Oran R. *The Intermediaries. Third Parties in International Crises* (Princeton, N.J.: Princeton University Press, 1967).

---. *The Politics of Force. Bargaining During International Crises* (Princeton, N.J.: Princeton University Press, 1968).

Zellentin, "Europäische Friedensordnung: Zielvorstellungen, Strategien und Handlungspotentiale," Jahrbuch für Friedens- und Konfliktforschung, II, 1972, pp. 72-86.

---. "Intersystemic regionalism and peace in Europe," JPR, 1973, No. 3, pp. 235-244.

Zinnes, Dina A. "The Expression and Perception of Hostility in Prewar Crisis: 1914," in: *Quantitative International Politics,* ed. Singer, pp. 85-119.

---, Robert C. North, and Howard E. Koch, Jr. "Capability, Threat, and the Outbreak of War," in: *International Politics and Foreign Policy,* ed. James N. Rosenau (New York: Free Press, 1961).

---, Joseph L. Zinnes and Robert D. McClure. "Hostility in Diplomatic Communication: A Study of the 1914 Crisis," in: *International Crisis,* ed. Hermann, pp. 139-162.

SUPPLEMENTARY BIBLIOGRAPHY

Alcock, Norman Z. "An empirical measure of internation threat: Some preliminary implications for the Middle East conflict," Peace Research Society (International), Papers, XV, 1970, pp. 51-72. (Hereinafter abbreviated PRSI)

——— and William Eckhardt. "Comparisons between the attitudes and behaviours of individuals and nations," Peace Research 5, No. 2, April 1974, pp. 33-44.

Alger, Chadwick F. "Decision-Making in Public Bodies of International Organizations (ILO, WHO, WMO, UN): A Preliminary Research Report," in: Dusan Sidjanski (ed.), *Political Decision Making Processes: Studies in National, Comparative and International Politics* (Amsterdam: Elsevier Scientific Publishing Company, 1973), pp. 205-229.

———. "Negotiation, regional groups, interaction and public debate in the development of consensus in the United Nations General Assembly," Transactions of the Sixth World Congress of Sociology, Evian 1966, (International Sociological Association, 1970), Vol. III, pp. 321-343.

———. "Research on research: A decade of quantitative and field research on international organizations," International Organization XXIV, No. 3, 1970, pp. 414-450.

——— and David Hoovler. "The Feudal Structure of Systems of International Organizations," paper prepared for the conference of the International Peace Research Association in Varanasi, India, 1974.

Alker, Hayward R., Jr. "Methodological Implications of Interdependence Controversies," paper prepared for the Annual Meeting of the International Studies Association in St. Louis, Mo., 1974.

——— and William J. Greenberg. "The UN Charter: Alternate Pasts and Alternate Futures," in: E. H. Fedder (ed.), *The United Nations: Problems and Prospects* (St. Louis: University of Missouri Press, 1971), pp. 113-142.

Axelrod, Robert. "Psycho-algebra: A mathematical theory of cognition and choice with an application to the British Eastern committee in 1918," PRSI, Papers, XVIII, 1972, pp. 113-131.

Azar, Edward E. "The dimensionality of violent conflict: A quantitative analysis," PRSI, Papers, XV, 1970, pp. 122-167.

Bailey, Sydney. "The veto in the Security Council," International Conciliation, No. 566, January 1968.

Bennett, James and Hayward R. Alker, Jr. "Restructuring Processes in the Global Stratification System: An Outline of a Simulation Model," paper prepared for the Annual Meeting of the International Studies Association in New York City, 1973.

van Benthem von den Bergh, Gottfried. "A note on time demarcation in conflict theory," Instant Research on Peace and Violence, IV, No. 2, 1974, pp. 110-113.

Bobrow, Davis B. "Ecology of international games: Requirement for a model of the international system," PRSI, Papers, XI, 1969, pp. 67-87.

Bonoma, Thomas V. "Deescalating Two-Party Conflict: Accommodation and Timing as Indices of Source Intent and Mediators of Target Compliance," (Chicago: Institute for Juvenile Research, 1974).

Bonoma, Thomas V. "A Social Psychological Perspective on the Escalation and Deescalation of Conflict: A Review and Reconceptualization," (Chicago: Institute for Juvenile Research, 1973).

——— and James T. Tedeschi. "The Relative Efficacies of Escalation and Deescalation for Compliance-Gaining in Two-Party Conflicts," 1974.

Boulding, Elise. "The Child and Non-Violent Social Change," in: Wulf (ed.), *Handbook on Peace Education,* pp. 101-132.

Boulding, Kenneth E. "The balance of peace," PRSI, Papers, XIII, 1970, pp. 59-65.

——— and Tapan Mukerjee. "Unprofitable empire: Britain in India, 1800-1967, a critique of the Hobson-Lenin thesis on imperialism," PRSI, Papers, XVI, 1971, pp. 1-21.

Bouthoul, Gaston. "Les baromètres polémologiques," Etudes Polémologiques, 4, April 1972, pp. 30-54.

———. "Définition et délimitation de la paix," Etudes Polémologiques, 11, January 1974, pp. 45-51.

———. *La Paix* (Que Sais-Je? No. 1600) (Paris: Presses Universitaires de France, 1974).

———. "Sociologie de l'aggressivité," Etudes Polémologiques, 7, January 1973, pp. 29-36.

Brady, Linda P. "Threat, Decision Time, and Awareness: The Impact of Situational Variables on Foreign Policy Behavior," Ph.D. thesis, Ohio State University, 1974.

Brecher, Michael. *Decisions in Israel's Foreign Policy* (London: Oxford University Press, 1974).

———. "Environmental Inputs and Decisions for War and Peace: The Israeli Experience," paper prepared for the Ninth World Congress of IPSA in Montreal, 1973.

Bremer, Stuart A. "An Appraisal of the Substantive Findings of the Inter-Nation Simulation Project," paper prepared for the Annual Meeting of the International Studies Association in St. Louis, 1974.

Burrowes, Robert and Jose Garriga-Pico. "The road to the Six Day War: Relational analysis of conflict and cooperation," Peace Science Society (International), Papers, XXII, 1974, pp. 47-74. (Hereinafter abbreviated PSSI)

Carrère, René. "Réflexions polémologiques sur la crise nucléaire de Cuba 1962," Etudes Polémologiques, 3, January 1972, pp. 25-54.

Choucri, Nazli. "Applications of econometric analysis to forecasting in international relations," PSSI, Papers, XXI, 1973, pp. 15-39.

——— and Robert C. North. "The determinants of international violence," PRSI, Papers, XII, 1969, pp. 33-63.

——— and ———. *Nations in Conflict; Population, Expansion, and War* (San Francisco: W. H. Freeman, 1974).

Darnton, Geoffrey. "The concept 'peace'," *Proceedings of the International Peace Research Association Fourth Conference,* pp. 105-116.

Dasgupta, Sugata. "Education for a Non-Violent Society," in: Wulf (ed.), *Handbook on Peace Education,* pp. 87-99.

———. "Peacelessness and Maldevelopment–A New Approach to Peace Research in Developing Nations," paper prepared for the International Peace Research Association Conference in Tallberg, Sweden, 1967.

Deutsch, Karl W. *Peace Research. The Need, the Problems, and the Prospects* (Middlebury, Vermont: Middlebury College, 1972).

———. "Theories of Imperialism and Neocolonialism," in: Steven J. Rosen and James R. Kurth (eds.), *Testing Theories of Economic Imperialism* (Lexington, Mass.: Lexington, 1974), pp. 15-34.

Deutsch, Karl W. and Dieter Senghaas. "The Steps to War: A Survey of System Levels, Decision Stages, and Research Results," in *Sage International Yearbook of Foreign Policy Studies,* ed. Partick J. McGowan (Beverly Hills, Calif.: Sage, 1973), pp. 275-329.

DGFK-Informationen, Sonderheft: Schwerpunkt II: Konflikte zwischen westeuropäischen Industriestaaten und Entwicklungsländern und deren friedliche Uberwindung (Bonn, West Germany: Deutsche Gesellschaft für Friedens- und Konfliktforschung).

Dolan, Michael B. "A Quantitative Analysis of the Neo-Functionalist and Systemic Approaches to the Study of Regional Integration," paper prepared for the Annual Meeting of the International Studies Association, St. Louis, 1974.

Dowty, Alan. "Conflict in war-potential politics: An approach to historical macroanalysis," PRSI, Papers, XIII, 1970, pp. 85-103.

East, Maurice A. "Rank-dependent interaction and mobility: Two aspects of international stratification," PRSI, Papers, XIV, 1970, pp. 113-127.

Ebert, Theodor. "Vermutungen über den dialektischen Prozess zur Sozialen Verteidigung," in: *Soziale Verteidigung,* pp. 2-17.

---. "Von agressiver Drohung zu defensiver Warnung. Das Konzept der sozialen Verteidigung," in: Senghaas (ed.), *Friedensforschung und Gesellschaftskritik,* pp. 152-200.

Eckhardt, William, Chris Young, Edward Azar, and Thomas Sloan. "Arab-Israeli perceptions of the Middle East conflict," Peace Research, 5, No. 3, July 1974.

Engelhardt, Klaus and Karl-Heinz Heise. *Militär-Industrie-Komplex im staatsmonopolistischen Herrschaftssystem* (Berlin: Staatsverlag der Deutschen Demokratischen Republik, 1974).

Etienne, Henri. "L'Emergence d'une Souveraineté Européenne," paper prepared for the Ninth World Congress of IPSA, Montreal, 1973.

Falk, Richard A. *A Study of Future Worlds* (New York: Free Press, 1975).

---. *This Endangered Planet: Prospects and Proposals for Human Survival* (New York: Random House, 1971).

---. "Toward a New World Order: Modest Methods and Drastic Visions," in: *On the Creation of a Just World Order,* ed. Mendlovitz, pp. 211-258.

--- and Saul H. Mendlovitz (eds.), *Regional Politics and World Order* (San Francisco: W. H. Freeman, 1973).

Frey, Bruno S. "An insurance system for peace," PSSI, Papers, XXII, 1974, pp. 111-128.

Galtung, Johan. "Nichtmilitärische Verteidigungsmassnahmen," in: *Soziale Verteidigung,* pp. 84-94.

---. "Nonterritorial Actors and the Problem of Peace," in: *On the Creation of a Just World Order,* ed. Mendlovitz, pp. 151-188.

---. "On Peace Education," in: Wulf (ed.), *Handbook on Peace Education,* pp. 153-171.

---. "Peace education for and with peace: Is it possible?" Proceedings of the International Peace Research Association Fourth Conference, pp. 169-187.

Gantzel, Klaus Jürgen. "Armament dynamics in the East-West conflict: An arms race?" PSSI, Papers, XX, 1973, pp. 1-24.

Goldmann, Kjell. "The Road to Peaceful Coexistence: Notes on the Analysis of European Tension, 1946-1970," paper prepared for the Ninth World Congress of the IPSA in Montreal, 1973.

Gurr, Ted Robert. "Social Change and the Interplay of Internal and International Political Conflicts," paper prepared for the Ninth World Congress of IPSA in Montreal, 1973.

Haas, Michael. "Communication factors in decision making," PRSI, Papers, XII, 1969, pp. 65-86.

Hare, A. P. and H. Blumberg (eds.), *Nonviolent Direct Action* (Washington, D.C.: Corpus Books, 1968).

Hermann, Margaret C. "Leader Personality and Foreign Policy Behavior," in: James N. Rosenau (ed.), *Comparing Foreign Policies: Theories, Findings, and Methods* (Beverly Hills, Calif.: Sage, 1974), pp. 1-58.

Hilton, Gordon. "The 1914 studies–A reassessment of the evidence and some further thoughts," PRSI, Papers, XIII, 1970, pp. 117-141.

Hoovler, David. "Structural Theories of Imperialism," paper prepared for the Annual Meeting of the International Studies Association in Washington, D.C., 1975.

Hopmann, P. Terrence and Charles Walcott. "Bargaining in International Negotiations," paper prepared for the Midwest meetings of the International Studies Association and the Peace Science Society (International), St. Louis, Mo., 1973.

Horn, Klaus. "Menschliche Aggressivität und internationale Politik. Vorklärungen," in: Senghaas (ed.), *Friedensforschung und Gesellschaftskritik,* pp. 116-151.

Howard, Nigel. "The Arab-Israeli conflict: A metagame analysis done in 1970," PRSI, Papers, XIX, 1972, pp. 35-60.

———. "Metagame analysis of Vietnam policy," PRSI, Papers, X, 1968, pp. 126-142.

Isard, Walter. "The veto-incremax procedure: Potential for Vietnam conflict resolution," PRSI, Papers, X, pp. 148-162.

——— and Panagis Liossatos. "The general equilibrium system for nations: The case of many small nations and one big power," PRSI, Papers, XIX, 1972, pp. 1-28.

——— and ———. "A small nation–Two big powers model," PRSI, Papers, XVIII, 1972, pp. 1-21.

——— and Tony E. Smith. "The major power confrontation in the Middle East: Some analyses of short-run, middle-run and long-run considerations," PRSI, Papers, XV, 1970, pp. 31-50.

Ishida, Takeshi. "Beyond the traditional concepts of peace in different cultures," JPR, 1969, No. 2, pp. 133-145.

Jahn, Egbert. "Civilian defense and civilian offensive," JPR, 1973, No. 3, pp. 285-294.

———. "Soziohistorische Voraussetzungen der Sozialen Verteidigung," in: *Soziale Verteidigung,* pp. 28-36.

Joenniemi, Pertti. "An analysis of the economic consequences of disarmament in Finland," PRSI, Papers, XIII, 1970, pp. 29-46.

——— and Adam Roberts. "Civil resistance and the law of military occupation," Instant Research on Peace and Violence, IV, No. 1, 1974, pp. 38-46.

Kelman, Herbert C. "International Interchanges: Some Contributions from Theories of Attitude Change," paper prepared for the Annual Meeting of the International Studies Association, St. Louis, Mo., 1973.

Kent, George. "Plan for designing the future," Bulletin of Peace Proposals, Vol. 3, 1972, pp. 280-285.

———. "Political Design," Research Report No. 63, The Dimensionality of Nations Project, University of Hawaii, July 1972.

Kent, George. "Prescribing Foreign Policy," Research Report No. 59, The Dimensionality of Nations Project, University of Hawaii, January 1972.

———. "World Order Design: What Could be More Practical?", unpublished manuscript.

Kothari, Rajni. *Footsteps into the Future: Diagnosis of the Present World and a Design for an Alternative* (New York: Free Press, 1975).

———. "World Politics and World Order: The Issue of Autonomy," in: *On the Creation of a Just World Order,* ed. Mendlovitz, pp. 39-69.

Krippendorff, Ekkehart. "The state as a focus of peace research," PRSI, Papers, XVI, 1971, pp. 47-60.

Kurth, James R. "Economic Systems, Hegemonial Policies and International Conflicts," paper prepared for the Ninth World Congress of IPSA, Montreal, 1973.

Lagos, Gustavo. "The Revolution of Being," in: *On the Creation of a Just World Order,* ed. Mendlovitz, pp. 71-109.

Lambelet, John C. "The Anglo-German dreadnought race, 1905-1914," PSSI, Papers, XXII, 1974, pp. 1-45.

Lee, Jong Ryool and Jeffrey S. Milstein. "A political economy of the Vietnam war, 1965-1972," PSSI, Papers, XXI, 1973, pp. 41-63.

Lentz, Theo. F. *Towards a Technology of Peace* (St. Louis, Mo.: Peace Research Laboratory, 1972).

Levine, Edward P. "Mediation in international politics. A universe and some observations," PRSI, Papers, XVIII, 1972, pp. 23-43.

Lin, Paul T.K. "Development Guided by Values: Comments on China's Road and Its Implications," in: *On the Creation of a Just World Order,* ed. Mendlovitz, pp. 259-296.

Lumsden, Malvern. "New military technology and the erosion of international law: The case of the dum-dum bullets today," Instant Research on Peace and Violence, IV, No. 1, 1974, pp. 15-20.

Masters, Roger D. "A Multi-Bloc Model of the International System," in: *Regional Politics and World Order,* ed. Falk and Mendlovitz, pp. 10-29.

Mazrui, Ali A. "World Culture and the Search for Human Consensus," in: *On the Creation of a Just World Order,* ed. Mendlovitz, pp. 1-37.

Mendlovitz, Saul H. (ed.), *On the Creation of a Just World Order. Preferred Worlds for the 1990's* (New York: Free Press, 1975).

——— and Thomas C. Weiss. "Toward Consensus. The World Order Models Project of the Institute for World Order," in: Grenville Clark and Louis Sohn. *Introduction to World Peace Through World Law* (Chicago: World Without War Publications, 1973), pp. 74-97.

Miller, Lynn H. "The Prospects for Order Through Regional Security," in: *Regional Politics and World Order,* ed. Falk and Mendlovitz, pp. 50-74.

Milstein, Jeffrey. "Soviet and American influences on the Arab-Israeli arms race: A quantitative analysis," PRSI, Papers, XV, 1970, pp. 6-27.

——— and William Charles Mitchell. "Computer simulation of international processes: The Vietnam war and the pre-World War I naval race," PRSI, Papers, XII, 1969, pp. 117-136.

——— and ———. "Dynamics of the Vietnam conflict: A quantitative analysis and predictive computer simulation," PRSI, Papers, X, 1968, pp. 163-213.

Mitchell, William C. "The role of stress in the war in Vietnam: An analysis of United States actions and public statements, 1964-1967," PRSI, Papers, XVII, 1971, pp. 47-60.

Modelski, George. "Conflict Stability and Intergovernmental Elite Networks: A Study of World Order in 1965," paper prepared for the Ninth World Congress of IPSA, Montreal, 1973.

---. "War and the great powers," PRSI, Papers, XVIII, 1972, pp. 45-59.

Morse, Edward L. "The politics of interdependence," International Organization, XXIII, No. 2, Spring 1969, pp. 311-326.

---. "Transnational economic processes," International Organization, XXV, No. 3, Summer 1971, pp. 23-47.

Mushakoji, Kinhide. "Peace Research and Education in a Global Perspective," in: Wulf (ed.), *Handbook on Peace Education,* pp. 3-18.

---. "Structures for peace in the North-South perspective," Proceedings of the International Peace Research Association Fourth Conference, pp. 223-238.

Mushkat, Marion. "Genèse et avenir du sous-développement," Etudes Polémologiques, 11, January 1974, pp. 30-35.

Myrdal, Gunnar. *Asian Drama. An Inquiry into the Poverty of Nations* (New York: Twentieth Century Fund and Pantheon, 1968).

---. *The Challenge of World Poverty. A World Anti-Poverty Program in Outline* (New York: Pantheon, 1970).

Newcombe, Alan. "The Inter-Nation Tensiometer and the Middle East," paper prepared for the Annual Meeting of the International Studies Association, St. Louis, Mo., 1974.

---. "Toward the development of an inter-nation tensiometer," PRSI, Papers, XIII, 1970, pp. 11-27.

---, John D. Barber, James Wert, Mark Haven, and Cathy Hiebert. "An improved inter-nation tensiometer for the prediction of war," Peace Research Reviews, V, No. 4, 1974.

---, Nora S. Newcombe, and Gary D. Landrus, "The development of an inter-nation tensiometer," International Interactions, I, No. 1, 1974, pp. 3-18.

---, and James Wert. "The use of an inter-nation tensiometer for the prediction of war," PSSI, Papers, XXI, 1973, pp. 73-83.

Newcombe, Hanna and Gernot Koehler. "The Balance of Peace: Predicting International Friendship and Hostility from Cognitive Balance Triangles," paper prepared for the Annual Meeting of the International Studies Association, St. Louis, Mo., 1974.

Nye, Joseph S. "Regional Institutions," in: *The Structure of the International Environment,* Vol. IV of Cyril E. Black and Richard A. Falk, *The Future of the International Legal Order* (Princeton, N.J.: Princeton University Press, 1972), pp. 425-447.

Ogley, Roderick. "Investigating the effects of threats," PRSI, Papers, XVI, 1971, pp. 61-93.

--- and David Thomas. "New hypotheses in game experiments," PSSI, Papers, XXII, 1974, pp. 75-110.

Osgood, Charles E. "GRIT for MFBR: A Proposal for Unfreezing Force-Level Postures in Europe," conference paper, 1974.

Pearson, Frederic. "Interaction in an international political sub-system: The 'Middle East,' 1963-1964," PRSI, Papers, XV, 1970, pp. 73-79.

Phillips, Warren R. "The dynamics of behavioral action and reaction in international conflict," PRSI, Papers, XVIII, 1971, pp. 31-46.

Poirier, Lucien. "Problématique polémologique et volonté de création," Etudes Polémologiques, 12, April 1974, pp. 3-24.

Puchala, Donald J. "Internal Order and Peace: An Integrated Europe in World Affairs," paper prepared for the Ninth World Congress of IPSA, Montreal, 1973.

––– and Stuart I. Fagan. "International politics in the 1970's: The search for a perspective," International Organization, XXVIII, No. 2, Spring 1974, pp. 247-266.

Rapoport, Anatol. "Problems of peace research," Proceedings of the International Peace Research Association Fourth Conference, pp. 253-275.

–––. "Various conceptions of peace research," PRSI, Papers, XIX, 1972, pp. 91-106.

Reinton, Per Olav. "Inequality in international systems of nations," PRSI, Papers, XI, 1969, pp. 47-55.

Rittberger, Volker. "Organized multinational cooperation within regional settings: A preliminary analysis," PRSI, Papers, XVII, 1971, pp. 93-118.

Roberts, Adam. "Civilian Defence Strategy," in: Roberts (ed.), *Civilian Resistance as a National Defence,* pp. 249-294.

––– (ed.), *Civilian Resistance as a National Defence* (Baltimore, Md.: Penguin, 1969).

Rosen, Steven. "Tolerance of human life costs for foreign policy goals," PRSI, Papers, XVII, 1971, pp. 61-73.

Rosencrance, Richard N. and Arthur A. Stein. "Interdependence: Myth or reality?" World Politics, XXVI, No. 1, October 1973, pp. 1-27.

Ruggie, John Gerard. "The structure of international organization: Contingency, complexity, and post-modern form," PRSI, Papers, XVIII, 1972, pp. 73-91.

Russett, Bruce M. *Power and Community in World Politics* (San Francisco: Freeman, 1974).

Sakamoto, Yoshikazu. "Toward Global Identity," in: *On the Creation of a Just World Order,* ed. Mendlovitz, pp. 189-210.

Salmore, Stephen A. and Charles F. Hermann. "The effect of size, development and accountability on foreign policy," PRSI, Papers, XIV, 1970, pp. 15-30.

Savon, Hervé. "Autour de la polémologie en Suisse," Etudes Polémologiques 7, January 1973, pp. 59-69.

–––. "Polémologie et peace research dans le monde (fin 1971)," Etudes Polémologiques, 4, April 1972, pp. 3-21.

–––. "Une méthode Britannique d'analyse des conflits," Etudes Polémologiques, 8, April 1973, pp. 58-63.

–––. "Une recherche sur la pathologie des relations internationales," Etudes Polémologiques, 5, July 1972, pp. 35-44.

Schelling, Thomas C. "Notes on policies, games, metagames, and Vietnam," PRSI, Papers, X, 1968, pp. 143-147.

Senghaas, Dieter. *Aggressivität und kollektive Gewalt* (Stuttgart: Kohlhammer, 1971).

–––. "Der alte Friedrich List und die Neue internationale ökonomische Ordnung," *Leviathan,* 1975.

–––. *Aufrüstung durch Rüstungskontrolle* (Stuttgart: Kohlhammer, 1972).

–––. "Die Dritte Welt als Gegenstand der Friedensforschung," DGFK-Hefte, No. 5, November 1974.

–––. "Diverse Anmerkungen zur forschungsstrategischen Diskussion über Rüstungsdynamik," unpublished manuscript, 1974.

–––. *Gewalt - Konflikt - Frieden. Essays zur Friedensforschung* (Hamburg: Hoffman und Campe, 1974).

–––. "The Impact of Domestic Interests and National Decision Systems in the post-1945 Arms Race: Some Reflections on Armament Dynamics," paper prepared for the Ninth World Congress of IPSA, Montreal, 1973.

Senghaas, Dieter (ed.), *Peripherer Kapitalismus. Analysen über Abhängigkeit und Unterentwicklung* (Frankfurt: Suhrkamp, 1974).

Shure, Gerald H. and Robert J. Meeker. "Bargaining processes in experimental territorial conflict situations," PRSI, Papers, XI, 1969, pp. 109-122.

Sigler, John H. "Cooperation and conflict in United States-Soviet-Chinese relations, 1966-1971: A quantitative analysis," PRSI, Papers, XIX, 1972, pp. 107-128.

Singer, J. David. "The peace researcher and foreign policy prediction," PSSI, Papers, XXI, 1973, pp. 1-23.

Sloan, Thomas, "Dynamics of Conflict Reduction in the Middle East: An Exploratory Study," paper prepared for the Annual Meeting of the International Studies Association, St. Louis, Mo., 1974.

Smoker, Paul. "Anarchism, peace and control: Some ideas for future experiment," PRSI, Papers, XVI, 1971, pp. 95-107.

Soziale Verteidigung. Friedens- und Sicherheitspolitik in den 80er Jahren. Herausgegeben von der Studiengruppe "Soziale Verteidigung" der Vereinigung deutscher Wissenschaftler e.V. (Gelnhausen/Berlin: Burckhardthaus-Verlag, 1972).

Spiro, Herbert J. "Interdependence: A Third Option Between National Sovereignty and Supra-national Integration," paper prepared for the Ninth World Congress of IPSA, Montreal, 1973.

Starr, Harvey. "An Appraisal of the Substantive Findings of the Correlates of War Project," paper prepared for the Annual Meeting of the International Studies Association, St. Louis, Mo., 1974.

Stohl, Michael. "Linkages Between War and Domestic Violence: A Quasi-Experimental Analysis," paper prepared for the Ninth World Congress of IPSA, Montreal, 1973.

Tanter, Raymond and William C. Potter. "Modelling alliance behavior: East-West conflict over Berlin," PSSI, Papers, XX, 1973, pp. 25-41.

Targ, Harry R. "Post-Industrial Societies in a Post-Revolutionary International System: A Futuristic Look at International Stability," paper prepared for the New England Meeting of the International Studies Association, 1975.

Vesa, Unto. "The development of Chinese thinking on disarmament," Instant Research on Peace and Violence, IV, No. 2, 1974, pp. 53-78.

Walbek, Norman V. and Thomas G. Weiss. *A World Order Framework for Teaching International Politics* (New York: Institute for World Order, 1974).

Weede, Erich. "Nation-environment relations as determinants of hostilities among nations," PSSI, Papers, XX, 1973, pp. 67-90.

Wehr, Paul. "Conflict Regulation." AAAS Study Guides on Contemporary Problems, No. 7 (Washington, D.C.: American Association for the Advancement of Science, 1975).

Weizsäcker, Carl-Friedrich von. "A Sceptical Contribution," in: *On the Creation of a Just World Order,* ed. Mendlovitz, pp. 111-150.

Werner, Victor. "Porrait-on maîtriser la violence?" Etudes Polémologiques 11, January 1974, pp. 5-15.

Wilkenfeld, Jonathan. "Domestic Conflict in the Middle East: An Analysis of International Inputs," paper prepared for the Ninth World Congress of IPSA, Montreal, 1973.

Young, Oran R. "Political Discontinuities in the International System," in: *Regional Politics and World Order,* ed. Falk and Mendlovitz, pp. 34-48.

INDEX

(Note: In general the index contains authors' names only if they appear in the text.)